The Charlatans

The Charlatans

The Authorised History

Words by Dominic Wills
Pictures by Tom Sheehan

With a foreword by Tim Burgess

This edition first published in 2000 by
Virgin Publishing Ltd
Thames Wharf Studios
Rainville Road
London W6 9HA

First published in Great Britain in 1999 by Virgin Publishing Ltd.

A catalogue record for this book is available from the British Library

ISBN 0 7535 0477 4

Photography by Tom Sheehan

Typeset by Phoenix Photosetting, Chatham, Kent
Printed and bound in Great Britain by
Mackays of Chatham plc, Chatham, Kent

Contents

Dedicated to Eileen-Rose, Jamie, Florence, Alex and Hollie.

Thanks to Steve Harrison, Tim Burgess, Martin Blunt, Jon Brookes, Mark Collins, Tony Rogers, John Baker and Rob Collins, Ben Mothersole, Typo, Clare, Nic and Linda at SHM, Dave Charles, Martin Mills, John Empson, Chris Sharp, Lesley and the Karens at Beggars, Ian Gittins, John McGee, Jane Taylor, Kim Peters, Chloe Walsh, Paul Mathur, Dave Haslam, Stuart Bailie, Stuart Maconie, John Gibbon and John Robb.

Foreword by Tim Burgess

FOREWORDS ARE COOL. I'm writing this one not by way of authorisation but out of respect – respect for the way the authors have understood us, sometimes disagreed with us, but always told us what they thought and shown us respect. Respect is deserved.

The process of the book coming together was pretty painless. It feels strange being interviewed sometimes but Dom and Tom have been around us for ten years, hanging about with us, watching us, so the research for this has been spread out over a long time. It's been fun – not like work because it wasn't always work. Until someone writes it down, you're not aware that you're part of a story, you're just doing what you do. We always tried to be natural rather than contrived but, with five very different people in the band, it was always complicated and sometimes you only realise what's going on when someone asks you about it in interview or writes about it in a feature.

This book puts down in words what we did in the past, and kind of solidifies what's happened – we did this, we did that, it says so right here.

So I like the idea of this book. For me, like the rest of the band, it's a chance to stop, look back at what's happened and then get on with the future, both with the band and in our own personal lives. I'm neither proud nor ashamed of the past, but I am glad it's over in that I'm glad to get over my teenage years, glad to get through it. I'm glad I can look back on what we did and tried to do and know that we did pretty well. I feel satisfied by what we've achieved, we enjoyed it at the time but now that part is done – chapter's over. I'm now thirty-one, I feel better on the inside and

I'm ready to get on with the pursuit of happiness. I think we're going to be good at that.

Looking back we've lost a lot, but I can't help thinking we've gained as much if not more. It's just life, really. We've lived our lives by the group, everything we've done has revolved around it. We've tried to keep the vision of the group intact, and struggled to make it and keep it a part of everybody else's life. Sometimes the vision alters, sometimes it breaks and fragments, and sometimes it's stronger than ever. You make mistakes, make bad decisions with lyrics or the music or anything else but none of that matters because it does all take you to the right place in the end. It's about action, you've got to try something or you're doing nothing, aren't you? And we tried. We made mistakes but we did try. Looking back over the albums we've made I see them all as flawed, but I still love them. It's like *Jaws* or *The Exorcist* – they're not perfect but they still work, they still do it for me – I repeat, forewords are cool.

For us, it's been about information, research and knowledge, the balance of foolish mistakes and greatness. We're prepared to admit to the mistakes and take the credit where it's due. Two members are gone and the music may be slightly different but that just goes to show the strength of the name of the group. The Charlatans go on, with or without us, and that's what this is all about.

I like this book – that's the weird thing about it.

Tim Burgess

Introduction

IT REALLY WAS AN extremely large mushroom. The man held it gently but firmly, thrusting it under the nose of anyone who, even for a second, turned his way. It was no prize-winner, that's for sure. A little battered from its rough journey in a crumpled Safeway carrier bag, it looked as if it had already served as lunch for several scuttling forest dwellers. But it was an impressive fungus, nevertheless, and the man was making sure that this summer lunchtime it was the talk of the pub.

Not that there were many in the pub to talk about it; just a couple of old lags hunched over the bar, engaging the barmaid in stilted conversation. Indeed, the whole of Middlewich was empty, the town easing grey and complacent into the warm afternoon. It seemed a fitting venue for a weird alien invasion, a perfect nest for Middlewich cuckoos. And maybe a fine bolthole for bespectacled white rabbits. In here, today, in July 1998, the big mushroom made good surreal sense.

At the end of the long, narrow bar-room, gathered around two beer-spattered tables, sat The Charlatans, their manager and their lawyer. This book's author and photographer believed the meeting had been called to give the band a chance to discuss how they might co-operate with the book, so the lawman's presence seemed a trifle unnecessary. There was clearly something else afoot. Earlier, as each member had drifted into the band's studio just round the corner, there had been a hard edge to their greetings, a funereal feeling, as if once again they were brothers in loss. Once complete as a unit, they had departed as one to some unknown destination – no outsiders, no exceptions. Business as usual, then.

Now, an hour later, the band were in the pub, telling stunned tales of massive embezzlement. They had just been told there was a very good chance that the man charged with handling their financial affairs, a Mr. Trevor Williams had, in fact, ripped them off for hundreds of thousands: approximately £50,000 per man. That was what they thought at the time anyway; by January 1999 the Serious Fraud Squad was involved and potential losses had risen to over a million in total. And it hadn't been just any old money, either: it was from the band's tax fund. Grim-faced men in dark suits, ears already deafened by daily excuses, would soon be coming after that money.

The Charlatans had received extraordinarily bad news that afternoon – but you'd never have guessed it. The band were in absurdly high spirits, joshing, questioning and swapping stinging insults. When they spoke of this new disaster, it was in comically overblown exclamations like 'I don't fookin' *believe* it' or 'What a *bastard*', each outburst leading to howls of laughter. Even bassist Martin Blunt, who would ordinarily be carrying the weight of the world on his shoulders and fretting about everything down to the frayed state of his beer mat, was pretty jolly. He even joined in the game of Guess The Mushroom's Weight (one pound ten-and-three-quarter ounces, as it happens).

Unbelievably, so soon after the theft had been discovered, there was even some sympathy for the perpetrator. Singer Tim Burgess had been round to the suspected fraudster's place the day before, accompanied by band manager Steve Harrison and assorted enforcers of the law. He sadly recounted how the hapless accused man, facing the music, had thrown himself upon their mercy in a pitiable 'you can kill me if you like, I deserve it' kind of way. As ever, Burgess's good nature overpowered the desire to accept his offer with extreme prejudice.

It was a blow – a bad one after all the work they'd put in – but you had to keep these things in perspective. No one was going to prison, or hospital. No one had died. More importantly, perhaps, it wouldn't really impede the making of the next album; might even *fuel* it. The Charlatans were well aware of their ability to pull forcefully away from the edge; to redeem themselves with music. So this setback was kind of funny, in a Victor Meldrew-type way;

just another kick in the balls. They would wipe their eyes and stagger on, recovering their composure in good time for the last-lap sprint.

It stayed funny too, for a while. A few days later, drummer Jon Brookes was milling about the studio when he saw a van parked outside the money man's place, just opposite. It seemed he was having a new kitchen installed. Unable to believe what he was seeing, Brookes stormed over and bluntly informed the workers that they had better pack up and leave because they wouldn't be getting paid for their toil. They wouldn't give him their names, or the name of their company, so later that day Harrison spent a few hours zooming around the area, on the lookout for a van that, based on Brookes' vague description, might be theirs. He never found them.

As the allegations emerged, it became clear that it really wasn't funny at all. It seemed the guy had started small in his deceptions, shifting tiny amounts from one of his accounts to another, covering his tracks. Not much: no one would notice. Slowly, though, his scamming had taken on a momentum of its own and the amounts had grown, the perpetrator locked in foolish denial. He could sort out the mess in the end, it would be OK. Yet now it wasn't OK. Consequently it looked like The Charlatans had taken it in the neck. The guy had begged forgiveness but didn't deserve it. After a nine-month investigation, Trevor Williams, 54 and of Middlewich, found himself up in court. He pleaded guilty to stealing £12,700 and £56,330 and asked for 21 other thefts to be taken into consideration. The total came in at just under £300,000. Harrison lost the chain of Omega Record shops he had built up, the biggest independent chain in the North-West, and had to work once more from home. Williams went down and, as is the case in such matters, the band would have to wait for his release before attempting to recover the missing funds.

In January 1999, there was a neat little summation of the band's attitude to all this. Harrison held a big clear-out at his office, Omega Music, in Northwich. A watercolour painting of flowers, lovingly daubed by the accountant and sent to Harrison in memory of Rob Collins, the band's keyboard player who had been killed in a car accident, turned up. A touching gift, it had hung for

3

a considerable period on Harrison's wall. Now he realised that, even at the time of Collins' death, the money man was probably operating his little scheme. He smashed the frame to pieces, took the painting and, with a black marker pen, scrawled the words 'Rot in hell, you bastard' across it. Then he returned it to sender, first class.

Dead flowers indeed. It's certain The Charlatans will not be putting roses on one particular gentleman's grave.

01 From Simple Hope Up The Indian Rope

TIMOTHY ALLAN BURGESS WAS born to Allan and Marion on 30 May 1967, within a couple of days of the release of The Beatles' *Sergeant Pepper's Lonely Hearts Club Band*. ('This is the age of Gemini,' he would later portentously declare on-stage, in reference to this date.) Hope Hospital, Salford, was the venue for the auspicious event. By lineage, his first claim to fame was that his father had once lived on Bolton Road, Pendlebury, home to the artist L.S. Lowry (and later Happy Mondays dancer Bez).

Burgess was a precocious child – charmed, charming and spacey even by ankle-biter standards. People recognised something oddly attractive about him, but they couldn't quite put their finger on it. He was somehow special, that was it, special. Tim remembers being described as special as early as age six, and again around ten. The point worked its way home and gave him a confidence and sense of self that would later work as a protective barrier against considerable difficulties.

Burgess also had the sense to be born good-looking. Coupled with a friendly temperament, this made him popular and certainly cushioned the shock of the family's move to Northwich. It had to be done: his father's work (his mother was a housewife) demanded a shift to the ICI plant just outside town where he was to be foreman. Moving can be a lonely experience for kids but there was no such trouble for Burgess. Yet to reach double figures, he was already waltzing through life, thrilled by the brilliance or bullshit of everything. Typically and tellingly, when he demanded a role in a school production of *Snow White*, he could not be denied, even though all parts were already filled; he was improbably cast as Snow White's best friend.

The Charlatans

In the first year of boys to attend classes with girls as the schools of the area combined, the young Burgess moved from Moulton Primary School to the new comprehensive Leftwich High School (formerly Leftwich Grammar) and his life just got better and better. He hung around with the big boys, who liked him because he was funny, enthusiastic and full of life without being arrogant or threatening. Tim, in turn, fitted in well and picked up their interests in music and clothes. At a ridiculously early age, Burgess was swanning around in 'Fila BJ tops, very pale jeans with the essential cut up the side, seventies Pumas or Adidas Wimbledons and Adidas Stan Smiths' (Stan Smith being the very contained, very cool American who pissed off the world by beating tennis clown prince Ilie Nastase in the 1972 Wimbledon final).

The music he loved was harder and rougher than anything you'd find in the seventies charts. The older guys he hung around with – some of whom would later be incarcerated after a local stabbing – were into punk and Burgess joined them. Its rush and simplicity suited him well. The first single he bought was The Vibrators' 'Automatic Lover', purchased by saving his holiday pocket-money. He also had a passion for UK Subs and race-along chants like 'Stranglehold'. Yet it was all rubbish really, dumbo speed anthems with no finesse or future, and Burgess was smarter than that. Ploughing his own course, looking for musical information with which to impress his big buddies, he greedily devoured the obscure tracks John Peel was pushing on Radio 1 between ten and twelve every weekday night (except Friday, Tommy Vance's metal night). He got into Killing Joke, with their complex blend of tribalism, mysticism and murderous anger. He even went to see them, aged eleven, still togged up in his school uniform (suitably fetishistic, under the circumstances).

Northwich, however, was not made for kids: the preponderance of signs pointing you towards the Salt Museum will tell you that. Salt mining was traditionally the town's *point*: the whole place was built on the stuff. Beneath the town centre run tunnels wide enough to drive a lorry through. Half the town could drop 50 feet without warning. And it's wet too; Manchester wet. The Charlatans have, over the years, made enquiries into buying premises in Northwich, to build a club for the kids and give something back. But it's too risky; it's just not safe. Though Lot might have disagreed, salt can suck big time.

So kids in Northwich, just as in olden times, had to make their own entertainment. Burgess would hang around the town centre with the others, often being closely scrutinised by giggling gaggles of very young women. He was caught smoking at eleven and sniffing glue at thirteen (these were the days before vendors realised that there hadn't *really* been a massive upswing in the popularity of model aeroplanes). Tim did a lot of glue, and petrol, and Genclean – a substance used for cleaning oil off motorbikes – but he wasn't, and has never been, addicted to anything.

Burgess went through the usual rites of passage – draw (expensive) and mushrooms (a gift from God), then alcohol and stomach pumps. He would loiter outside the off licences, getting drunk on cider, barley wine and, when in the money, Southern Comfort, smoke Peter Stuyvesants, smash windows and indulge in petty theft. He and his mates took to shooting pigeons with air rifles, then they'd shoot each other, usually aiming for the buttocks or the meaty tops of the legs, in order to cause maximum pain but no lasting damage – the kiddy equivalent of Brad Davis stabbing his annoying cell mate in the arse in *Midnight Express*. Burgess himself was shot many times and when asked about it today will nod sagely, sternly advise you that if you go out shooting people you should expect to be fired upon yourself, then literally crease up, bent almost double, arms flailing, fingers popping Manchester-style, hacking out that brief, uncontrollable laugh of his.

Burgess left school in 1983, at sixteen, with one O Level in English to his name. School was never his thing. He wasn't a big reader, once proudly claiming that *Watership Down* was the only book he had ever completed. Today, though, he possesses a fair few shelves of literature, mostly cult classics by the likes of Kerouac and Irvine Welsh, and revered rock texts concerning Boy George, Jim Morrison, the Stones and Bob Dylan bootlegs – anything providing titillation and soul food, really.

He immediately found employment with ICI, first in Northwich then Runcorn, beginning work at an excruciating 6.30 in the morning. It was one-in-the-eye for the teacher who'd told him,

'Burgess, you've got no chance.' Northwich ICI is a bizarre place, an industrial Gormenghast stretching across the fields with no thought to structure or style. At night, or in the early morning, with its glaring lights and menacing shadows, it's like Tina Turner's corral in *Mad Max – Beyond Thunderdome*.

Burgess began as a push-bike messenger between offices. 'If I'd had a Lambretta, I'd have been in *Quadrophenia*,' he recalls. He liked to wreck the bikes whenever possible, then think up the most outlandish excuses. It was a good life; enough to provide him with beer and records, which was all he wanted really. Promotion was unwanted, but came anyway. Burgess was moved up to cleaning toilets (no, *really*), then after that endured contract work as a fitter's mate, a period involving carrying tools, putting up scaffolding, bricklaying, carpentry and a long period scrubbing asbestos-coated ceilings and the nauseating insides of chemical tanks ('I had to sign a contract so that if I die of asbestosis, my mum and dad or my sister can have a four-year legal battle for a load of dosh'). Each Thursday when he got his wages, he'd buy tunes. He'd rarely go out, except to watch Witton Albion on a Saturday, but instead sit in and listen to the new tracks, suck in their spirit and read anything he could find about them. A few years later, Liam Gallagher would lead a very similar young life.

He soon realised he wanted to be in a band. Burgess had an uncle who was a bassist and remembers him talking about music and his life in a group. He particularly recalls an occasion when he came round in a truly buoyant mood, excitedly explaining that he had found a manager. So Burgess got into the idea. He tried to learn guitar, then the bass, but lacked the patience for either. It was clear he'd have to be a singer.

He joined and left a series of nondescript outfits in and around Northwich. None of them were remotely serious or even managed to get a gig together. Then came The Electric Crayons. Psychedelia informed the work and, in particular, the names of many bands around the north-west at this time (The Charlatans' early guitarist, John Baker, was presently playing in Liquid Egg Box), hence The Electric Crayons. Burgess liked the name, though he would have preferred The Electric Crayon Set. He liked the rhythm and feel of the psychedelic era, the way they would use adjectives to make 'ordinary' objects marvellous and magical, like The Pigeon-Toed Orange Peel from Clint Eastwood's *Coogan's Bluff*. He regarded psychedelia as a prodding of people's imaginations that could lead to a genuine expanding of consciousness. This was a notion quite in keeping with the deliberate personal and musical openness prevalent around the north-west, and particularly Manchester in the mid-eighties.

Burgess was into anything out of the ordinary. He loved Joy Division and The Fall, especially the latter's 'Slates' EP with its staccato classics 'Prole Art Threat' and 'An Older Lover Etc'. He was very taken with singer Mark E. Smith's cut-up technique, the irrepressible rush of words reminding him of what happened every time he tried to impress a girl. He ended up blurting nonsensically but honestly, making total and zero sense, not being able to stop *being himself*. Burgess was also into the colourful American folk and psychedelia of REM, The Long Ryders and The Rain Parade (an early outing for Mazzy Star's David Roback).

At sixteen, as soon as he had some cash, he took to hanging around a little music import store in Winsford called Omega Music, which was run by Steve Harrison. Harrison was quickly impressed by Burgess's musical knowledge and took him under his wing, introducing him to sixties pop, folk and garage, Northern Soul and West Coast experimentalism – his own favourites, really. The pair became closer still when Harrison moved Omega to Northwich.

Harrison says now he always recognised Burgess's star quality, claiming he saw it shining out of him from day one. He started taking him to gigs, and tried to hook him a career in rock.

'Tim always had star potential,' says Harrison, 'even when he was in terrible bands round here. He always looked the part, and he always had this amazing talent for seeking out and absorbing great music. I was really desperate for him to do well, and I found a couple of jobs for him. The first was with this band I'd heard of, Inspiral Carpets.'

Harrison had called the Inspirals a few times, trying to get gigs for the pre-Burgess Charlatans, whom he was already managing. Inspirals' singer Stephen Holt had acrimoniously left the band after their debut 'Planecrash' EP and they needed a replacement.

Harrison persuaded Burgess to try out for the placement, saying he would drive him to the audition and everything. Also up for the job was Chris Griffiths, now tour manager for Manic Street Preachers, but on the day of his audition he went to see Manchester City instead. The runway was clear for Burgess but by the time he plucked up courage, Tom Hingley had got the job.

Next came indie icons and greatcoat rockers Echo And The Bunnymen. Ian McCulloch had gone solo in the summer of 1988, and the band (who wouldn't suffer the death of their drummer Pete De Freitas in a motorcycle accident till June the next year) needed a new mouth. Burgess liked the idea, feeling The Bunnymen certainly had the requisite psychedelic edge, but he wasn't *really* up for it. He was enjoying himelf too much with The Electric Crayons, raucously shouting out Led Zeppelin and Iggy Pop covers (he says he didn't actually realise he could sing till he was told to by The Charlatans), haring about the stage and mooning at the audience. The Electric Crayons were two longhairs and a couple of big quiffs, Burgess looking not unlike Gripper Stebson from *Grange Hill*. 'They were popular in Northwich,' says Harrison, 'but God knows why. I thought they were *fucking awful*.' Awful or not, Burgess was enjoying himself immensely. He was also fully availing himself of the various intoxicating benefits of the emerging Madchester scene.

Acid house was exploding. Inspired by the club scene in Ibiza, a few DJs had returned to the UK and set up clubs of their own (Danny Rampling's Shoom being a legendary example). Any music could be seized, mixed and pumped up to the max – indie eccentrics The Woodentops, oddball situationists The Residents; absolutely anything could be a part of what was termed Balearic Beat. Psychedelia informed the music and the lighting systems. Hippy drugs dope and acid were back on the agenda after years of punky amphetamines. And now there was Ecstasy too. The infant scene pulsated with an open, loving groove.

The late eighties were exciting and eclectic times for music. On the fringes, there were the slamming, sample-heavy Teutonic beats of Front 242 and Belgian New Beat (touched by the hand of Kraftwerk), added to the burgeoning and massively celebratory

Chicago House sounds of Marshall Jefferson and Robert Owens. Then there was the simplistic, trippy weirdness of Detroit techno and the advanced industrial mayhem of Canada's Skinny Puppy, Front Line Assembly and Psyche. All of these helped to shape a fascinating clubland and create 1988's countrywide summer of love. House stormed the charts and entered the vernacular. Everyone was at it.

And Manchester, with its long history of musical open-mindedness, became the centre of it all, the Hacienda a Mecca for clubbers across the UK. The place was packed and stomping, the atmosphere a revelation. Manchester stuck to the Balearic ideal. DJs would mix dance and indie, West Coast folk and acid rock. In fact, the dance thing actually got people into rock: 'Sympathy For The Devil' was a club staple. You had to have the first Pink Floyd album, *Piper At The Gates Of Dawn* (Charlatans guitarist Mark Collins had *Dark Side Of The Moon* too). You needed some Byrds stuff – *Younger Than Yesterday* probably,' says Burgess now, 'because it's so trippy' – and of course some Hendrix – 'probably *Axis – Bold As Love* because it's the most acidy.' And soon Manchester had its own music, its own band, with the shuffling beats and big rock of The Stone Roses, kings of the indie-dance crossover soon to become known as 'baggy'.

Burgess was there throughout, dreaming of the big time. Invariably off his face, he thrilled to the togetherness of it all, the way this culture and these drugs irrevocably changed the way people spent their leisure time (no kicking out at eleven o'clock here). It made everyone feel special, and Burgess (*special, so special*) even more so. He was never happier than when fronting The Electric Crayons. He loved being up there. He was hooked.

The Crayons, riding their Northwich popularity, recorded a single, 'Hip Shake Junkie', a tin-pot blast of garage, backed by the punky silliness of 'Happy To Be Hated'. It was produced by a member of Liverpool psychedelic band Dr Phibes And The House Of Wax Equations, who would later be jailed for killing his own mother. They played often and uproariously, usually at the Vic, a club attached to the local perennially under-achieving football side Northwich Victoria. It was there that, on 30 September 1988, they supported the emergent Charlatans. Burgess remembers that, during The Charlatans' set, Martin Blunt urged him to get up on-stage and join in on backing vocals.

It wasn't long before Tim Burgess did a great deal more than that.

The make-up of The Charlatans today, and in many ways the sound, is down to Martin Blunt (nickname Tunes). Born on 21 May 1964, in the Portobello area of Willenhall, just west of Walsall, he was, like Burgess, not good at school. But Blunt got punk, and punk got Blunt. He'd been taken to gigs by his older brother, and consequently formed an interest in black music – reggae and especially soul.

He also loved scooters. Between 1980 and 1983, Blunt spend his weekends on the big runs being organised at the time. It would be very easy to describe Martin Blunt as a mod – he's certainly always been the sharpest of The Charlatans in his clothes and haircuts and he's the only one of them who's never entertained the notion of scruffiness – but there's more to it than that.

'It wasn't so much a mod thing,' he explains. 'People were into Northern Soul, Joy Division, Echo And The Bunnymen, The B-52s and Dexy's, all sorts. If there were discos they'd play everything. It was a bit like the rave thing – you'd be listening to Northern Soul and then The Smiths would come on. I loved it, used to listen to a lot of old stuff because I thought most of the new stuff at the time was dire.

'We'd do runs to Scarborough, Morecambe, Weymouth. It was something to do at the weekend. We'd get down there and meet up with people from all over the country, all different social and musical persuasions, all going to the seaside. There'd be Perry boys from the north-west, and the psychobillies and flat-tops from London, all on scooters. It was like a melting pot, you know, with scooters the only thing people really had in common – other than *being people*. I think it was a big influence on the Manchester scene. And then when E came on the scene in the summer of '88, it was all there, a link for everyone.'

Blunt really took to this *mélange* of styles. He'd attend funk all-nighters at Birmingham's Locarno, as well as Northern Soul all-dayers. He was into Stax, Atlantic and Motown, the traditional mod soundtrack, and also mod style prototypes The Small Faces. Blunt, like Burgess, was a denizen of Steve Harrison's scruffy little Omega shop – he was after Northern Soul. And, once in there, just as The Small Faces in 1968 moved into psychedelia with their *Ogden's Nut Gone Flake* album, so Blunt progressed too – Quicksilver Messenger Service, leading to The Church, Dream Syndicate and Rain Parade, then back into sixties beat and garage, then 13th Floor Elevators and back through The Action and The Creation. Blunt went back and forth through the years and the styles: he even checked out electro, where Afrika Bambaataa and Grandmaster Flash were sowing the seeds of the hip-hop phenomenon.

Harrison knew Blunt well: in fact, Blunt had stayed over a few times with Harrison and his new wife, Judith. He recognised Blunt as an oddity. 'A lot of mods were very narrow,' he says. 'They didn't seem to want to expand their minds in any way. But Martin was wide open to exploring things – that always struck me about him.'

By the age of nineteen, while working in various record shops (he'd later slog away on building sites), Blunt was in his first serious band, Makin' Time. Having seen his father spend the last eight years of his working life on the dole – his dad had been a printer, as were his mother and brother – he was more than keen to make a go of music. Poverty, he had realised, is not ennobling: it is to be avoided at all costs.

Makin' Time formed in 1984 ('well after the second wave of mod had died down,' says Blunt). After a few line-up changes, they settled on a membership comprising Fay Hallam, Mark McGouden, drummer Neil Clitheroe (who now works in an adult comic shop in Mannheim, Germany) and Blunt. McGouden, nicknamed Sid after Sid Vicious, had changed his name from Gouden by deed poll – something to do with Patrick McGoohan, apparently. He's now just finishing his last year of training to be a psychiatric nurse.

Makin' Time were originally a down-the-line blues band but quickly widened their sound with the introduction of front-of-the-mix organ, Hallam having been drawn by Blunt to the work of artists like Brian Auger And The Trinity. At the time, they were very influenced by the Medway scene, where The Prisoners and Billy Childish's Thee Milkshakes were fusing punk, out-there garage rock and, in the case of Childish, anything that came into his head.

Makin' Time's idea was to reintroduce soul to music. With New Romantics dominating the mid-eighties, seen by them to be the ultimate in plastic pap, they looked back for deeper inspirations and, with Hallam and McGouden sharing and swapping vocals idiosyncratically, came up with a poppy combination of soul and R&B. Playing extensively around the north-west and the Midlands, particularly the Wolverhampton/ Walsall axis, they built up a strong live following that soon saw them signed to Stiff's Countdown indie imprint, the same label as The Prisoners signed to for their fourth album.

The tellingly titled album *Rhythm 'N' Soul*, was released in June 1985, and the band continued pushing and touring across the UK and Europe. But they had a major problem: they kept getting tied in with, and weighed down by, the flailing corpse of that mod scene. Consequently, the press wouldn't touch them and the public weren't too keen either. They toughened up their sound, covering Elvis Costello's 'Pump It Up' and The Kinks' 'I Gotta Move', but were then accused of ripping off The Prisoners (the two bands were closely linked – Hallam would later marry The Prisoners' Graham Day). It was a deeply unhappy situation, and probably unjust.

'To be honest,' says Steve Harrison, 'I always thought it was the other way round; that The Prisoners took something from Makin' Time. Makin' Time started more as a pop outfit with a mod feel, and The Prisoners were a garage band, but then they kind of collided, because Makin' Time were going more for garage and The Prisoners went more pop. The Prisoners certainly came out of it all with more credibility, which was unfair because Makin' Time were a deep band, very well versed in soul and well respected by people who were really into black music. I always thought Makin' Time could have crossed over like The Housemartins or something. Some of it was pretty cheesy, but they had good soulful pop songs.'

Countdown didn't have the clout to overcome these problems

and would soon be shut down and reincarnated as Acid Jazz. Then everything got a little messy. The Prisoners split in 1986 with a farewell gig at London's 100 Club, their relationship with Countdown ending badly with three penniless members throwing T-shirts out of the window of Stiff's offices while the other wrestled on the floor with two Stiff officials, desperately trying to retrieve demos and the master tape of their fourth, horribly overproduced album, *In From The Cold*. The band reformed ten years later, partly due to The Charlatans having repopularised the idea of organ-driven garage rock (neat, given that many observers believe Blunt saw The Prisoners as a prototype for The Charlatans).

Makin' Time didn't last much longer. The label ran out of money, the press were unforgiving, and their variety of stylistic influences went unnoticed. A mod band they were and a mod band they would stay, no matter what they sounded like. They did fairly well in Germany where there was a strong mod scene, but that kind of following, just as in the UK, would never grow or last.

Makin' Time finally split in September 1986, after the failure of their second album, *No Lumps Of Fat Or Gristle Guaranteed*, the title a reference to a TV advert for Tyne Brand canned meat pie filling. They meant there was no bullshit. In fact, there was way too much.

'I think Makin' Time was killed by the mod thing,' says Harrison. 'It always happens when you're tarred with the brush of a very insular scene. With The Charlatans I think Martin was very keen to not have that happen again; almost paranoid. It was a shame because I thought Fay was a bit like Dusty Springfield. She had a really good voice.'

Makin' Time were dead and Blunt set about beginning again. He formed The Gift Horses, with Fay Hallam on vocals, Graham Day on guitar and a new drummer, Jon Brookes.

With his two brothers, Brookes had grown up in West Bromwich, in the Fox and Dogs, a pub run by his parents. Pub life can be intimidating for a kid but Brookes sailed through it, building the abrasive but thoroughly personable character he has today. Like the other Charlatans, he was no hotshot in the classroom, and was told as much by his teachers who seemed to have no interest in boosting the young lad's confidence.

'I want people to take notice of me,' he says, looking back with pride and some degree of bitterness, 'and I want to enjoy everything that comes my way. The last thing I was supposed to do, according to everybody, was do something good. I was always gonna fucking fail. The careers teachers at Wednesbury Comprehensive never bothered looking at me. I knew it at the time and I'm reacting to it now. Sticking two fingers up to them all was a main motivation for me from the start, and it still is.'

Brookes has faced this attitude over and over again. Maybe it's to do with his accent. You can't help feeling that if Albert Einstein had spoken in a West Bromwich accent, he would have been laughed out of every lecture theatre in the world. It's an accent that calls for friendly resolve in the face of innate and foolish disrespect, and Brookes has that in buckets.

At the age of seven or eight, Brookes discovered drumming. The Fox and Dogs had a resident dance band and their drummer, a decent sort named Harvey, would help Brookes pick up the gist of different musical forms. Whenever Harvey took a break, Brookes would get up and play till he returned. He must have been pretty good, despite never having had formal lessons; after all, people's tolerance for enthusiastic but incompetent children stretches only so far.

'I think I might have got into it for all the wrong reasons,' remembers Brookes. 'I mean, I was into all the rock 'n' roll stuff – Ozzy Osbourne biting bats' heads off and all that. But I also used to listen to records to learn how to be a drummer. That's all I ever wanted to do. I remember seeing Cozy Powell on *Top of the Pops* [drummer with, among others, Ritchie Blackmore's Rainbow, who died in a car crash in 1998, his last words on his mobile being, 'Oh, *shit*']. My brother had his "Dance With The Devil" single and I played the shit out of that. I must have been about eight then. I was eleven when I got my first drum kit. I used to imagine being in a heavy rock band and pounding away at these colossal gigs.

'All I ever wanted was to be respected as a drummer and to be famous and known to everyone on the planet. The thought that you might be able to make a good living out of it only came later.'

While Brookes learnt from Harvey in the evenings, his brothers came through with inspiration during the day. One was into reggae (Third World, Bob Marley and Peter Tosh), enabling Brookes to work on a drumming style that was both loose and rock solid. The other used to blast out Motorhead, Thin Lizzy and Rush, teaching Brookes power and advanced technique (Rush's Neil Peart being widely and often cited as the most gifted and inventive drummer in rock).

Eventually, he came upon his great loves: Mitch Mitchell from The Jimi Hendrix Experience and Led Zeppelin's John Bonham. Brookes identified with Bonham deeply, in terms of his birthplace, style and physical shape. 'Bonham came from the West Midlands,' he says proudly. 'He had big shoulders and he played his drums like he was digging the garden.'

On leaving school, Brookes took a job in a sawmill, slicing his fingers open every other day. When no one was looking, he'd knock out pairs of increasingly well-weighted drumsticks. He thought of nothing but drumming. He even played in a band, briefly, when he was sixteen, with a keyboard player called Rob Collins.

When a chance came, Brookes took it, immediately shooting down to London when he received a call from two friends who had scored themselves a publishing deal. He lived with them for a while in a caravan in Crystal Palace, but nothing happened. They were too finicky; pissing about with the sound when he desperately wanted to be hitting something (*them*, eventually). He went back north, hacked off his hair and dyed what remained yellow, and joined a covers band, supporting himself with a gardening job.

There's an old story that claims that at this point Brookes was a street sweeper. Apparently, he encountered Blunt lying face down in the gutter, covered in vomit. 'You'd better get up,' said Brookes. 'I'm in a band,' replied Blunt, and so came about a ten-year creative liaison. It's a great story, and not that unlikely given Brookes's pragmatism and Blunt's obsession. Sadly, though, it's not true.

Blunt knew a local character called Rob Collins from hanging around the Trough pub in Walsall, the area's main haunt for bikers, indie kids and all types of scumbag (The Charlatans' early guitarist John Baker drank there too). Brookes knew Collins from that band back when he was sixteen. One evening in the pub, Brookes introduced himself to Blunt. Blunt liked him immediately. He'd seen him play and knew he was good. And, Christ, with *that* barnet, he was in.

The Gift Horses, just like Makin' Time, were an ill-fated crew. A harsher version of that earlier incarnation (how could they not be with a drummer into Motorhead?), they fitted in nowhere. They tried it on in Germany, hoping to pick up on the relative success of Makin' Time, but they just attracted the same mod crowd, only now ten times smaller. They released one single, the brassy 'Rosemary', for the German label Pop-I, and that was it. After a tour of Holland, Day departed with Hallam to form The Prime Movers with Simon Howard and Alan Crooks from The James Taylor Quartet, an offshoot of The Prisoners.

The deserted Blunt knew he had to act. He made contact with Baz Ketley. Born in Malvern, Ketley had moved to Wolverhampton in 1978 and was a dyed-in-the-wool punker whose tastes had widened into Joy Division and Echo And The Bunnymen. Playing bass in The Andy Leek Band (Leek having played keyboards for Dexy's Midnight Runners), he quickly began to write his own material and, feeling like taking on vocal duties too, left to form The Blue Toys, pausing only to poach Pete Barton, an early drummer with Blunt's Makin' Time. Blunt and Ketley had got to know each other well, Ketley renting Blunt his lights whenever Makin' Time played in his area.

As The Gift Horses were falling apart, Graham Day quit for a while. In his absence, Blunt had got Ketley in to play guitar, something he'd never done onstage before. He played two or three gigs with them in London, then Day returned.

So when the band split for good, Ketley was at the forefront of Blunt's mind. Ketley was into the idea; Brookes was up for it too. Now Blunt needed a keyboard player, someone to match James Taylor from The Prisoners for panache and power. They auditioned a few candidates and rapidly came up with their man. For four or five rehearsals it was going great – and then, suddenly, he was dead.

According to Blunt, the guy had been on anti-depressants and somehow OD'd. He may have been drinking, or so consumed by his own thoughts he forgot what he'd taken, but he lay dead in his flat for two days before he was found. Blunt remembers taking the day off work to attend his funeral, then getting lost around Aldridge, near Walsall, and missing the ceremony altogether.

The death of one keyboard player, however, brought them to another – Rob Collins. At the time, Collins was playing in what he himself described as 'a naff rock band'. Absolutely no one remembers their name, and Rob would certainly never say. Blunt and Collins had chatted a few times, but Blunt found making the first approach tricky. Luckily, he also knew the naff rock band's guitarist and went to see them with that as an excuse. Afterwards, he got talking with Collins again and Rob, even without the knowledge that his old mucker Brookes was involved, agreed to go along for a jam.

Rob Collins was born in Sedgley in the West Midlands on 23 February 1963. February 29 would have suited his contrary nature better. He attended Queen Mary's Grammar School but his big loves were not academic in nature. They were fishing and playing the piano, the latter being taken up as a small child and continuing through school bands and a couple of local groups.

Collins was very English and very working class. He loved a quiet pint or ten. He was often in trouble, once being caught stealing lead from a church roof (a clichéd crime if ever there was one). He was also done for D&D (drunk and disorderly) and claimed to have been charged with GBH. After school, he became a toolmaker for five years. He was good with his hands, was Rob.

And he was contrary. He could be affable but was just as likely to maintain a stony and deliberately excruciating silence. He wasn't very communicative at the best of times. He would fish seriously, with Mani, bassist with The Stone Roses, and producer Steve Hillage, but he would do it on E too (Tim Burgess recalls riverside conversations running along the lines of, 'Is it a chub?', 'Dunno... Who cares?', 'Er, dunno'). He'd confuse Burgess by changing his handwriting and signature. Sometimes he'd be crueller. But he would always stand up for him if the going got rough. He would threaten or bash anyone who tried it on. Good with his hands, was Rob.

Musically, Rob trod a difficult path too. All his keyboard heroes were pre-punk, proper artistes who were supposed to have been swept away by the angry tide of 1977. Collins didn't give a flying one – for him it was Brian Auger, Jon Lord, Keith Emerson and Billy Preston. He paid no mind to any idea of 'hipness'. He loved The Beatles, The Who and Bob Marley. You could love what you liked; this was *his* thing.

And then there was his choice of instrument, the Hammond organ. Where most kids would bowl around their rooms, posing and thrashing on invisible six-strings, or pout and shout with their fist clenched to their mouth, Collins was a Hammond player. And that was utterly appropriate because the Hammond itself could be quiet or crazy, supportive or dominating. It was weird and important and interesting right from the earliest years of rock 'n' roll.

The addition of Collins completed this new line-up, and Blunt was eager to name the band The Law Lords. Ketley, however thought The Charlatans was a better moniker. It had a pleasing ambiguity and, let's face it, wouldn't *you* expect a band called The Law Lords to be wearing leather lederhosen and rubber masks with zips? Knowing Blunt's implacability, it was a sign of Ketley's strength of character that the decision came down to the toss of a coin. Blunt called wrong. The Charlatans it was.

By now, Ketley had become a fairly accomplished songwriter, and was also increasingly well read. A diehard fan of The Clash with a penchant for Joy Division, his songs were heavily melodic, soulful and kind of punky, with a hugely romantic sensibility. The infant Charlatans recorded two sets of demos, slowly drawing together the disparate elements of powering funk bass, clattering percussion and keyboards, growing ambition and aggression. Ketley was feeding off both Joe Strummer *and* Henry Miller, delivering anti-materialist anthems and yearning love songs. The songs' titles, like 'Tropic Of Love', 'Nothing's Left', 'Drowning In A River Of Tears' and 'Angelica', are clear pointers to their content. Ketley was a songwriter, not a stylemonger.

With the tunes beginning to flow, they now needed a manager. They required a man with a love of music (so he would understand them), an acceptable personality (so he wouldn't piss them off) and a canny business sense (so the Makin' Time nightmare scenario would never ever befall them). Blunt thought hard but not too long. He already knew one person with all those qualities and more. It had to be Steve Harrison.

Harrison had known Blunt by sight back in the days of those scooter runs, although they were only on nodding terms then. Blunt ran with the Stockport Crusaders, while Harrison was closer to another crew, the Cheshire Midnight Runners. His scooter buddies included Peter Hook and Bernard Albrecht of New Order, and John Squire and Ian Brown, now of The Stone Roses. So Harrison was not just a music lover (he'd been guitarist for The Nice Guys, supporting The Fall a couple of times), he had connections, too, and as the owner of a vital record outlet, he was a pretty important figure. Gareth Evans, manager of the International club in Manchester, sold tickets through Omega, visiting regularly to collect the money. One day, he went down to Witton Street with a tape of a band he was thinking of managing. He wanted Harrison's opinion. On hearing it, Harrison reckoned it was a bit like The Rain Parade but nevertheless fabulous stuff, and advised Evans to jump at the chance, like, *yesterday*. Steve couldn't believe it when Evans told him it was The Stone Roses (it was actually the 'Sally Cinnamon' demo). He'd seen the Roses in their early days, supporting Plain Jayne at the International, and considered them to be essentially dodgy goths.

From here, Harrison's relationship with Evans and the Roses grew tighter. Evans would invite him to gigs, encouraging him to aim higher: 'You don't want to be working in an *office*, man.' Harrison wasn't sure – his Omega business was going great guns – but he listened hard and picked up management tips whenever they were offered. Evans had plenty of ideas about how to make friends and influence people, once asking if he could borrow Harrison's day-old Mercedes to attend a meeting with a record company interested in the Roses. The Roses themselves would come down to Omega too, Harrison once sorting them out with hi-fi equipment.

So when he received a call from Blunt asking him to pop down to the Overstrand club in Walsall to see his band play, Harrison was already considering a move into management. He just hadn't realised that he was gong to start that night. 'Bring your cheque book,' Blunt had said. Always was a cheeky bastard, always will be, was Harrison's first thought.

But Harrison went to the Walsall gig and was mightily impressed. They were the best band he had seen at that level in years. And, after an evening's coaxing and coercion (Harrison buying all the beers, naturally), he agreed to take on their management. As soon as the words had left his mouth, he discovered why he had been asked to bring his cheque book. Blunt turned to him and, wholly businesslike now, asked if he would buy them a van. In fact, would he buy them the white Bedford that was sitting outside – the owner wanted the money tonight and they had a gig the next day. Cheeky bastard, always was, always will be. But Harrison coughed up, regardless. He walked away £275 lighter and with his future changed.

Looking back at that gig, Harrison says: 'It was a lot more punky than it was later, a lot less groove orientated, a *lot* less. It wasn't as funky, more power pop, much more song orientated. Martin looked good, but the others ...' He pauses, visibly grimacing at the memory. 'Oh, Rob looked terrible, with this big moustache, like Carlos Santana or a Mexican bandit. He might have got away with it if he'd had long hair, but he didn't. It was amazing, considering how cool he later became. No, Martin was definitely the style guru then, and it wasn't rubbing off on the others, that's for sure.'

Harrison immediately set about promoting his new protégés, proving to be a natural blagger. He badgered promoters all over the north-west for gigs and plastered posters on every available wall-space proclaiming that The Charlatans, presented by the Transworld Consortium, would be appearing soon at *a venue near you*. The Transworld Consortium didn't actually exist, but it sure sounded good, lending the band extra much-needed weight. 'It was Martin's idea,' explains Harrison. 'Just to add a bit of intrigue. It's actually from a James Bond film. *Dr No*, I think.' He also took great care in his press releases, ensuring they were adequately descriptive and well written so that local newspapers would print them almost verbatim, thus saying exactly what he wanted them to say.

Best of all, he had the contact with Gareth Evans and The Stone Roses. By now they'd released 'Sally Cinnamon' on FM Revolver and then signed to Silvertone, putting out the superb 'Elephant Stone'. Though they wouldn't explode nationally till the next year, they were already preposterously big in Manchester. Spurred on, they had begun to tour more widely, and Harrison latched on to this, getting The Charlatans so many back-up slots they became known as 'The Stone Roses' favourite support act'. This was invaluable, reputation-wise, and also as far as technique was concerned. Brookes in particular would learn something new, something looser, from Reni, the Roses' drummer. He still considers him to be one of the finest ever.

It once worked the other way too. Harrison used a contact at London's LSE to get a gig, and the Roses came too.

'It was a horrible night,' says Harrison, 'a really horrible night. We were dead jealous because we were in the Bedford van and they had a transit from Stamford Van Hire.' Much worse, no one watched the gig. All the industry types remained in the bar, missing their big chance to snare the Roses – all except the people from Zomba/Silvertone. Their attentiveness would serve them well.

The Roses were always good to The Charlatans, though, ensuring the stage was clear for them and treating them to beer and sandwiches when they had no rider.

There were other gigs, too, without the Roses. One in particular, with Goodbye Mr Mackenzie (featuring the pre-Garbage Shirley Manson on vocals) at International 2 in Manchester, was notable for its carnage. Harrison remembers having to pay off the headliner's sound guy, monitor guy and lighting guy for the use of their equipment and expertise. Goodbye Mr Mackenzie wouldn't let The Charlatans share their dressing room (quite right, too, with ladies present), and Rob Collins was trying to provoke guitarist 'Big John' Duncan (formerly of The Exploited, later a live guest of Nirvana) by calling him a fat bastard.

No one was there to see The Charlatans, so Ketley walked off the front of the stage to get a pint while the rest of the band booted over the equipment. The staff went mental, memorably telling Steve, 'That microphone's worth more than your whole fucking drum kit.' The promoter told Harrison that The Charlatans would never work in Manchester again. When Harrison returned to his car, parked outside, the windows had been smashed but nothing was stolen. Naturally, security didn't have a clue who'd done it.

Smashing stuff was a bit of a Charlatans speciality at this time. With Ketley's roots deep in The Clash, he was almost born to it, and the rest were keen to follow suit. There were reasons for real annoyance too. Though 'Angelica' had received favourable local reviews when sent around on tape (this sells for a fortune now to people who mistakenly think it's an early recording with Burgess), the band's only appearance in the national press came when they supported the God-awful Stones-wannabes Broken English in August 1988. They were described as 'standard rock': not even Ketley's literary bent could save them.

Within the band, though, things were changing. Blunt was coming more to the fore, pushing the sound towards that groove-orientated funky soul. Brookes was going with him and getting dancier still (he'd already been off to sample the musical and chemical wares of Ibiza), and Collins was starting to (Jon) lord it over the tracks. Ketley, the songwriter, was no longer quite the force in the band he had been at the start.

'Baz Ketley was a songwriter, first and foremost,' says Harrison. 'He's a nice bloke, but songwriting was what he wanted to do, rather than develop a bigger picture or a style. Martin came from a completely different background – though he'd deny it, the mod thing always had that sense of style. That's where any conflict lay. We worked hard, played the gigs, but it wasn't to be. It wasn't bubbling over, but I think there were frustrations on both sides.'

Ketley saw it differently. He thought the band, including himself, were all picking up on the Manchester groove. The sound was evolving and he was evolving with it. Mind you, when it was mooted that the band go a little more sixties he came up with the classic line, 'If we go any more sixties we'll be fookin' *fifties*, man.' He had a lip on him, that Baz.

But eventually it made no difference. Ketley suffered a personal loss that took him out of the picture. His girlfriend, the soul of much of his writing, left him and relocated to Germany. It was a choker. He couldn't deal with that and the band at the same time, so he bailed out. No hard feelings, just goodbye. He would later reappear in The Hedonics.

A new singer was required. And now, with the music moving towards an up-front collision of funk, dance and psychedelia, they needed a face to suit the times. Not just a songwriter, not just a singer. Now they needed a frontman.

Thoughts turned back to that gig at Northwich Vic in September 1988 when the fresh-faced guy from The Electric Crayons had sung backing vocals with them. What about *that* guy?

The Electric Crayons were on the verge of releasing 'Hip Shake Junkie' and were thought to be on their way. But Burgess remembered well both his early encounters with The Charlatans – with the Roses at the International, and at the Vic. Still does. 'I remember going with Steve to see them with the Roses at International Two,' he says, 'and I remember Martin walking off-stage and saying he really liked my leather jacket. He wanted to buy it off me, basically. I was a legend already! My main memory of that night is Jon Brookes and how he was the most impressive thing I'd ever seen. Steve Harrison asked me what I thought and I said I thought The Charlatans were better than the Roses. Later The Electric Crayons supported The Charlatans at Northwich Victoria. I took my top off and I was being all Iggy, and they thought I was a fucking *dude*, man.'

Again, as with Collins, there would be no overt poaching. The Charlatans knew Burgess was their man and asked Harrison to work his magic. He put up a Vocalist Required sign in Omega and made sure Burgess had a close look. Burgess was a little surprised – he hadn't realised there was a chance of Ketley leaving – but he went along to audition anyway.

'From what I could make out with them at the time,' he says, 'they were happy with their singer but they didn't think he was happy with them. They thought he didn't have any belief in the rest of the group; he thought his material was the way forward. That was the story I got, anyway. I didn't want to get involved in all that. You know: "Oh my God, I'm replacing Baz" – this guy I'd seen, who I'd said hello to.'

At the audition jam, Burgess hurled himself into the tunes, taking the others aback. Well, apart from Collins. With him it was a point of honour to never be taken aback. Blunt recalls his own impression of Tim's enthusiastic performance: 'He was just up for everything; he was everything we could have wanted from anyone.'

From that very first session Burgess felt something special. He left The Electric Crayons forthwith (one of them would later turn up in the superbly named Tomatomatic) and threw himself into what was his first serious venture into music. And now that he was under pressure to be a good singer, he realised that he could actually become one.

As Ketley had doubled as both singer and guitarist, The Charlatans also needed another new member. They knew who they wanted for that position, too. John Baker had been in a garage band called The Violet Slides and, through trying to get them gigs, later became the booker for the Walsall Overstrand. Blunt was a regular there and had asked Baker the year before if he would try out for The Charlatans. Baker wouldn't; he was happy with his present outfit, Liquid Egg Box. When the call came again, this time in 1989, he refused once more, suggesting another guitarist who was available at the time. He was tried out, found wanting, and Baker was asked yet again. This time he said he'd go down to help them out. The first rehearsals went well, and he stayed on.

Harrison wasn't so sure. 'It may seem a little cruel,' he says, 'because John's an incredibly lovely guy, but I think it was felt that it was a coup getting the singer we'd got, so we jumped into finalising the guitarist a little quickly.'

Nevertheless, he was in. And Tim Burgess made five – band complete.

The Charlatans' early days weren't easy ones. They tried to keep hold of a few old songs but Baker couldn't play them easily (Ketley actually went down to help out) and Burgess was finding the old repertoire difficult to perform. They involved someone else's emotions so he struggled to connect, and they were a little too, well, *written* for his liking. His feelings towards the work of singer-songwriters, and the point of their observational narratives, would change drastically over the next three or four years. One of these was a track called 'Hey Teen', which was soon dropped along with the others but would become a very successful T-shirt slogan for the band before the end of the year.

By now the north-west was buzzing. The Stone Roses had just released their debut album (it only reached Number 32, but would keep selling for over a year), they'd sold out the 6,000-capacity Empress Ballroom in Blackpool and the good press they were getting was close to obscene. Happy Mondays had received similar plaudits the year before for *Bummed,* and now had the single 'Lazyitis', remixed by Paul Oakenfold, on turntables across the country. This was a new lack of preciousness towards personal art, in keeping with hip-hop and dance's idea of what was 'fresh'; an idea that kept those genres moving remorselessly onward. It was a genuinely exciting time, which reminded many observers of the creative explosion of punk. Things were hotting up too for Inspiral Carpets.

Harrison was sure The Charlatans were on to something. 'We thought we could have a piece of this,' he says. 'That with our new frontman and the good band we already had, we could really go somewhere.'

The line-up looked strong and the band's enthusiasm seemed justified, but what they needed more than anything were some good songs (many of the best-looking bands simply forget this part). Amazingly, one day very soon after they had begun searching, the songs just turned up. And three at once – like buses, but without the waiting. With Brookes vanished to Ibiza once more, they were down in their rehearsal space in Wednesbury, taping on to a ghetto-blaster, amps arranged with the loudest the furthest away from the machine, when it just *happened.*

'We actually wrote "Indian Rope", "The Only One I Know" and "Sproston Green" all in the same weekend,' says Burgess, 'when Jon Brookes had gone off with his mates to Ibiza. I'd read that John Lennon had tried singing through a biscuit tin, so I drilled a hole in the top and bottom of a tin and put my mike inside, and got this "I Am The Walrus"-type effect. I think it was a shortbread tin.'

This crucial weekend delivered a single to boost the band, a single to break them and a track that would still be a show-stopper a decade later. At last the band had pulled together all their influences and the best of their abilities and hit the contemporary nail dead on the head. The rhythm was merciless, aimed straight at the legs and groin, the vocals were soft, sweetly melodious and exceptionally vulnerable (though belied by the confidence of the lyrics), and as for the keyboards, God, Collins had pulled out all the stops. Suddenly, he was no longer just a texturalist and purveyor of complex solos. It was as if he'd looked back over the history of the Hammond and rediscovered why he chose his particular models. He had become a bona fide riff machine, using the organ like a metal guitar – to *attack*.

Even then, though, Burgess was unsure of quite what they had. He just didn't know if it was brilliant or crap. Or both.

'Three pivotal moments for us in the same day,' he says. 'It proved to us that we had something, that we could do something. We weren't that sure about "The Only One I Know". I remember some mates telling us that it was a top tune, but we weren't convinced till later.

'With "Indian Rope" which was probably the fifth song we ever wrote, I remember being really pleased. I remember saying to Martin, "Do you think this'll be the best song we'll ever write?" and him saying, "No. No way. We can do much better than this." I was really confident in myself, but when we put out "Indian Rope" as our first single, I was a bit worried that we'd put our best song out first.'

Everything had to be right, though. Even with the stylish Blunt and Burgess in place, they needed to look the part too.

'I don't know if the idea was to tailor the group,' says Harrison, 'but the look is integral to any pop group and you have to take care of that. People have got to want to be like the band. And something I tried to instill into the band was that mindset. Like, "Stop thinking about yourself as working for ICI, start thinking about being in this band. Wake up in the morning thinking you're in The Charlatans, go to bed at night thinking you're in The Charlatans." You have to drill it into them, make them feel special. Because they *were* special, they had the charisma, they just needed to feel confident with it all. You know, Tim would have looked good in a paper bag, but you need to dress up, and you need to feel comfortable with dressing up. All bands have to do that, whatever kind of music they play.

'As far as being lumped with the Manchester thing went, well, we'd set ourselves up here in Northwich, I had contacts in Manchester for getting gigs or whatever; we were just reflecting everything that was happening around us. We weren't subscribing to a particular look, just trying to look like a professional band.'

Harrison arranged for some 'proper' photos to be taken, shots that would allow them to be the living-it, breathing-it band he knew they were – or, at least, soon would be. A clothing fund was organised, with money put forward by Harrison and Burgess (they'd be paid back rapidly), because some snappy new duds were called for. The Charlatans needed to put on the Ritz, dress for success, all of that.

But if the idea was to look smart, they blew it badly. Burgess was cherubic, but a right urchin, his tatty black flares folding and scuffing over the cobblestones. He was unshaven, with an untidy growth shadowing his chin, temples and upper lip. It was a rough adolescent sprouting, its distinctly separate hairs dark and glistening with short, fast, vital life like the stubby legs of insects buried upside-down in his skin. His haircut was a strange, double-faceted pudding bowl with a straight fringe and the back cut high, arching wilfully down to his temples. It was a weirdly inventive helmet effect, like Louise Brooks in a hall of mirrors, or Robert Wagner in *Prince Valiant* had James Mason been a tad more accurate in his broadsword assault. It was an intuitively aggressive look, experimentally slovenly, and defiantly anti-adult.

Brookes was street-cool in red kickers, button-up sweatshirt, 24-inch flares and hair grown to shoulder length. Blunt and Baker were smarter in smooth roundnecks, baggy jeans and pristine trainers, with almost mid-parted bobs, the mod feel still in effect (not that different from Ocean Colour Scene today, as it happens).

But it was Collins who was really *out there* in scruffy half-baggies, trainers that seemed to have lived for real the transcendentally hectic first twenty minutes of *Saving Private Ryan* and a psychedelic sweatshirt slashed with wild pinks, purples and yellows. Then there was the short, tight hussar-style jacket. Convincingly odd, engaging but a little dangerous, he had you thinking of those welcoming automaton dolls in *Blade Runner*.

Collins' expression was effective, too – he could really turn it on when he felt like it. He'd turn away, head down, cigarette cupped and hidden within curled fingers in that classic surreptitious smoker's pose from old war films or prison dramas. Either that or he'd stare to camera, challenging and curious, eyes wide and inno-cent, lips slightly parted, like a pretty, partially self-aware pre-pubescent taunting some dirty, desirous old man.

Blunt had that boyish, slightly scornful Small Faces look. And Burgess – well, Burgess clearly couldn't stand still long enough for all this. There he was, messing about, mischievously chuckling with arms outstretched, less a hoary Jesus Christ rocker than a playfully buzzing Cessna. He gazed dreamily into the middle dis-tance as if thoughts of pin-up status were present but flitting quickly across an easily distracted mind.

To those outside Manchester, who weren't acquainted with the togs that went with the scene (many of them introduced by Cressa, a sartorial law unto himself, who was a clubland hero and occa-sional dancer for the Roses – Charlatans guitarist Mark Collins says that being passed by him on the street was like having an Elizabethan galleon scud by at full sail), The Charlatans looked really odd. Their style was annoying in its deliberate perversity, intimidating in its exclusivity. But this was what was being worn. Roundnecks for sixties garage, flares for the psychedelic edge, Parkas for mod, name trainers for hip-hop and hooded tops for sheer shadiness. It all made sense when you thought about the music at the same time.

So now The Charlatans really were go. Gigs were arranged at the Overstrand in Walsall, Winnington Rec in Northwich and JB's in Dudley. The band and their manager went into overdrive. Everything, absolutely everything, must be right. These shows were to be more than gigs, they were to be *events* (the Roses were now doing something similar but on a much larger scale). Harrison – or the Transworld Consortium – suffocated Northwich with posters. Everyone was alerted that something was about to come alive.

In particular, deep thought was put into the band's stage show. There would be projectors loaded with stills from *A Clockwork Orange* (still notorious, and little seen since Stanley Kubrick withdrew it in the early seventies), psychedelic lighting and, best of all, oil lamp projections, sending coloured blobs across the halls. These would prove so popular that, by July the next year, Liquid Wheels Lightshow Projectors would be advertised all over. The band also employed moiré effects: those shifting wavy patterns seen when two surfaces covered with regular lines are superimposed.

These gigs were to be termed 'happenings'. The Charlatans' DJs would be known as The Groovey Sound System. People would be encouraged to come in and stay – for good. Fans would be looked after, picked up and transported around. The band knew they needed a grassroots following fast, and intended to deserve one. The first few gigs were great; really encouraging.

Now they had to get the record together.

There was £3,000 available for recording, pressing, printing and distribution. It needed to be done on the cheap and produced by someone inexpensive. Chris Nagle, the house engineer at Strawberry Studios, Stockport, was their man, offering his services and the graveyard slot at the studio. Nagle was a veteran of those classic Joy Division sessions, having been producer Martin Hannett's engineer.

Burgess was blown away by the prospect. 'Things were such a buzz then,' he recalls, developing the point with his trademark enthusiasm. 'I know it doesn't sound like much now, but then it was like, "Chris Nagle! Joy Division! Fucking New Order! Let's *have* it!"'

'Indian Rope' was cut in one night's session, between midnight on Sunday and 8 a.m. on Monday morning, and mixed the next night. It all happened in a bit of a panic – Burgess had only 30 minutes to lay down the vocals – but, for the most part, it worked. Burgess claims some of the edge was lost through Nagle's insistence on using a click for timing (probably fair enough – this was hardly an act experienced in studio work), but he wasn't displeased with the result. 'Looking back now,' he says, 'it seems a bit twee, but live it was brilliant.'

An instrumental version of 'Indian Rope' was also recorded and mixed, but never released.

To keep the costs down further, when the single was released, at the beginning of 1990, the sleeve would be artwork by Kim Peters, a fan of the band. Peters would go on to shoot many of their videos. This also helped to keep everything in-house and among friends, something they would try – and often, for assorted reasons, fail – to achieve over the years. The Charlatans were already revealing a fiercely independent spirit.

Now it was all happening at once. The north-west was so hot and The Charlatans' gigs so successful, with such ecstatic reactions to their new material, that it was hard to keep tabs on it all. They bulldozed past a schizophrenic review in the *Manchester Evening News* that said their demo tape (containing 'Indian Rope', 'White Shirt' and 'You Can Talk To Me') was 'more Georgie Fame than Inspiral Carpets' and accused them of stealing 'White Shirt''s bassline from the Roses' 'She Bangs The Drums', yet still ended by urging the readers to see them live. The demo would be briefly sold at gigs for a very reasonable £2 a throw.

Harrison sent out promo packs, including tapes, photos and a thoroughly bizarre staccato cut-up press release, to anyone and everyone who might be remotely interested. There were no takers. Though The Stone Roses, Happy Mondays and Inspirals were now press darlings, this was not a London scene and so labels, for another couple of months at least, remained wary.

But The Charlatans couldn't wait for London to catch up. They felt their momentum was such that they had to make something happen, something *special*. So Harrison started his own label, Dead Dead Good, to put out 'Indian Rope'. It was intended to be a label just for The Charlatans, to make them look like they were in total control of their own destiny, not kowtowing to the majors or anyone else. Dead Dead Good was meant to be a brand name for Charlatans products (an echo of the mysterious Transworld Consortium) and synonymous with them, a guarantee of absolute quality. It was not intended to be like The Beatles' Apple imprint, or Led Zeppelin's Swan Song. Later, however, there would be other releases on the label, much to the chagrin of the band, who felt the fans would consider them in some way to be endorsing the acts involved.

For now, Dead Dead Good was theirs and theirs alone, and the label's name became a hit T-shirt slogan for them too (there would be smart and well-made sweatshirts, too). T-shirts were big news in Manchester at this time: James, and Inspiral Carpets with their 'Cool As Fuck' and cow logos, were making a mint (in fact, James would have gone under without their merchandising revenue). The Charlatans knew this and developed a few lines: 'Hey Teen' was one logo, then 'Dead Dead Good' and 'Looking For The Orange One', the last being a line from a new song, 'Polar Bear'. This was taken by some to be a reference to some kind of pill, though Burgess claimed he was using a greedy search through a packet of Revels as a metaphor for living with righteous ambition (it would also very soon be the name of the first major Charlatans fanzine).

The band shirts were soon selling merrily alongside Guns N'Roses' *Appetite For Destruction* and the many hilariously tasteless designs generated by *Viz*. There were six different Charlatans designs. And this, remember, before The Charlatans even had a record in the shops. Harrison had been proved correct – people wanted to buy into the music *and* the look.

It all seemed so easy, but you needed to be careful. Before very long, Inspiral Carpets would forget themselves, take sponsorship from Joe Bloggs and, having to wear all their gear all the time, be caught looking naff, undignified and far from independent, especially when Joe Bloggs blithely stated that they were to clothes what McDonald's were to food. Not very cool, that. Along with their appearances on children's TV, it would be the end of the Inspirals.

It was at the end of November 1989 that the Manchester bubble began to expand to outrageous proportions. Anyone could join in with these 24-hour party people, enjoy euphoria despite the fear of unemployment and the scorn of an uncaring government. The Stone Roses and Happy Mondays appeared on the same edition of *Top of the Pops*. The Roses' double A-side 'Fool's Gold/What The World Is Waiting For' reached Number 8 in the charts while the Mondays' 'Madchester Rave On' EP, officially giving another name (beyond 'baggy') to this north-western phenomenon, entered the Top Twenty too.

By the beginning of 1990, that classic debut album, *The Stone Roses* would be tearing from the racks. March would see the Roses playing to an elated and reverential crowd of 30,000 at Spike Island, near Widnes. They would go from a modest headliner at the tiny Camden Dingwalls to hosting their own party at Alexandra Palace in a matter of months. So very quickly they would change the dress sense, the dance styles and even partially the language of hundreds of thousands. In its effect this was very rare, in its sheer speed it was almost unprecedented.

Of course, it would all go wrong. There would be drug trouble in Manchester, with God's cop, James Anderton, attempting to close the Hacienda. The Roses would be fatally held up by injunctions as they left Silvertone for Geffen, and when they were sued after sacking Gareth Evans. After that they would be paralysed by the weight of expectation, and disappointed in their arrogant assumption that America would dutifully fall at their feet. The Mondays would be torn by internal strife and pulled down by drugs, then rise again, only to fall harder. But at the end of 1989 the image of Ian Brown sauntering across the stage, bell in hand, was the very picture of cool.

The Charlatans were coming through too. At a gig on 15 November they supported Cactus World News at Manchester Boardwalk. Two hundred and fifty people had watched The Charlatans; only twenty-five remained when the headliners took the stage. (Aside from one terrible occasion, The Charlatans would never support anyone again.)

Well versed in the history of rock, the band were also on the ball with the newest beats and used to this mixing and remixing lark: Burgess's beloved New Order, for example, had their 'Confusion' remixed by Arthur Baker, who had earlier worked on the seminal 'Planet Rock' with Afrika Bambaataa. It seemed certain that they would be next to ascend; that they would grab a piece of the action while the Roses and the Mondays were limbering up for Wembley Stadium.

But for now, questions had to be asked; hard questions. The five

Charlatans were being required to give themselves wholeheartedly to the cause. Should they give up their jobs or not? Burgess was so convinced it was going to happen that he was gone from ICI like a shot. Collins had bigger responsibilities, having got married that year. Brookes asked, 'Steve, is this gonna happen or what? Should I pack my job in? Because I'm sick of making excuses.' He was told to hold on, just in case it was slower than predicted. As it turned out, Brookes would hold his job for only a few more weeks.

On Friday 15 December the band played a big home town gig (Burgess's home town, anyway) at Northwich's Winnington Rec. Entry was £3 only. This place had once served as a social club for ICI, with its bowls, hockey and Subbuteo football (with a green strip for Northwich Victoria and red and white for Witton Albion). Before the gig, the Fifth Dimension's 'The Age Of Aquarius' was blared out, setting the scene for that endearing but none the less effective DIY light show. The fans (even here, at only the band's sixth show, they were already *fans*) near rioted. They loved The Charlatans. The band talked to them and made themselves available. They looked after them and clearly cared what they thought. They might be part of a bigger scene, but this band was theirs.

Throughout the show, all the visual techniques were employed: the oil lamp projections, the wandering blobs of colour, the infamous and slightly sick stills. With this swirling, pumping music, this band that no one else had seen, these pretty, crazy lights and (for some) these fabulous drugs, the Winnington Rec became a magical tabernacle containing everything you could ever want from a band. For years, the people in the audience would follow them anywhere.

In the last week of 1989, the national tabloid press would tip The Charlatans as Those Most Likely To in 1990 – along with the Inspirals, Social Kaos, Hollow Sunday (who made up dances to go with their songs) and Stop Laughing (a Steely Dan-style two-piece provided with a cellar studio by London Records and given a year to 'get on with it').

Seldom has a prediction been so speedily and magnificently proved accurate.

In the second week of January, 1990, 'Indian Rope' appeared in the Turn On staff favourite list in the *New Musical Express*, alongside releases by Ride, Carter USM and The Sundays. There was now plenty of press coverage for Manchester bands, or bands deemed to be part of the Madchester scene. The list of bands being name checked was vast. There were Ruthless Rap Assassins (with rapper Kermit, later of Black Grape), Yargo, Social Kaos, Paris Angels, Northside, The Bodines (still), A Guy Called Gerald, Dirty Tryx, Johnny Dangerously, Krispy 3, Rig, Asia Fields, The Bedflowers, Technosis, First Offence, Tunnel Frenzies, The Loft (as in 'Fuck off, we're The Loft!'), Mirrors Over Kiev, DRRB featuring Lavorne... even A Certain Ratio were enjoying a renaissance. Of course, there were The Fall and Bernard Albrecht's Electronic. But The Charlatans had leapfrogged them all and very soon would replace Inspirals Carpets in the baggy triumvirate.

Steve Harrison had realised the importance of a tour. The band needed to be out in people's faces. Gigs were hastily arranged, a great many considering promoters only knew of the band by a very vague word of mouth. At Stoke-On-Trent Wheatsheaf on 10 January (the first night of a stop-start tour), the band had two coaches full of fans turn up, one from Northwich, one from Manchester. Harrison had spoken to the promoter and arranged for coach passengers to be allowed into the gig at half-price. On arrival, this agreement seemed to have been conveniently forgotten about, but Harrison raged until it was reinstated, and he did the same when the band were denied their promised hot food. They refused to take the stage until supplied with fish, chips and peas. They didn't want it, or eat it, but there was a principle at stake here.

At the Aldershot Buzz Club, three nights later, Harrison nabbed the band's first bootlegger. The guy said the tape was just for his own personal use: even so, recordings from this tour would be advertised for sale in the music press within weeks.

The impressive showing in that *NME* Turn On chart was immediately superseded by 'Indian Rope's entry into the Independent Charts at Number 13. Remorselessly it climbed to Number 1, beating off challenges from current indie superstars Ride, Birdland

and The Telescopes, plus Depeche Mode, Renegade Soundwave and Silverfish's caustic anthem 'Total Fucking Asshole'. Despite the band's confidence in 'Indian Rope', no one had expected recognition to come *this* fast.

Harrison, in particular, was taken by surprise. In forming Dead Dead Good to release the single, he'd signed The Charlatans for three singles and an album. This was partly for the sake of form, and also to up the stakes for any other labels interested. There was a gentleman's agreement between them that, should any label come up with an adequate offer, he would allow the band to renege on their deal with Dead Dead Good.

As label boss, though, he was responsible for funding 'Indian Rope' – for its distribution and manufacturing – and now the copies he'd had printed up had sold out. More were needed, that was imperative, but he didn't have the cash. He brought his sister in on the deal – and put his own house up against the value of his expanding overdraft. Still the single kept selling, till the house was no longer worth enough to cover the debt. Were it not for an unusually funky bank manager who accepted Harrison's guarantee that money would be forthcoming within six months (it takes that long to get a sales statement through), Harrison would have gone under. And if that *had* happened, it would have been down to simple ignorance: Harrison had listened closely to Gareth Evans but was still very green.

'It didn't occur to me to ask the distributors if they'd press them for me,' he admits, a decade later. 'I didn't know it worked like that.'

On 27 January The Charlatans hit London, playing the Powerhaus in Islington. This was the big one. Though only the band's twelfth show, they would have to be impressive far beyond their experience. Everything was set in place to make it work: all those vital peripherals. The Orb would DJ, Alex Patterson contributing his own super-hip take on Pink Floyd-style psychedelics. The crowd was organised too. This time, for this special show, there would be four coaches – two from Northwich, one from Manchester and one from Wolverhampton, Brookes' and Blunt's neck of the woods – a total of 150 hardcore Charlatans fiends.

The Charlatans

The industry buzz was doing its job. A host of music business insiders descended on the place, keen to know what they'd been missing and even more keen to be able to say with authority that they knew what this Madchester thing was all about. It's always exciting for prospective financiers to see a band with an already established following. It makes their job so much easier; can even make up their mind for them. But this was on a completely different level. All those sweaty kids in baggy jeans and flares, their purposefully chosen T-shirts hanging loose over their backsides. The laughter, the togetherness, the hum of the place, the loud and raucous chant of 'Manchester, la-la-la!' Something was clearly going off here.

The reviews were tremendous. The *NME*, still the untouchable bestseller of the weekly music press, said, 'The five mop-tops played their teenage psycho-delia with passion and confidence.' They praised The Charlatans' energised version of acid rock, calling it 'clear drug music minus the narcissism or drudgery'.

'Indian Rope' seemed unstoppable. It couldn't, just couldn't, be this easy... and it wasn't. In his column in the *Manchester Evening News*, Terry Christian said of the single that he found it derivative of The Stone Roses and Inspiral Carpets, no doubt due to the soft vocals, up-front melodics and the very presence of a Hammond. This was a little unfair. Though there were similarities in style and instrumentation, compared to the Roses, The Charlatans were much more a rush of colours and images, and Blunt's Prisoners influence, allied with his penchant for funk, set the band apart from the standard baggy shuffle. As for the organ, next to Rob Collins' shrieking monster the Inspirals sounded like they'd obtained their Hammond with one of those little crane-claws at a funfair.

Terry Christian also warned the band to expect trouble from the south: he knew they would not receive a favourable reaction from a jealous music press that had already grudgingly gone for the Roses and the Mondays. In some respects he was right. The backlash against The Charlatans would begin within days of their debut release. And the criticisms were unanimous: the band were a pale imitation of The Stone Roses. No one really went into detail: it was just understood that The Charlatans were former no-hopers who'd leapt voraciously upon the Madchester bandwagon. There was no soul here, everything about them was a sham. They were simply filling a gap while the big boys were away. They were The Stone Roses' *Favourite Support Band*, for God's sake.

Blunt's background was not investigated. Baker's psychedelic garage credentials were not checked out. The ambition of Brookes and Collins to become rock behemoths went unmentioned. It was Burgess who was latched on to and held up to ridicule. He looked and danced like Ian Brown, he moved and talked like Ian Brown, he sang, pouted and sneered like Ian Brown. Ian Brown. Ian Brown. Ian Brown. Even for the disinterested, the one-point sniping became dull to read.

'We very quickly started getting stick from critics for being like the Roses,' says Burgess. 'They were saying that we really *were* charlatans. But we kept at it. It used to really wind me up, but Martin was always so solid about it.'

It was true that Burgess had seen The Stone Roses, but so had everybody else in Manchester. Ian Brown's beatific gaze and cocksure swagger seemed to be replicated everywhere. That was another thing about the apparent power of The Stone Roses – they even seemed to have changed the way people *walked*. But Brown hadn't invented the attitude or the posture. That was a Manchester thing. Mancs always seemed to be cocky: that's why the rest of the country so revelled in Manchester United not having won the League in 25 years. It was an inner city thing, a northern pose, to do with working-class pride and bravado. Brown was a product of his surroundings, just as Burgess was now.

It's undeniably true that Burgess walked the baggy walk. But, young and impressionable, with a natural and mostly subconscious desire to fit in, he hadn't got it from Brown, he'd got it from everyone else. That's peer pressure, that is. It's a bastard. This meant that the attacks on Burgess were not simply personal; he was the major scapegoat as people began to set upon anyone from the Madchester scene who wasn't a member of the two 'grudgingly' accepted forerunners.

Beyond this, there was the elitist idea in the music press that the Madchester phenomenon, now sweeping the nation, was the revenge of 'ordinary' against the sophisticated artistry of present-day pop.

These bands were simply yobs with no purpose but to drag you down to their grimy level. They needed to be sent packing back to their estates and northern terraces as soon as possible.

The Charlatans did their best to answer the critics and distance themselves from a scene they knew would, inevitably, come crashing down as suddenly as it had sprung up. They weren't from Manchester, they said, they were from Northwich, Wolverhampton and Crewe (true, though their connections with Manchester were stronger than those of most). They pointed to a set of influences radically different from the ones attributed to them – the *Nuggets* compilations, The Prisoners, Thee Milkshakes, The Small Faces and *Piper At The Gates Of Dawn*. All true, just as it was true that Burgess sang softly because he was too nervous to do otherwise: he'd only been singing 'properly' for six months. 'It wasn't about flares,' the band would say later. 'It was about *having flair*.'

'We're not trying to jump on any bandwagon,' said Burgess to the press at the time. 'We're just trying to do what The Charlatans have been doing for the last eighteen months, but we're getting it right now.'

He also revealed a silly, surreal side to his nature (as if singing about Revels was not enough) by lauding his band in the most preposterous terms. 'The Charlatans are the most danceable band in the universe,' he opined, bizarrely. 'Even sheep can dance to us.'

Though they appeared to be unfazed, the accusation of being real-life charlatans cut the band deeply. Blunt had now spent years struggling to make soulful music and, in attempting to emulate their musical heroes, the others felt exactly the same way. They had just begun a long journey towards self-discovery, the place where a group soul is found, and while these jibes were motivating – they gave the band more to prove than anyone else – it was clear already that it wasn't going to be easy.

Nevertheless, things were good for now. 'Indian Rope' was still selling, a fanzine dedicated solely to the band had been started (*Looking For the Orange One*) and audiences at their shows were clearly paying no heed whatsoever to press criticism. Gigs were sold out and chaotic. Rob Collins' Hammond, despite being a heavyweight sod to move, was having to be welded to its stand as stage invaders threatened to pull it into the crowd. At St Helen's Citadel, on 10 February – still in Burgess's top three gigs as this was where he first realised the band really *meant* something to those present – fans were swarming in through the fire escapes. At Birmingham Burberries, Burgess swept condensation from the ceiling on to the gasping, heaving throng. With all gigs prefaced with 'Age Of Aquarius' and 'Across The Universe', many were attended by news film-crews, usually asking fans to 'do something laddish' for the camera. You know, Manchester-like. A month after release (a point when most singles are on their way out), 'Indian Rope' actually made it into the national Top 100.

Now even The Charlatans, notoriously hard to convince of anything, recognised this as a bona fide phenomenon.

'None of the people who usually confirm that you're doing something right were telling us anything,' says Harrison. 'It was only when "Indian Rope" went into the chart and it got radio play and we were being asked to do interviews that we suspected anything. It was only when we played London, the Powerhaus, that it all went barmy. Then everyone was coming up the motorway, to the shop or to Wednesbury, offering us everything.

'I vividly remember the first time we made a profit on a gig. It was in Southampton [Joiners Arms, 8 February]. We had enough money to buy three curries to share between the six of us.'

After the Powerhaus gig, representatives of the Beggars Banquet label had asked for a meeting the next day and put The Charlatans up in the fairly swanky Ryan Hotel. Harrison pretended he was taking the band to a guest house, made out like he couldn't find it then, parked in front of the Ryan, declared, 'Oh, *this'll* have to do.' The band were elated, the restaurant in particular being a joyously otherwordly experience for chaps more used to slouching around in ropey cafes and pumping coagulated ketchup out of red plastic tomatoes (although this excitement wouldn't last – The Charlatans have never really been into the flash wining-and-dining side of the process).

With all these A&R types buzzing about (Phonogram, Island, pretty much the lot), offers to The Charlatans were rising all the time. The top money on the table was half a million from

Polygram. Their chairman, Maurice Oberstein, offered to fly up to Manchester or fly Harrison down.

'I suppose in some ways I couldn't relate to all that money,' says Harrison, 'but eventually it didn't matter anyway. The lads were really motivated and working hard. They had the next single and pretty much enough material for the first LP. They weren't thinking about anything else.'

All potential deals would go through Harrison first. 'Call it a vetting process, if you like,' he says, 'but it's always been this way. The band, and especially Tim, are very uncomfortable meeting with record companies, in the big-sell environment.'

The big sell was coming. It was now just a question of *how* big.

02 From Beggars Banquet To Dog's Dinner

FOR A BAND AS bloody-mindedly independent as The Charlatans, signing to Beggars Banquet made a great deal of sense. Formed by Martin Mills and Nick Austin in 1974, Beggars Banquet had begun life as a funky little record store in London's Earl's Court (today a fully fledged Australian colony). By the time punk broke, Mills had expanded his horizons, taking on the management of The Lurkers, a rough gang of none-too-serious roustabouts best known for their buffoonish anthem 'I'm On Heat'. Naturally, no major label would touch them. The Sex Pistols' rucks with A&M and EMI had shown punks to be a dodgy option and, besides, The Lurkers were considered to be resolutely second division. This didn't stop the resourceful Mills who, taking the name of his shop, started up his own label, just as The Charlatans and Omega boss Harrison would do a decade later.

Success came quickly for Beggars Banquet. Though The Lurkers predictably proved themselves to be half-arsed no-hopers, Mills was fortunate enough to sign up Gary Numan's Kraftwerk-inspired Tubeway Army, setting the new label on its way with the Number 1 hits 'Are Friends Electric?' and 'Cars'. Soon the label offshoots 4AD and Situation Two were set up, and premises found in Alma Road, Wandsworth, South London, deliberately distanced from the swanky West End bases of the majors. Distribution was performed by the indier-than-thou Rough Trade, till it miserably folded, then the Vital/RTM alliance. The coffers were kept filled by Bauhaus, The Icicle Works, the flamboyant, purposefully sophisticated Associates and, most importantly, The Cult. Having advanced from vaguely tribal, heavily melodic goth beginnings to the clipped Rick Rubin-inspired mega-rock of *Electric* and *Sonic*

Temple, by 1990 The Cult were a very big deal indeed. A very silly deal, certainly, but a big one nonetheless.

The thoroughly contemporary Charlatans were of course no respecters of The Cult, finding their rock posing laughable and bridling at Ian Astbury's sanctimonious rants about the plight of Native Americans (in that affair, history should be kind to poor Astbury – a little over-earnest perhaps, but his only real mistake was misjudging the placement of his soapbox by 5,000 miles). In fact, when asked these days why they signed to Beggars, Tim Burgess will suddenly revert to his monstrously self-glorifying 1990 persona, claiming unkindly that The Charlatans wished to be an unquestioned priority, the only 'important' band on what would otherwise be the 'naffest label in the country'.

If Burgess's flip pronouncements are to be taken seriously, then The Charlatans' choice of stable was extremely foolhardy: it wasn't as if there was no room at the inn. But there were more practical reasons for choosing Beggars Banquet. For a start, as a supplier Beggars had always been unusually straight up in their dealings with Harrison's Omega outlets. They had also, with The Cult, proven themselves capable of breaking and maintaining a sizeable act.

Beyond this, Martin Mills seemed to have a firm grasp of the meaning of independence and the spirit and principles of the diehard indie band. One of punk's few notable legacies was to give young bands and wannabe industry entrepreneurs a sense of self-reliance. It was truly believed that anyone could do it: form a band, start a label, storm the charts, *go!* In 1990, a host of vital and inventive British bands were combining with their American counterparts to make the UK indie charts seem gratifyingly challenging. There were Primal Scream, My Bloody Valentine, Pixies, Dinosaur Jr, Throwing Muses, Butthole Surfers, Sonic Youth and Big Black, plus the spiky likes of The Sugarcubes, Front 242 and The Young Gods from the European mainland. Really, The Charlatans needed to look no further than their own Mancunian backyard. Aside from the socially crucial Hacienda, Factory Records had brought them Joy Division, New Order and now Happy Mondays.

The Charlatans figured the soft southern majors hadn't cottoned on to Manchester, so fuck 'em. This was about class, northern working men's pride. Where the Pistols had aimed for EMI, The Clash for CBS and Siouxsie And The Banshees for Polydor (all of them either suckers, art school ponces, or both), the Roses were on FM Revolver, then Silvertone, the Inspirals on Playtime then Mute, The Bodines on Creation. For The Charlatans, the indie runway was brightly lit. Beggars looked good.

Even the label's name – Beggars Banquet – seemed a good omen. With the *Their Satanic Majesties Request* album, the Rolling Stones had attempted to match the surreal innovations of The Beatles' *Sgt Pepper* but so awful was the result (Christ, there's even a song written by Bill Wyman) that they were accused of simply being sorry-arsed bandwagon-jumpers. Like The Charlatans, in fact. The *Beggars Banquet* album was the Stones battling back. They'd been publicly rubbished, they'd even been jailed, but *Beggars Banquet* was infused with the revolutionary spirit of 1968.

Now building up towards the tragedy of Altamont, the Stones at last had the devil in them. 'Street Fighting Man' was the theme tune for student riots in Paris and right across Europe and the USA. And then there was 'Sympathy For The Devil', not simply an undeniable classic but also a track habitually played at outdoor raves to herald the breaking of the dawn, its clattering percussion acting as the death rattle of the night. It was very dark, very deep and very, very *now*. It was *the Stones*, for God's sake, a band so passionate, so powerful they could take any musical style under the sun – blues, R&B, soul, pop, reggae, disco, swamp rock, voodoo shit, anything – and make it absolutely their own. A 'proper' band, built to last. *And* there was the *Beggars Banquet* sleeve – the outrageously flash duds, that sickeningly decadent party. *That* might be nice.

Yes, Beggars Banquet was a major buzz-phrase for a band already much concerned with their place in rock's pantheon. It would also become an ever more appropriate stamp as the band's sound progressively veered towards countrified rock 'n' roll.

Even at this very early stage, The Charlatans were hugely concerned with maintaining control; *creative control* – the very essence of the pro-indie argument. For Blunt, whose wounds from

Makin' Time, The Gift Horses and the pre-Burgess Charlatans were still raw, the prospect of further failure was hellish. To blow it now, with Madchester at full pelt, with 'Indian Rope' kicking up a storm and the world and his mother scrapping to get on The Charlatans' guest list, would be unthinkable. And to blow it because of the foolish, thoughtless, power-crazed demands of an interfering record company would be a catastrophe from which he would surely never recover. The rest, including Harrison, were increasingly full of themselves. They put the burgeoning success of 'Indian Rope' completely down to an unholy talent and the impossible precision of their planning and execution. In short, *they would not be told*.

As an obvious fan of music, a record seller and a manager, Martin Mills seemed sensitive to the needs of his artistes. His CV also declared him to be a professional bloody-minded Indie-Head. A deal with Beggars would allow for reasonable negotiation and hand the band powers of veto. Nothing would be released without their say-so. They would dutifully, even gratefully, listen to the company's advice, yet be coerced into nothing. The relationship would be one of pragmatic, forward-looking inter-reliance: a Thing Of Beauty.

Mills scored immeasurable brownie points with the band when they played a gig at Manchester University on 17 May 1990. This show was to be the first triumphant homecoming, a blow-out party guaranteed to have the eyes bugging, the pores pumping and the kidneys screaming for mercy. The A&R turnout was expected to be obscene. But the weather that day was atrocious, grim even by the elevated standards of the north. Conditions were dreadful on the M4; on the M6 downright dangerous. No one from London made it – except for Martin Mills who impressed the band by labouring through the abysmal conditions. This may sound like an air-headed, irresponsible way of making life-changing decisions but with The Charlatans it's *always personal*. Mills had got there when no one else had, revealing the vital qualities of persistence, respect and nerve. He'd probably never make it into the Charlatans gang but he'd shown the loyalty required of an affiliate member.

It also made him look great beside his competitors, especially after Harrison had called EMI to ask if they were going to see the band, only to have them reply that they'd seen them in Aylesbury the night before and 'they were really average'. That would be quite hurtful under normal circumstances but two nights previously there had been an enormous fight at that venue and The Charlatans' show had been cancelled due to the owners having to refurbish the place.

Oh, and then there was The Fall. The Fall were on Beggars Banquet and, starting with the scintillating *This Nation's Saving Grace*, were on an incredible run of form. Burgess had secret plans to raid the Beggars basement and liberate all those top twelve-inches. As ever, *having it*. The Beggars deal was signed at the band's rehearsal space in Wednesbury. As label boss, Harrison would not enforce the three singles/one album deal the band had signed with Dead Dead Good, though the label's logo would appear on their records for a while (alongside Beggars' Situation Two stamp) to keep up the brand profile and also make the band seem double-indie. The Charlatans would have the control they had demanded and were so convinced they could properly use.

It's clear in hindsight that the band were being utterly naive and wholly unrealistic. For the most part, independent labels stick their oar into the creative process just as much as the majors – maybe more, as their relative lack of funds mean one serious misjudgement can bring them to the edge of extinction. It's well documented how close My Bloody Valentine's epic studio costs came to bankrupting Creation Records. On top of this, The Charlatans' much-vaunted democracy brought its own problems. With each member buzzing with ideas as well as carrying a veto on decisions, they would often find themselves in utter stasis or, worse, aiming both barrels at their long-suffering feet. Before too long, when it came to matters like concepts for videos, they would occasionally become so embroiled in the endless possibilities that they'd eventually hand the reins over to the label, just to get something, *anything*, done.

'Everything that we've done – videos, album sleeves, records, producers, posters, venues, support groups – everything has been what we've chosen or what we've wanted,' says Burgess, 'and the danger is sometimes it becomes bigger than the music. Even the manager always asks what we want to do. So this total control thing – I sometimes think I'd advise everyone just to be exploited, completely! Don't have any control at all!'

A video was needed for the next single, 'The Only One I Know', to be released through the Beggars subsidiary imprint Situation Two. The band decided to replicate a Charlatans gig, lights and blobs and all, in a Sandbach warehouse owned by a long-standing friend of Harrison's. Kim Peters, who'd done the artwork for the 'Indian Rope' sleeve, would be in charge of the shoot.

The band prepared during the day, setting up the equipment (not that there was too much of that), then at night let loose. A big gang of friends and fans had been invited to play the crowd. They were naturals. The band had a ball, joking and larking about with no one to impress and the pressure off.

Before long, inevitably, the police showed up. They'd received a call informing them there was a rave going on in the warehouse. This was highly feasible, as Sandbach services were a well-known meeting place for kids looking for all-night outdoor parties. As the cops pulled up, they thought that was exactly what was going on. Music was booming and gaudy lights were shooting up into the sky: the only difference was that this time the ravers had what looked like £1m worth of Carling Black Label to keep them going.

It took a while to persuade the police otherwise. Look closely at the video and you can see the bemusement on their faces.

This wasn't the only police activity inspired by the band around this time. The residents of the hamlet of Sproston, 250 yards from Junction 18 of the M6, had awoken to discover that the sign marking Sproston Green Lane had disappeared. Twice. After that, locals decided not to bother replacing it. It was thought that Charlatans fans were involved, sneaking in from all over the country to purloin a memento of their track 'Sproston Green'. It later transpired that the crimes were actually perpetrated by the same guy, who'd slipped down there under cover of darkness with a mate and a small power-drill. He was later tracked down by the band's official *109* fanzine.

The place has since become another stop on The Charlatans' pilgrimage – one poor fellow who stood around for too long taking pictures of the surrounding fields (there's not much else there) was followed home by the police and accused of being the horse molester who'd recently been terrorising the local equine inhabitants.

On went the tour, now in a mini-bus and Harrison's car (the white Bedford having long since passed away) and with it the relentless rush of new success. The Charlatans returned to London, this time to the Boston Arms in Tufnell Park, in the north of the city. More coaches were organised but, where the fans bussed to the Powerhaus show had been a vital tool to help give the impression of a buzz around the band, the only motivation this time was a great party. A recurring motif in the band's career was to be the trips to see them in Europe and America, organised by Hit By Hit Travel and Harrison's Omega outlets in Northwich, Altrincham, Crewe, Wigan and Macclesfield (Omega was then the largest independent record chain in the north of England). This was partly because the extra volume and bonhomie these fans provided made the atmosphere more conducive to a storming set, but it was also to do with Blunt's treasured memories of those scooter runs to the seaside. He had loved those excursions, and felt everyone should have the chance to experience something like that.

This time there were three coaches, one each from Northwich, Manchester and Wolverhampton.

'We're getting all the coaches to meet up at Watford Gap services,' said Burgess. 'The fans all get on together and that's quite fresh, quite nice, because there are too many partisan Manchester people already following bands. We're bridging that gap.'

It seemed like big things were in store for The Charlatans. They were certainly now too popular to play the likes of Winnington Rec, so they decided to leave their old life with grace. On 26 April, they played a secret thank you gig at Manchester International, a benefit for Piccadilly Records who'd been helpful in pushing their records and T-shirts during those long, hard, er, weeks. There was no support, just DJ Philippa playing a suitably eclectic mix of Soho, Hendrix and Augustus Pablo.

On 4 May, it was back to Northwich, the place where, in so many respects, it had all begun. They couldn't play the Vic, that was obvious: the fatalities would be horrific. So, at the Memorial Hall, they said their thank-yous and goodbyes and played their last Northwich gig. It had gone too far now. There was no turning back.

At this point it's worth noting that a few rules had been laid down. Two, to be precise, The Charlatans (with the exception of Blunt) not being ones to overburden themselves or limit their freedom. The first rule came from Blunt himself, the one with the experience in these matters. He decreed that the band could say what they liked to each other. They could take the piss, have a laugh at each other's expense, even row until the cows came home, but they must never *ever* argue about money. He knew from bitter experience that such rows could break up the closest friendships – and this thing they had was way too precious to take that risk.

The other golden rule was that there was to be no piss-taking in the studio. None of them, not even Blunt, were so brilliant that they wouldn't make mistakes, and it wouldn't help the band's cause if fragile confidence was further damaged by careless remarks. Furthermore, if members were ever put down for coming up with stupid ideas they might clam up, think twice about saying anything the next time, and consequently all their good ideas would be lost too. They could never have enough good ideas: they all needed to be protected.

One further stipulation was discussed with Beggars Banquet right at the start. There was to be no abuse of formatting. Obviously, some Charlatans fans preferred CDs, some twelve-inches, some cassettes. Some diehard indie kids still wanted seven-inches (The Charlatans amongst them). But they should never have to buy more than one version of any given single, just because the band had put different B-sides on each. That was a sneaky trick, and many of their loyal followers were either poor or on the dole. They needed to be protected too. This was a big deal for The Charlatans. They were convinced that if they were good to people, then people would be good to them. You shouldn't mess with that – karma comedians got their comeuppance in the end.

So far they had been proved correct in this. 'Indian Rope' had sold upward of 15,000 copies, much to the delight of Harrison's hip shake bank manager. That more than made up for the increasing number of disrespectful comments about them in the music press. Actually, some were quite funny. Burgess in particular got a big kick out of being in 'the appalling Charlatans'.

When the band's second single, 'The Only One I Know', was released in the second week of May, they began to get the creeping suspicion that all their worries might soon be over. It was backed by 'Everything Changed' and a surprisingly tasteful instrumental called 'Imperial 109'. (This was the track from which the official fanzine took its name. Paid for by The Charlatans, it usually includes exclusive and often revealing interviews with the band by its writer and organiser, John McGee. Now well past its twentieth issue, it has never cost its readers a penny.)

With the release of 'The Only One I Know', it became noticeable that the band's attention to detail extended to the run-out grooves of their records. They'd scratched into its A-side 'There's no messages, just pure politics', a reference to their shared belief that *everything* is political – politics being about the way people choose to live their lives. This would prove to be a lyrical theme throughout their career. On the B-side there was a simple and irritatingly accurate question: 'Good, Aren't We?' The 'Indian Rope' run-outs had been just as interesting, with a prophetic 'Everybody will want to know me soon' and a rather unnecessary '5-1, 6-4', the 5-1 referring to a severe drubbing Manchester City had given to their United rivals. This could only have been Harrison's doing.

And the lead track itself was a revelation. A burbling bass suddenly fired into a tumbling run as Collins climaxed repeatedly and Burgess floated serenely above it all, his chorus line, 'Everyone has been burned before,' being a straightish steal from The Byrds' 'Everybody's Been Burned' and recalling those early days spent rummaging through Harrison's import racks at Omega. It became quite clear in conversations with dissenters at the time that they were forcing themselves not to like this one, or at least keeping the truth to themselves. The bass and Hammond were so much the song's focal points, it was certainly hard to see the logic behind yet more Stone Roses comparisons. Burgess is fairly to-the-point about why it was chosen as the follow-up single: 'It was picked for the organ stabs, really – we thought it'd make people go mental at the gigs.' Reviews began to mention the Spencer Davis Group, though Burgess's vocal sensitivity made that one hard to see. Most critics were simply lukewarm.

The Charlatans were given a chance to help the single's progress when they were invited twice on to *Top of the Pops*. Both were turned down for a predictable reason: they refused to cancel gigs and so disappoint their fans.

Despite losing 15,000 sales to a chart computer cock-up, 'The Only One I Know' charted at Number 24. The band continued with the tour, now travelling in a new Toyota Spacecruiser they had christened Scooby because of its resemblance to the Mystery Bus in the TV cartoon *Scooby Doo*. There was also a supporting van, for either the fast-selling T-shirts or the band, depending on which was needed at venues first.

The single kept rising, up to Number 10. At the Bristol Bierkeller, where 'The Age Of Aquarius' could not be found and the rather more mod-flavoured 'Theme From The Persuaders' introduced the band, it was noted that The Charlatans were surprisingly quick to hug one another, a touchy-feely trait not expected in the leading lights of the "laddish" Madchester scene. Burgess was keen to point out that the band were in it for the duration, and hoped to peak in around five years.

This is interesting, as it shows how routinely he would flit from being thoughtful and aware of his limitations and potential patterns of growth to lipping off grandly about how fantastic he was *right now*. But that was Burgess for a good four years. On the one hand, he was a musician striving for excellence, on the other he was loving the camera as much as it loved him. He announced that he was no longer prepared to explain his lyrics, as his attempts to do so had recently caused a disappointed fan to flee in tears.

Outside London's Town and Country Club on 3 June, the band having reached one of the capital's larger venues less than six months after their debut, Burgess met an old girlfriend he'd 'idiotically' dumped. He was moved to hear her proud congratulations: 'Tim, you've done it, you've made it.' On-stage that night, nonchalant and dancing loose-limbed, he came out with a neat 'Welcome to the Age of Aquari-Us and Them' a snipe back at constant press criticism. Within the space of a few days, they had been called 'a dodgy mod band' and been compared disparagingly to both prog-rockers Procul Harum and Flowered Up, supposedly London's answer to Happy Mondays. It was confusing. They could either do no wrong or no right.

But The Charlatans had had Single Of The Week on Radio 1, and music press front covers too. And, to their utter amazement, 'The Only One I Know' went up *again*.

'It was at Number Ten when we were coming towards the end of the tour,' says Burgess, 'and we thought we'd made it. Then it went up to nine, so we walked out on-stage going, "Number Nine, Number Nine, we're fookin' Number Nine, us." It was great; we really thought we were starting to mean something.'

In order to be allowed into Northern Ireland to play Belfast's Limelight, they were forced to thrust their singles' front covers at deeply suspicious customs officials. They still looked like the scruffy delinquents they were in those initial press shots.

'The Only One I Know' went on to sell 150,000 copies, yet when the band celebrated it was with curry, not champagne. Ever cautious, at this stage they were paying themselves £65 each a week – and there were no arguments.

After the success of 'The Only One I Know', The Charlatans truly felt as if everything was possible. Prematurely, maybe foolishly, they even felt ready to take on America without having finished recording their debut album. Via Beggars Banquet, they were signed to RCA in the States, and Steve Harrison went over to check the lie of the land. Everything seemed ready. As ever, America had been keeping a beady eye on the UK, and RCA executives were aware of Madchester and felt that their market was more than ready for a slice of psychedelic pop.

There was a major problem, however. There was already a band called The Charlatans operating in the US. The British band would have to change their name. Knowing the band's attitude as he did (he actually shared it), Harrison could predict what their reaction would be. No, and who the fuck *are* these other Charlatans, anyway?

The original Charlatans were in fact the first San Franciscan underground rock band, prime movers in igniting the psychedelic explosion of the mid-sixties. Formed in 1964 by autoharpist George Hunter, guitarist Mike Wilhelm and bassist Richard Olsen, they were quickly joined by pianist Michael Ferguson (whom Hunter had bumped into in a dole queue) and drummer Sam Linde, who just as quickly departed, making way for Dan Hicks. Their image was well thought out: they dressed as outlaw dandies from the late 1800s, their swanky duds matching the Edwardian mansions found all over the Haight area of San Francisco.

The US Charlatans' embroidered waistcoats, stiff-necked collars, tall boots and flowing locks (think Jeff Bridges in *Wild Bill* or Dennis Quaid in *Wyatt Earp*) so impressed the proprietor of the Red Dog Saloon in Virginia City, Nevada, that in 1965 he gave them a residency in his bar. It was here, throughout that burning summer, that they gradually melded together a hugely influential sound encompassing heavy folk and blues, the then massively popular R&B, and kick-ass, pistols-in-the-air boogie. Perhaps even more influential were the self-designed adverts for their performances: Ferguson's effort for their debut show is widely accepted to be America's very first psychedelic poster.

Returning to San Francisco towards the end of '65, The Charlatans found themselves hailed at the peak of the Haight hierarchy, one third of a triumvirate also featuring Jefferson Airplane and The Grateful Dead. Unfortunately, unlike their illustrious peers, they just couldn't capture that wild groove on record. Autumn Records rejected their demos, while Kama Sutra refused to release an album the band had completed for them, so the only release by this classic line-up was a single, 'The Shadow Knows', which they didn't even want out.

Disillusioned and roundly suspecting that they were bobbing listlessly on a river of excrement without a paddle between them, Hunter, Ferguson and Hicks left. Olsen and Wilhelm though, proud of their influence and dreaming hard of a brighter future, stuck to the task like obsessive-compulsive limpets and in 1969 finally got an album, simply titled *The Charlatans*, released by Philips. It didn't quite burn with the ferocity of those shows at the Red Dog but 'Fulsom Prison Blues' and 'Alabama Bound' came close and, anyway, it was some kind of testament to The Charlatans' vital contribution.

ermany, 1992

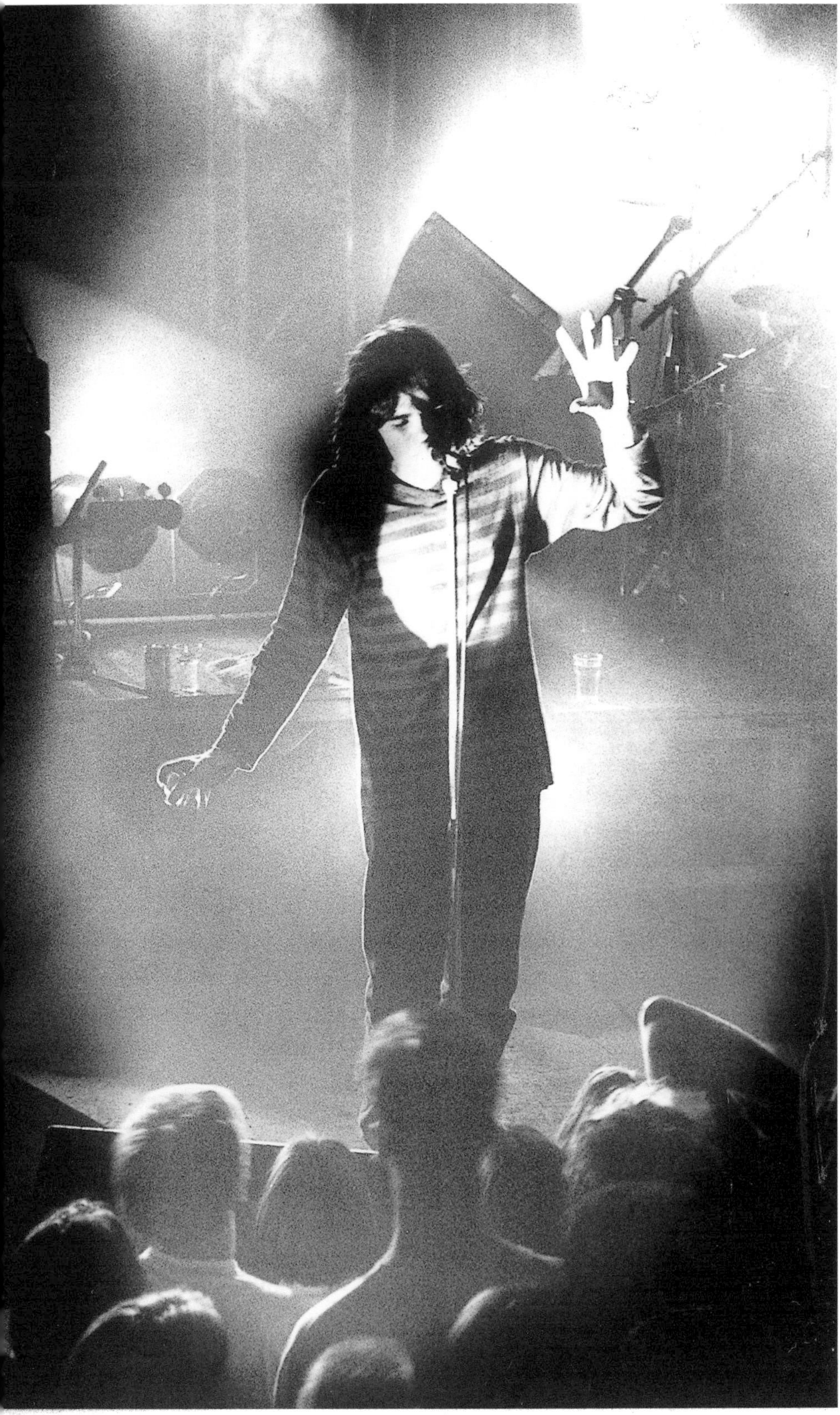

Mil

Martin, Germany

Tim and Mark, Germany

Milan

Germany

Holborn, London, 1994

Monnow Valley, 1995

Job done, Olsen and Wilhelm packed it in (for now, at least). An album of demos would be released in 1982, and later a couple of messy compilations, but this was the end of it. The US Charlatans were all over, the members all over the place. Wilhelm was in Loose Gravel (he was later to join Flamin' Groovies in their 'Shake Some Action' period), Ferguson in Tongue And Groove, Hicks in Dan Hicks And His Hot Licks. Hunter, continuing on the band's graphic trajectory, got into cover art, producing such renowned sleeves as Canned Heat's 'Hallelujah' and Quicksilver Messenger Service's 'Happy Trails'. And Olsen – well, Olsen moved into production at Pacific High Studios, keeping his hand in and, it soon transpired, his ear to the ground.

Come May 1990, the American music industry had been closely scrutinising this Madchester phenomenon for some months. Talk was of another British invasion, maybe not as awe-inspiring as the attack led by The Beatles and The Rolling Stones, but certainly up there with the glam assault of Bowie, T. Rex and Gary Glitter or the New Romantic vision of Culture Club and Duran Duran ten years later. These things are cyclical, it was thought: early sixties, early seventies, early eighties, here comes baggy. Let's face it, it really takes something to break down that sad-ass limey fag reserve, and this time the Brits were fuckin' *losing* it.

So The Charlatans, The Stone Roses and Happy Mondays were news in the US before they'd even reached the baggage conveyor belt at JFK. They hadn't happened yet, but word was out that they surely would. RCA America were ahead of the game, already spreading the gospel according to Madchester and preparing the way for their Northwich certs. Which was how Richard Olsen got to hear about them. He picked up on the pre-publicity: The Charlatans this, The Charlatans that, they're young, they're stylish, they're witty and pretty, they've got great tunes but they still rock and they're *so psychedelic*, they've only been together a year but they're going all the way...

Having worked so hard to ensure the original Charlatans would be regarded as seminal and never be forgotten, Olsen could only resent a band attempting to appropriate their name. *Especially* a band who were supposedly part of a psychedelic fad and to whom everything was coming easy. This could only devalue the original act and would probably, if these loud predictions of another Brit invasion proved accurate, go a long way towards wiping his own band from the pages of rock history altogether. Quite reasonably, under the circumstances, Olsen resolved to sue their lily-white limey arses off.

The rest of the US sixties combo weren't so bothered about the new pretenders. In fact, in the summer of 1990, while in New York to interview Nine Inch Nails, Ice Cube and Living Colour, the photographer of this book dragged the author down to see Hicks play a club date with his new band, Electric Warriors. When asked afterwards what he thought of the British Charlatans, Hicks expressed no interest whatsoever.

The new Charlatans had already been made very aware of the old as a French label had recently reissued two of the original band's albums. Such was the Brit band's overweening confidence that they had dismissed their forerunners with the cute warning: 'Fans should note there is no similarity in our trouser width.' But this Olsen business was different: a violent attack on their chances and their cool.

Such disagreements are a fairly regular occurrence in the music industry. When Vince Clark and Alison Moyet changed their Yazoo moniker to Yaz for America, everyone was thrown into fatal confusion by the release of Coldcut's single 'Yazz And The Plastic Population'. The Beat were forced to become The English Beat and The Mission were touring as The Mission UK. Such changes tended to damage the bands' mystique (important to The Charlatans, that) by specifying and thus making important their birthplaces, and also by adding a flavour of patriotism that, given the behaviour of some Brits abroad, was not always going to be welcome. Most of all, though, The Charlatans resented being ordered to change their name and having their independence undermined. So, fuck 'em. No way. Charlatans *forever*.

Steve Harrison flew over to New York City, along with lawyers representing both the band and Beggars Banquet, to sort the mess out. Though The Charlatans themselves had not heard of the originals when they took the name, Harrison, a big fan of Quicksilver Messenger Service, had certainly come across them during his days as an import retailer. Yet he predicted no problems as they'd 'unfortunately never transcended that folky psychedelic scene' and, anyway, they'd broken up before half of his band were even toilet trained. Piece of piss, this legal lark.

So Harrison – resourceful and committed but nevertheless still just a business innocent managing his equally inexperienced mates – found himself sat in a major league boardroom with the president of RCA plus lawyers acting for RCA, Beggars and both sets of Charlatans. Harrison laughingly recalls his own ignorant disregard of the originals' historical influence: how he took on Burgess's mantle and kept stressing that his band were so much bigger already and set to go global, how he confused the Americans present by repeating how 'pissed off' he was and how he demanded to know if the originals were still working, because if they weren't they were nothing.

Annoyingly for the soon-to-be Charlatans UK, the US band *were* still active. Posters were produced proving that the original Charlatans (featuring Richard Olsen) were playing bar mitzvahs in the San Francisco area. It was bizarre and infuriating, but nonetheless it was game over. Almost.

'Over a period of time it all started making sense,' says Harrison. 'The American band had a lot of pride in what they'd achieved, you know, and they were hanging on to a bit of their past. Later, in the Hall of Fame, we saw a poster that had Jefferson Airplane, The Grateful Dead, Quicksilver Messenger Service and The Charlatans on it, and it really struck home. They were an important group.

'But at the time we were fucking furious, really disrespectful, because we didn't have the knowledge we have now. We hated the name Charlatans UK, and we even dropped the UK when we went over there later.'

At the end of July, it was announced in a rather face-saving manner that, when Stateside, the band would be known as Charlatans UK 'more to disassociate the bands than for any legal reason'.

But that wouldn't be the end of it. There was more to come. The Charlatans UK were not prepared to go down without a fight.

On the 13 July the band played at the Manchester Ritz. The show was for a Granada TV special celebrating youth culture and thus recorded for posterity. Walking on-stage, Burgess arrogantly dead-panned 'Get them fookin' cameras on *me*,' then allowed the floor manager to take his fag off him. No one was allowed to smoke, drink or take photos and security guards escorted people to the toilets.

Despite these restrictions, somehow the gig was bootlegged on video and offered for sale. The band sent off for one and received it almost immediately. It had been shot from the balcony, leading to a visit to a house in Manchester with their lawyer. They thought it might be a kid, a fan or a student supplementing their dole with a little resourceful scally activity, and they'd stop it and stop him getting nailed by Granada. Then they found duplicating equipment stashed in the ceiling and the perpetrator showed them order forms from all over the country for 'Charlatans: Live At The Ritz'. Despite this, he was not prosecuted.

Throughout the summer the band nipped back and forth between their homes, the studio where they were recording the debut album, and various unconnected concerts. In August, they played their first European date at Sweden's Hultsfed Festival, alongside The Waterboys, Hothouse Flowers, Jungle Brothers, Soul Asylum and The Buzzcocks. They also played Warrington Legends, another steam room of a gig that was way too pokey for a band of their present stature. They played it purely by way of returning a favour. Legends had supported them when they were nothing. It was the only gig they would play around their third single, 'Then', released on 3 September.

This single, described in the press as being 'like ELP with a cocaine enema' (that was supposed to be an insult) caused tremendous arguments between band and record company, and among the band members themselves. At one point Burgess even aimed a punch at Brookes, receiving a fight-finishing blow in return.

The problems were manifold. First, as they were recording and immediately releasing new material, everything was rushed. It was also assumed that the material they were laying down was for the album. Assuming 'The Only One I Know' was to be on the album, this would make two singles from the same record, which they still regarded as ripping-off the fans. Michael Jackson did that kind of thing, not The Charlatans. It was eventually agreed that 'The Only One' would *not* be on the album, or at least not on the vinyl version which the band, most of them old-school vinyl junkies, considered to be the real thing.

The actual decision to release 'Then' proved to be a terrible headache, with the band's democratic voting system not agreeing with Blunt at all.

'"Then" represented the second part of the first LP,' says Burgess, 'where the sound had started to become more commercial. We were trying to improve and "Then" was recorded along with "Polar Bear', and there was an argument as to which should be the second single. Everyone was saying "Polar Bear" and Martin walked out in protest and he was fucking right because it was a live favourite but we'd overproduced it and destroyed it in the studio. Martin realised that, but I didn't.

'I remember going down to the pub to find him and he was just sitting there with a full pint. He'd been there for an hour without touching a drop, almost catatonic. He said, 'If "Polar Bear" comes out, I'm leaving.'

'So we put out "Then" and it went to Number Twelve. Everyone complained that the vocals weren't high enough, but I think that just added to its intrigue. And it had a great groove which we perfected live later.'

For the video for 'Then', another party was organised, this time in a cave Kim Peters had found on a hillside. On the day of the shoot, Rob Collins was taken ill with food poisoning and remained in bed in a hotel nearby and was replaced by a friend and fan chosen 'because he had a pretty good haircut'. The stand-in would mime bent over double in classic Collins pose, then turn away as the camera zoomed in, the oil lamp lighting helping in the deception.

Meanwhile, the music press began to surmise that the Madchester phenomenon was on the wane. Letters to the *NME* and *Melody Maker* claimed there were police cameras at the Hacienda, there had been a crackdown on smoking in the city centre and the police were persistent in their attempts to close clubs down. For a movement based on freedom of influence and expression, it really didn't sound good at all.

For now, though, The Charlatans had left Manchester behind. America was calling, and Burgess and Brookes flew over for a pre-tour (or, hopefully, invasion) press trip. It looked like the US was ready. The Stone Roses seemed to have decided they couldn't be arsed to conquer the States, but The Charlatans' attitude was why not?

The first North American tour (it was only a fleeting visit, really) began on 2 October at Toronto's Horseshoe Tavern. This place was run by an immense biker named X-Ray, a good friend of the late comedian John Belushi. X-Ray treated them well, feeling he was getting early on to the Next Big Thing. The band liked him, too: they made it their business to get on with all types.

From here The Charlatans dropped down to New York's Marquee. The east and west coasts of the States are always the quickest to "get" happening bands and The Charlatans found they were well known already. The singles went down fantastically well, causing a quite frightening commotion, but unfamiliarity with the other tracks saw the heat die down until the crowd was stoked up again by 'Sproston Green'.

Then it was on to the Gathering Of The Tribes, held over two days at San Francisco's Costa Mesa Pacific Amphitheatre and the Mountain View Shoreline Amphitheatre in Los Angeles. This was a travelling festival organised by The Cult's Ian Astbury (who was consequently nicknamed Ian 'Haight' Astbury). Though the original site was unavailable, Astbury's idea was to recreate the spirit of 1967's Monterey Pop.

Gathering Of The Tribes was to be a two-day celebration of music, unity, consciousness and communication, though given the pungent whiff of fine hashish emanating from the sites, it was more a celebration of *unconsciousness*. There would be displays by environmental and social groups (this made it an obvious precursor to the massively lucrative Lollapalooza tours), and especially by Astbury's beloved Native Americans.

Gathering Of The Tribes' intention was stated in a fabulously pompous press release which deserves to be reprinted here:

'We need to communicate on a very basic level to recognise each other's uniqueness and understand how we can educate each other.

The main purpose of this festival is to find and celebrate a common ground. We must embrace the need to wake up to the issues, both environmental and social. By inviting a cross-cultural group of musical performing artists from rap to rock, country to pop, we hope to realise this vision.'

The bill, given Astbury's penchant for staying on top of any new fashion and music, was suitably varied. There would be The Cramps, Ice-T, Indigo Girls, Queen Latifah, The Mission, The Charlatans and a host of others.

Given the charitable nature of the proceedings, it was only natural that The Charlatans should get into trouble immediately.

'They told us we could play for twenty minutes,' says Harrison, 'but the band wanted to play for forty. So the arrangement was that I would disappear and mingle with the crowd, so no one could complain to me when they overran. The stage guys went mental and started to dismantle Jon's drum kit while he was actually playing "Sproston Green"! The crowd loved it.

'I got back to the dressing room and found the stage guys pouring all our beer into the sinks, saying they'd been instructed not to let me or the band in there. It was like, "You guys fuck with us, you're gonna get it!" They were pushing us out of the way and everything. Then Ice-T came over, who we'd been talking to earlier, and started telling the stage guys, "You're messin' with my boys, my homies," and this big confrontation started going off. It was getting really mad. Ice-T asked us if we wanted his Rhyme Syndicate to get involved and we were going, "No, no, we've had enough of these bastards. We're going home." We were there with all the guitars under our arms, all ready to go.

'So I went off for a fight with the promoter and, when I got into his office, he turned out to be the biggest bloke I'd ever seen in my life. He had hands like shovels. I thought, Oh shit. Then he said, "That performance was fucking brilliant, and I've got something to ask you. Public Enemy haven't been allowed into California state, so would you play before Iggy Pop, right at the end of the night?" I said, "Don't you know what's been going on here? The band have come off-stage and you've kicked us out of the venue!" The guy went berserk, offering to double our money, give us bigger dressing rooms, everything.

'So we went back to ask the lads and it'd gone really crazy. Apparently, Wayne Hussey from The Mission had gone up to Rob Collins acting like Mr Weird, going, "Woo, woo, woo," in his face or something, and Rob had him up against the wall. I'm going "Rob! Rob! Put him down! Put him down!" Everyone was really fried. We went through the whole thing, like, let's play it, it'll be 20,000 people, but the band wanted to make a statement about the way they'd been treated. They picked up the guitars and walked out.'

A typical Charlatans attitude: dignity before fame. Luckily, the LA gig was staffed by a completely different set of stage hands.

Over three sessions during the course of 1990, The Charlatans recorded their debut album, *Some Friendly*. This was done, again with Chris Nagle, at The Windings, near Wrexham, in the Ffrwd Valley (formerly coal-mining country). Dating back to the early 1900s, the studio was originally an old winding shed used to bring the main cage up from the coal surface. The 660 foot live room sits above the main shaft which stretches about 400 feet down inside the mountains.

Initial stories emanating from the place claimed that the sessions had been unhappy ones, even that the band had engaged in bouts of wanton destruction.

'The place was a bit hippyish,' says Burgess, 'and I don't think we left on very friendly terms. It was one of those studio bust-ups between the owners and the group. Rob and Martin were up to their tricks, smashing stuff up and that.'

Harrison doesn't recall any wrongdoing, but adds that he wouldn't be surprised if Blunt and Collins hadn't indeed 'been up to their tricks', breaking things and concealing it from him till he inevitably found out later.

The band's main problem, however, was not the behaviour of their individual members: it was that they had been together for so short a time that they hadn't had a chance to build the stockpile of songs most bands enjoy when coming to record their first album.

'It was like that to begin with,' says Burgess. 'Everything happened so quick. We'd write songs, then record them, then get to play them live and work on them. So most things would sound better about two years after they were recorded. Most people get to do it the other way round.

'I thought "Indian Rope" was brilliant. I thought "The Only One I Know" was brilliant, even better. And the third one, "Then". As a band's first three singles, they were unique, the best thing that came out at the time, because they were weird as anything and they all charted. But I don't think we were really ready to make that first LP.

'We had some great stuff, but also some stuff that had to go on there just to make up the numbers. Martin always said we rushed it. But if we hadn't rushed it, we wouldn't have had an LP at all, and if we hadn't gone through the second LP in the way we did we'd never have got to the third LP, so I can't feel too bad about it all.

'Mate, you know me,' Burgess summarises, with his trademark endearing self-deprecation. 'I don't have any idea of what we're doing at any moment in my life. Ever. I just fucking *do* it.'

In some respects, The Charlatans were under the same pressures for their debut album as most bands are for their second. One thing that was on their side, though, was their sheer enthusiasm for the process. They regarded being in a 'proper' studio with a 'proper' producer as a major step on the road to historical significance and they each recognised the need to rise to the occasion.

The pressure of the situation gave rise to the album's main charm: its evident desire to make something of itself, the way it loses momentum then claws its way back into the groove. Though some of it, in retrospect, is a little thin-sounding and overly twee – Burgess's love of psychedelic sixties pop getting the better of him – most of it was raised to a great height by Rob Collins. He played like a big cat waiting to pounce, his Hammond hovering over Blunt's funky rumble until the perfect moment to strike, then charging in with unanswerable force.

Collins made the most of 'Opportunity', seven minutes of looming trouble, and showed admirable restraint during 'Flower', a malicious little pop song owing much to Baker's thorny guitar. Despite its sweet title, this one saw Burgess wishing painful death on those who had slighted him. 'Opportunity', Burgess said, concerned a post-rehearsal visit to London when, getting off the tube at Goodge Street due to Tottenham Court Road being closed, he found himself walking through the final throes of the Poll Tax riots – people running, police on horseback, windows smashed and being smashed, unashamed daylight looting, the lot. He remembered being 'overawed by the violence'.

The band members themselves felt that some of the album, particularly the live favourites 'Polar Bear' and 'White Shirt', were spoiled by overproduction. The bass, they felt, was underpronounced. And they had a point: *Some Friendly* does lack the underpinning force of their other, later offerings. It *moves* rather than *drives*, showing its influences clearly without taking them on to another level. Even the introduction to the mighty 'Sproston Green' is changed into 'Won't Get Fooled Again' rather than the drawn-out live experience, where its overbearing solemnity hides a sense of crazed anticipation.

One review proffered the opinion that the album 'reawakens deeply embedded memories of glorious pop moments crackling from radios in childhood' and that's very accurate. With hindsight, there's something quite dreamy about it, sleepy even, but it's a level of sleep where you're not quite ready to feel the full pleasure or terror of dreams.

The CD and cassette versions of *Some Friendly* – its cover a fuzzy picture of the band, chosen over a depiction of melting wax models of them – did indeed include 'The Only One I Know' and 'Then'. There was also a limited 'special deluxe' LP in a white plastic sleeve – but that was a treat for the fans.

Looking back now, The Charlatans' determination only to take one single from each album seems wilfully perverse and unrealistic. The argument that they should be included to draw people in to the other, perhaps more testing material is often a good one. But The Charlatans had their principles.

'The thing about having just one single on each album was like our first statement,' says Burgess. 'Having "The Only One I

Know" on the CD was a phoney compromise, and I still feel bitter about that. Then again, I didn't even want there to *be* a CD.'

The album was released on 8 October and, overproduced or not, went straight into the chart at Number 1, knocking The Three Tenors, Pavarotti, Domingo and Carreras, from that perch. Aside from solo albums by former members of hit-making groups, this made The Charlatans the first new act to debut at the top of the album charts for three years (since Johnny Hates Jazz in January 1988). Sales were good all over the world, from France through Greece to Australia. It quickly shifted 140,000 in the States.

Reviews were mixed, with most stressing the band's influences rather than the contemporary nature of their sound. Collins' input was mostly lauded, with Burgess the one to suffer the most attacks. The Doors were mentioned, as were Traffic and Pink Floyd. There was one quite poetic description, describing the album as being like a frieze in a primary school classroom, where hints and thoughts and pictures of varying size and quality are all pieced together in a cute and curious fashion.

That was the truth of it. As Burgess says, The Charlatans weren't quite *ready*.

For The Stone Roses, their legendary Spike Island show had been both a triumph and a disaster. A triumph because it showed their sudden and powerful drawing power, a disaster because, in their performance, they had seemed lacklustre, even lazy.

As The Charlatans ended the year with their first full-length UK tour, they came to Glasgow's Barrowland. This tumultuous date showed the band that, even though their popularity would wax and wane nationally over the next three years, they would always be assured of rabid support north of the border. Significantly, *Melody Maker*'s review of the Barrowland gig said that, just as The Stone Roses had thrust Morrissey from the top of the indie tree, so The Charlatans would displace them. The review continued to say that The Charlatans were this night so wired, so firmly entrenched in club culture, that they made the Roses look 'opportunistic'. So who were the charlatans *now*?

After headlining a festival in Paris, playing with James and the

Velvet Underground's John Cale, the band had opened the tour at the Birmingham Hummingbird, where they introduced into the set 'Can't Even Be Bothered', eventually to appear on their second album. At Leeds University, 1,800 people were crammed into the refectory and one girl collapsed with a crushed windpipe. Only sharp-eyed security and prompt first aid saved her life. At the first of two shows at London's Kilburn National Ballroom (7/8 November), they were described by *Melody Maker*'s Ian Gittins as 'absolutely state-of-the-art, taking psychedelic pop back to its basics'. And the two shows at Manchester Academy were personal highlights for the band, yet more proof that they really *had* come this far.

By now, it was taken as read that the band would put on a great show, and their fans would ensure a grin-inducing party atmosphere. But the idea of the gig as an event was still at the forefront of The Charlatans' minds. They wanted to continue to evolve their live performances, vary them and add to them, maintaining that sense of being something special. It was to this end that they introduced the UK to Captain Whizzo.

Captain Whizzo, rumoured to have been living in a tree-house in California, was a psychedelic survivor from back when it all started. He was Joshua of the famous Joshua Light Show back in the sixties, the man who produced the head-spinning effects at Bill Graham's Fillmores East and West. Whizzo's techniques were secret but the optical miracles he performed were legendary. He'd have overlapping grids assaulted by violent flashes as they dissolved into weird viscera, then swirled off as gaudy tornadoes. He'd blend colours and darkness to draw the audience in, then let them have it with a crimson lightning strike. He'd worked for The Chocolate Watch Band, Hendrix, Quicksilver Messenger Service and the Jefferson Airplane spin-off Hot Tuna. The guy was unbelievable, a true one-off.

Steve Harrison had stumbled upon Whizzo on one of his fact-seeking missions to New York. He'd gone to see Deee-Lite in a club where, coincidentally, Whizzo was blowing people's minds on a weekly basis. Harrison was stunned, and loved the fact that Whizzo had worked with The Chocolate Watch Band when he himself had cited the same act as influencing The Charlatans in his early press releases. He had to have him, and he persuaded the good captain to go out on UK tour with the band to ensure that no one left with their brain stationary. Whizzo got on fabulously with the band, becoming known for a while as 'the sixth Charlatan'.

The Charlatans' glorious first full year together, 1990, ended as it had started. Their fans adored them, yet the critics' jibes kept coming. It was endlessly repeated that they would be nowhere near their present position if their superior precursors were fully active. They were half-arsed doppelgängers, just as Aerosmith had been to the Stones.

The band weren't overly vexed, sure that time would sort this misconception out. More worrying was an interview quote from John Baker, in which he said, 'I'm not terribly eager to be recognised in Safeway, signing autographs at the checkout.' It seemed unlikely, then, that he would enjoy what was intended to come next: the domination of America.

On 10 February 1991, The Charlatans began their US invasion at the Tower Theater in Houston, Texas. At least, RCA hoped it would be an invasion. The band themselves weren't so sure. All this touring was getting to them. It wasn't that they didn't enjoy it. On the contrary, each night was a welcome self-justification, they loved to experience new people, and the drink and the drugs were certainly more readily available than they had been back at Walsall Overstrand. No, touring was generally cool.

The problem was that they'd found that they also loved to write and record, and were missing the opportunity to do so. That bright and beautiful weekend when they'd come up with those three indubitable corkers was now a distant memory, the buzz long gone. And after the rushed recording of *Some Friendly*, Number 1 or not, that was the buzz they were after. They didn't really want to keep promoting the same album and playing the same set (they've never been able to write on the road). They'd written a few tracks for the next single during breaks in the last tour, but it wasn't enough to sate their craving. They didn't really understand why they should have to do this tour now.

The halls they played in the States were of some considerable size. At San Diego's Montezuma Hall, Burgess threw his mike at a kid who'd aimed a bottle at him, and stormed off-stage. At the Ackerman Ballroom in Los Angeles, Ecstasy T-shirts abounded. The gigs were storming – the band owed the crowds that much – and one of the best was at the Metro, near the Cubs' Wrigley Field in the heart of Chicago's bohemia (Smashing Pumpkins' Billy Corgan lived just round the corner). This show was recorded and became the band's most well-known bootleg: Isolation 21.2.91. Except that it wasn't a bootleg.

'This has always been a grey area,' explains Harrison, 'and we always liked to shroud it in mystery, but what happened was that we were getting bootlegged all over the place and were getting a bit paranoid about how much stuff was out there. Beggars Banquet were too. So we recorded that gig and I concocted a story that we'd seized these records in America and, to get our money back for the legal costs, we were going to bring them back to the UK and sell them.

'It was a great story, but Beggars did it so professionally, printing it up and giving it a catalogue number, that it didn't look like a bootleg, it looked semi-legitimate, and that wasn't the idea. It was supposed to be a cool quality bootleg recording that people could get instead of the terrible quality stuff that was circulating. Eventually we sold it through the fan club, and in a few shops that Beggars had good contact with.'

The New York show, at the Ritz on 28 February, was an unhappy experience presswise. Before the gig, many of the press corps had gone to see Oliver Stone's rock biopic *The Doors*. At the gig, the hacks made a tenuous psychedelic connection and criticised the band for not ripping off their clothes and leading the crowd in a snake-dance round the hall (thereby bringing down the government and its hoary systems of outdated morality). It was absurd.

By now 'Sproston Green' had been released as a US single, the idea being that it would be 'weird enough' to bubble under and 'introduce them to radio stations properly'. Unexpectedly, the track began to take off. The band were so fearful that this unwanted success would mean an extension of the tour and a further delay in recording, they demanded that the single be pulled.

Perhaps unsurprisingly, this request had repercussions for their relationship with the American label. This was at least the second time the band had seriously pissed off RCA. They'd done it in 1990 when they'd failed to get out of bed for an interview with, of all magazines, *Rolling Stone* (it was for the cover, too). The furious journalist had complained to the label, calling them the most unprofessional band he'd ever worked with.

'I think the band had a hard time getting to grips with the way things are done in America,' says Harrison. 'All the pressing the flesh and meet-and-greets. They were very concerned with preserving their dignity and, above all, doing things on their own terms.'

Their refusal to take more than one single from *Some Friendly* gave their record label grief worldwide. Harrison says now that 'it compromised us in just about every territory on the planet'.

Worst of all, Burgess had opened his big mouth once too often. Americans don't usually take kindly to limeys larging it about how glamorous, sexy and talented they are. But people do sometimes get away with it, if they can really play. No one, however, gets away with slagging off America itself – and Burgess had the poor sense to do just that. Purely for the sake of being contrary, and for a moment forgetting his own influences, he had stated, quite clearly, that no good bands had ever come out of North America.

'I was a typical naive rock 'n' roll-head,' he says, 'saying, "Oh, we're gonna be bigger than the Pistols and bigger than The Beatles." All this stuff was coming out of my mouth, all of it from years of reading about it all in magazines. It was just textbook shit, really, but I thought I'd get away with it because I didn't think I'd ever go there again, and no one would ever see me. And now, eight years later, it's like, "You remember in 1991?" I mean, I just wanted to make a mark. I hate to think what I was like, but I always meant it.'

The *faux pas* was hugely foolish, almost up there with Primal Scream's Confederate flag on the sleeve of *Give Out, But Don't Give Up*, and it wasn't even from Tim's heart, whatever he says about meaning it.

'The reason I first started going down to Steve Harrison's record shop when I was a kid,' he continues, 'was because they sold American imports there. Before it was cool, you know, around the time of REM's first album, around 1983. In the mid-eighties, when it was all Heaven 17 and stuff, you had to search for something different, and I looked to America.'

So this wasn't to be the year The Charlatans broke America. People had been saying that it was *bound* to happen; that the arrogance of The Stone Roses in not bothering to cross the Atlantic, as if they could take the States whenever they pleased, would leave the door open for Burgess and the gang. Now it would be neither band. There *would* still be a British invasion this year, as it happened. It just wasn't anything to do with Madchester.

Incredibly, the UK assault on the States in '91 was a tin-pot electro invasion. In July, EMF's 'Unbelievable' would go US Number 1. The very next week, the Number 2 spot would be filled by Jesus Jones's 'Right Here, Right Now', a song only kept from the top by Bryan Adams' inescapable '(Everything I Do) I Do It For You'. Truly, wonders never cease.

Harrison now says that The Charlatans' tactical withdrawal from the States, when *Some Friendly* had sold half a million and could so easily have doubled that, was eventually the right course of action. He doesn't think the group could have taken it.

'With hindsight,' he says, 'I don't think we could have coped with it, or at least we would have found it extremely hard, but fortunately, because we were with Beggars and not a major label, we were allowed to back off and just put out an interim single in the UK while we recovered.'

The added pressure, the increased attention and the accompanying extra duties might well have finished the band off. Though not averse to hard work, they were also in a band to enjoy themselves, and they would not have enjoyed doubling their workload.

It was better to get out while the going was still not bad.

The 'interim single' was to be the 'Over Rising' EP. Recorded at Konk, the Kinks' old studio in Hornsey, London N8, this was to be clear evidence of the band's resolution to move on, away from "baggy", away from everyone else. To help them in this endeavour, they employed a new producer. Chris Nagle had acquitted himself heroically but now they needed someone who could prod them in another direction.

The choice they made was perverse in the extreme: David M. Allen, best known for co-producing *Disintegration*, The Cure's most depressing album. It would be mixed by Mark Stent (Massive Attack). The results were as predictable as things ever get with The Charlatans, a gloomy psychedelia moving slightly onward (but not far) from the darker moments of *Some Friendly*. The band were deeply unsure about the whole experience.

'We had fourteen mixes of "Over Rising",' says Burgess. 'Like, the "Guitar Up Slightly Mix" and the "Organ Down Slightly Mix". It was hard to tell the difference. We actually chose the mix we wanted on the way to the video shoot for it, so we'd be able to mime.'

In fact, 'Over Rising' was never intended to be the single's featured track.

'"Happen To Die" was going to be the main track,' explains Burgess, 'but then the Gulf War happened. Lots of people were affected by that; Massive Attack changed their name to Massive for a while. So we thought a track called "Happen To Die" wouldn't get played on the radio. There was an official list circulating of supposedly offensive band names and song titles. So we went with "Over Rising" and that didn't get played on the radio either.'

Also on the EP was 'Way Up There' (from which another of The Charlatans' consistently entertaining fanzines took its name). It was baleful and gently hypnotising, with flares of blistering guitar and punching Hammond from Collins. Though it was 'Happen To Die' that would become the live favourite, this was arguably the EP's best track.

The video was an intriguing affair. The screen was split vertically in three and showed intermingled footage of the band playing, car headlights, Collins eating spaghetti, people dressed as penguins stumbling around the countryside, the band smearing each other with paint and bishops and gymnasts, while Burgess prowled between the three strips. The split screen was reminiscent of *The Thomas Crown Affair*, Blunt being a fan of the super-sharp Steve McQueen.

There was one more track on this EP, and it was probably the most important of the four. 'Opportunity 3' was a remix by Flood of *Some Friendly*'s 'Opportunity'. Three hundred and fifty copies of it were mailed out to clubs. It would be the first calculated dance crossover of many.

A month after returning from the USA, the band made a three-date trip to Japan. They would later come to enjoy the country but at this point the culture shock and unfamiliar super-politeness were the last things they wanted. They lost their edge for the first time and loathed the whole experience. It was getting too much like a job, the thing they'd partly joined the band to avoid. They just *had* to get back to the UK.

Once back, there was the briefest chance to relax and write before a summer tour of the UK began. Just before it did, they re-released 'Indian Rope' on CD. This wasn't a cash-in but a generous gesture to save new fans from paying upward of £40 for foreign reprints which were being touted as original copies from 1990. They even attempted to release it with no bar code or catalogue number so it couldn't register for the charts but that, apparently, is against the rules.

Rehearsals for the tour, which was to begin on 11 June, took place in Scarborough's Futurist Theatre. The band's plans to host a two-day show at Stafford Bingley Hall – their own mini Gathering Of The Tribes – had already been scuppered by the local authority's refusal to grant them a licence. It was a shame: that would have been special. Still, there were other special moments to come, the gig at Manchester Free Trade Hall for one. Burgess now has a particular affection for the place, having read C.P. Lee's *Like The Night*, the tale of how Bob Dylan's famous *Live At The Albert Hall* bootleg was discovered to actually have been recorded at the Free Trade Hall. Then there was the Royal Albert Hall itself.

This gig was as much a statement of intent as a celebration of the band's arrival in the upper reaches of the charts. Though 'alternative' bands such as Siouxsie And The Banshees and The Sisters Of Mercy had famously played the place, they were not cast as barbarian ·invaders: indeed, their gothic solemnity seeming perfectly in keeping with the building's grand tradition. Still, the band were aware that the Royal Albert Hall was more used to rocking to the partisan strains of 'Jerusalem' at the Last Night Of The Proms.

The Charlatans were keen to give their fans a big day out, and planned the Albert Hall gig as a classy alternative to Blackpool illuminations. The trouble was (and still is) that the Albert Hall remains a cavernous, all-seated, Excuse-me-Your-Grace-but-you-appear-to-be-sitting-on-my-binoculars temple of decorum. Blocks and boxes are tastefully separated, making it gloriously suitable for those wishing to drift off into private reverie as orchestral grandeur sweeps over them, but horrifically inappropriate for anyone well up for a bangin' party. The arena just doesn't lend itself to a true sense of togetherness.

The Charlatans tried, they really did try. Performing with as much intensity as they could muster, given the album-interrupting inconvenience of these tours, they dug deep. Burgess, still unused to dominating such intimidating surrounds, stalked the stage, sometimes aloof and remote (very much *de rigueur*, that), more often pouting and posing outrageously. The light show was reasonably effective too, with blinding flashes and coloured blobs bounding from tier to tier. It felt a little like lying prostrate and face down on a particularly attention-hungry pinball machine.

But, lights aside, up in the gods it was all too far away. The heady, heaving atmosphere generated in the stalls could not translate to the back. Row upon row of recently befringed kids, shiny and smart in their pristine white long sleeves and scuff-free flares, gazed longingly and adoringly down on the stage, willing their heroes on yet – jerking and twitching – not finding themselves quite able to fully join in the dance.

This continued throughout the show, the people rapt but slightly frustrated. Until, that is, the rumble and detonation of 'The Only One I Know' shattered the tension and turned the Albert Hall into a swarming ant-hill of desperate motion. The sprawling, pulsing 'Sproston Green' would be a similarly invigorating catharsis.

The strobe-light warnings in the foyers proved unnecessary, but a point was made. Even in the process of finding their feet, The Charlatans would risk humiliation in an effort to offer something new and identifiably their own.

It was during this UK tour that John Baker finally reached his personal crisis point. He'd enjoyed the writing, rehearsing and seeing the group grow in status. He'd even enjoyed the dreaming and, very briefly, the furore of the initial success. But now (like the others) he was bored senseless by the long-running promotion of *Some Friendly*, where the gigs blurred into one another and constant touring made fresh songwriting problematic if not downright impossible. This life also brought with it extended periods of down time naturally filled with bouts of heavy drinking and the impassioned pursuit of pharmaceutical kicks. It all added to Baker's feeling of displacement.

'He didn't want a record contract,' says Burgess. 'Didn't want any of the hassles. You know, the touring, the interviews. He just wanted to be in a group, play a few little gigs, release records, but not really be signed to anyone, which is fine, it's what he's doing now. The only bad thing is I haven't seen him since he left, and he's a good mate.'

Beyond his creeping discomfort with the trappings of success, Baker was also finding that his musical contributions did not carry the weight he would have liked (he'd already only been credited on five of the eleven tracks on *Some Friendly*). With the band deciding that their debut had already been flogged to an undignified degree, all thoughts were turned to a follow-up which would take them in a new direction. Internal squabbles were beginning to break out – Blunt versus Rob Collins, Burgess and Brookes against the world – while in the background, management, label and assorted insiders were all ready and willing to suggest where The Charlatans should go next.

In this harsh and unruly atmosphere, Baker was overwhelmed. Described by Blunt as 'always subdued', and with his unwanted lifestyle pushing him deeper into isolation, he was never going to shout the others down. Having joined at the same time as Burgess but lacking a singer's automatic claim to importance, even leadership, he was doomed to remain at the bottom of the creative and social pecking order. As the touring went on and on, he felt the original members were becoming a clique and pushing him to one side. The inter-band rivalry seemed to be taking on a harsher edge. It was looking increasingly like Baker no longer fitted.

Perhaps if he'd produced a few killer riffs, some exceptional material it might have been different. Perhaps it wouldn't have made any odds. The truth was that his personal isolation and the constant rejection of his ideas had finally shot Baker's confidence to pieces. For him (aside from the shows – the Albert Hall being a personal high point), much of the fun of being in a band was gone. The purity, unity and exuberance of recording on to portable tape-decks in scuzzy backrooms had been replaced by suspicion, strife and growing demands for compromise.

The Charlatans' official story was that towards the end of the tour Baker approached the others and explained that he felt he had little left to contribute, he was holding the band back, and it would be better for everyone if he left. They claimed they thought his decision was brave, as he could easily have said nothing and milked the situation for some considerable time yet. For honour's sake, he would delay his departure until after the band had ful-filled their commitment to play the end-of-June Roskilde and Belfort festivals in Denmark and France.

The truth was rather different. Life on the road had been a laugh but The Charlatans have never written well on tour. Things started to go wrong when they were back in the studio and under pressure to deliver new material. Baker was feeling inadequate and insecure and asked Blunt if anything was wrong. Blunt replied that everything was OK, yet the reply was a touch half-hearted. Blunt claims that his intention was to encourage Baker and lift his confidence, yet if this was the aim, his efforts were a consummate failure.

As the sessions continued, at Rich Bitch studios in Birmingham, the band began to feel that where they required progression, Baker was rehashing the sounds of *Some Friendly*. Baker himself began to recognise that this was so. Then again, though his lack of confidence had him naturally falling back on what he knew he could do well, that *was* his style, it *had* worked before, and he would continue with it once he had left the band.

Eventually, it was Rob Collins who suggested that something had to give. They had to move on and they were going nowhere. He spoke to Blunt and the others and it was agreed that Baker, the outsider, would have to be sacrificed for the sake of the future.

With Brookes and Burgess out of the studio for some, probably diplomatic, reason, Blunt and Collins called Baker in and told him he was no longer required.

At the time, John took it well. It was a surprise, coming so soon after those big gigs and tours of America and Japan, but he knew his part in the recording process was under question and that he hadn't been able to give of his best. Indeed, he was now so paranoid in the studio that he was afraid to suggest much at all. He had also been perturbed and (quite reasonably) annoyed when Blunt and Collins had taken to 'bashing stuff out' on the guitar. He just didn't think it would come to this and, given the terse nature of communication between the band (and blokes in general, really), there was no way he could have known that matters had gone this far.

Unfortunately for Baker, it was all to do with time – there wasn't any.

'In some ways,' says Blunt, 'it was Morning After Syndrome. We'd come from such a high, and we had the belief that you're only as good as your last single, and "Over Rising" was a dud. We'd always had this feeling of momentum, and we felt that John was stuck in a rut. It had turned into me and Rob making the music and we really wanted him to fit in with our ideas, but it wasn't happening. I don't want to character assassinate the bloke, because he's a really deep, genuinely nice man, but you can tell from the stuff he's done since. It still sounds a little like *Some Friendly*. We just couldn't let it drag on. You can't, can you?'

Once he'd left the band, Baker fell into deep shock. Stepping from a buzzing chart act into absolutely nothing was hard to cope with. Feeling that he'd been given no good reason for the sacking, he could only assume that his contributions were not up to standard – maybe never had been. First marginalised, now pushed out entirely, he felt useless. He'd also just got a mortgage that he could no longer keep up. On the road, with the band, he'd been drinking for fun. Now that became hardcore, a hiding place.

It took him a year to get over, but he proved resilient. Eventually, he formed a new band called Spin Playground and a while later returned to college to study Advanced Media and Communications. By 1997, he would be garnering reviews once more, as a member of Walsall band Polanski. There are no grudges held; in fact, Baker has since stated his belief that the sacking, though rough for him personally, was probably the best move for all concerned.

Back with The Charlatans, prospective European dates that autumn were now shelved and the release date for the next album put back to March 1992 – at the earliest. A now typically cagey press release on Baker's departure was issued, with the band 'not prepared to comment at the moment', though everyone was 'still the best of friends'. Those notorious 'musical differences' were cited too, a grim cliché that whitewashes all manner of beastliness, although the group did exhibit a rare grace in acknowledging Baker's contention that his songwriting input had become negligible.

They also knew that they needed a replacement urgently – and they found one, fast, in Mark Collins.

In many ways, Mark Collins was obviously perfect for The Charlatans in that he added even more personal chaos to their mix. The son of two teachers, he was born and brought up with three brothers and two sisters in Whalley Range, Manchester, thus giving the band an undeniable (and now damaging) blood connection to the Madchester scene. Also, he was *strange*, odd even by their warped standards, and so added a further set of complexities to their fraught internal workings.

Collins was an outsider, had been for years. It was partly a size thing. As a boy he'd grown as the other boys did, then, for some reason, his upward curve bottomed out at a meagre four feet six inches, a height he stayed at till around the age of sixteen. Faced with this constant humiliation, he simply disappeared into himself. It wasn't that he was absolutely solitary or friendless, just palpably distant from everyone else. Though he shared Burgess's habit of shooting people in the arse with air rifles, he never suffered for it. Bullies never came for him, despite him being the easiest of targets. It was as if, being so self-possessed, so separate from the norm, he did not qualify as a victim.

Other people noted his oddness, too. At fourteen, Collins was checked out by social workers and taken out of school. They

thought him backward, disturbed, incapable of communication
and ingesting information – he certainly reacted badly to prompt-
ing. An intelligence test proved him to be well above average and
showed he was clearly taking everything in, so he was taken back,
with his teachers being instructed not to hound him but to offer
gentle encouragement.

This new liberal strategy worked. Far from being clinically catatonic, Collins was actually a little bundle of energy, and to this day
a keen soccer player. It was just that he felt, like so many others,
that the education system had nothing to offer him. He was particularly alienated by the strict Catholic school he found himself
in, with its black-clad, disciplinarian Brothers offering a wide
range of violent, vaguely sexual experiences (Collins still recalls
how he, like the other boys, would sometimes be called into the
headmaster's office 'for a hug').

But it was music that moved Mark Collins. Having an older
brother not averse to conning him out of his pocket money in
order to buy Neil Young's latest (Mark's own affection for Young
came much later), Collins was blitzed with rock from a very early
age. The guitar was his thing. He loved the chiming twelve-string
melodics of The Byrds' Roger McGuinn, but also the sharp look
and vicious downward slashes of Paul Weller in The Jam. These
led, unsurprisingly, to a major admiration for Johnny Marr, Pete
Townshend and, of course, Jimi Hendrix.

Collins took up the instrument seriously at sixteen – quite late
when you consider how many respected guitarists could play Van
Halen's 'Eruption' with their teeth by that age. Once he'd taken it
up, however, he wouldn't put it down. His guitar became an integral part of his strange, insular world. No one would bother him
while practising; he could step in and step out at will. His family
and teachers would leave him alone, grateful that at least he was
interested in *something*. It would bring him his own form of
expression and the respect of others, and all on his own terms. He
was bolshy like that, always had been: another reason why he'd fit
so well into The Charlatans.

From school, it was straight to that musician's haven, the dole,
where Collins would stay, on and off, for the next eight years. For
a short while he cleaned carpets but quickly tired of visiting peo-

ple's houses and taking away their hair, skin and general filth. He also toiled briefly in a kebab shop. It was a dismal job, but he at least found a point to it all. Crushing frozen mince with his bare hands, he moulded little bloody balls into bigger bloody balls until, ever the perfectionist, he'd created the ultimate spicy-meat-kebab-thing.

Finally, fame of a sort came knocking. Collins had been in various dodgy combos but now he joined The Waltones, a Manchester four-piece also comprising Alex Fyans (drums) and Manny Lee (bass), with James Knox on vocals. The band were heavily marked by the mid-to-late eighties' obsession with simple songwriting, their main influences being The Smiths, the Merseybeat groups of the mid-sixties and classic American pop from the period immediately afterwards. Various singles were released, including 'She Looks Right Through Me' (1987) and 'Spell It Out' (1988), as well as one album, *Deeper,* that took as its cover Millais' 'Ophelia' (1851-2), a Pre-Raphaelite classic wherein a frighteningly pale woman lies, both stately and yearning, in a flower-strewn pool. The use of the painting was testament to Knox's advanced romanticism, yet musically the band were little more than run-of-the-mill jangle pop, with occasional keyboard bursts courtesy of Clint Boon from Inspiral Carpets. Collins' efforts were adequate but as yet uninspired, though the effective slide guitar featured on the single 'The Deepest' was a strong pointer to the future. It's also perhaps worth noting that despite the quiffs, chunky shirts and furry Robots-style footwear of The Waltones' earlier phase, Collins very rapidly achieved the purposefully casual look he'd carry on into The Charlatans.

Reviews were fairly positive, but The Waltones didn't last. Collins joined Medalark XI who were picked up by Creation. There would later be official releases, but while the band were at the rehearsal and demo stage (paid for by Creation's Alan McGee), Collins left with the band's drummer to concentrate on their own project, Candlestick Park. An album was recorded for Midnight Music, but canned when the label went bust.

Collins took to hanging around 23 New Mount Street in Manchester, at the time the centre of the city's musical operations. The Fall and James had offices there, as did regional pluggers Red

Alert. It was also the official home of Inspiral Carpets, then pretty much matching The Stone Roses and Happy Mondays hit for hit (if falling miles behind in terms of credibility). The Inspirals knew The Waltones pretty well, having attempted to borrow – if not steal – their manager, Anthony Boggiano. Collins picked up a few odd jobs from them, for a time becoming their driver. Before and after soundchecks he'd use the empty venues for impromptu soccer matches which often involved Noel Gallagher, then on the Inspirals' backline.

When the call came from The Charlatans, a word having been put in by a mutual acquaintance, Alison Martin of Red Alert, Collins was more than interested and auditioned for them at a rehearsal room in Birmingham. This, he thought, would be an easy gig since, as far as he knew, they were looking for a second guitarist, but it was immediately impressed upon him that he was required to fully contribute to songwriting; to 'perform and not conform'.

The call had come on a Monday. By that Wednesday, he was on trial. If he gave his all, and his all was enough, he was in.

Martin Blunt saw that John Baker had to go, but was still upset by his departure. Burgess and Brookes took The Charlatans intensely seriously – it's hard to think of a point in the last nine years when Burgess has talked about anything but The Charlatans – but were capable of switching off now and then or lifting themselves with thoughts of a rosy future for the band.

Blunt, though, was different. Far from irrepressible, he had suffered from serious depression before. Indeed, he had described himself as 'a partial schizophrenic'. Where the others were new to band life and able to treat every problem as surmountable, even as a new adventure, Blunt had learned in Makin' Time that talent, effort and confidence were not always a guarantee of continued success. Fashion was important too: the mood of the country, your money men, your pluggers, promoters, press officers and distributors, not to mention the music media. Were your band too closely aligned with a scene, as Makin' Time had been with mod and The Charlatans now were with baggy, then you would eventually be tossed into its open grave no matter how transcendent you considered yourselves to be.

Blunt wanted a sure future in music, not simply because that would provide security for himself and his prospective new wife, Toni (they were to marry early the next year), but also because it would make sense of a near-decade's worth of escape attempts. But he knew only too well the many pitfalls, and found it nigh on impossible to delegate responsibility. He was all too aware of how the music industry is devilishly ingenious in finding new ways to fuck things up.

Blunt thought hard about his responsibilities as the only experienced band member, and thought about everyone else's contributions too. He thought about the way things could go horribly wrong. Above all, he thought with dread about *going back*, back to a dignity-draining life in a household nailed to the breadline.

So for Blunt, John Baker's departure came as a major blow. In his mind, all the great bands had stuck together – it was one of the things that made them great. Baker leaving had weakened The Charlatans at the least opportune moment, with Madchester beginning to fade and the band coming to realise that in stubbornly signing to the indie Beggars they had denied themselves the higher budget (and consequently the *time*) to ride out any storm. It didn't feel good to Blunt. Change scared him, it made him think more, and when he thought he always thought the worst.

Blunt's fear that the loss of Baker had taken away the gang mentality that was its best hope of survival was heightened by reports in the press, of which Blunt was a keen reader. Though Mark Collins had been taken on board and band shots released with him, pointedly placed at the front, still the rumour abounded that no permanent guitarist could be found. More problematic was the intensely pressurised scheduling for the second album. There just wasn't going to be enough time to experiment with all the options – and there were plenty of those. While most people agreed that The Charlatans should take a long and carefully considered stride away from baggy, it was also noted that too big a step would alienate their burgeoning fan base.

Creatively, this was an extremely confusing time. The band was wracked by the need to stay true to themselves, yet if their natural impulses led them to writing only a more advanced version of *Some Friendly* (as most bands would be permitted to do) they'd be critically slaughtered. Conversely, they knew they couldn't veer *too* far from their winning formula. Each band member had something to say on the subject and, as you'd expect from such a collection of mavericks, everyone had a different idea of what they should collectively be staying true to.

Mark Collins' musical input also made things worse for Blunt. Collins' penchant was for a jangling racket that veered off into sweeping rock, a direction that aligned him with Burgess, Brookes and Rob Collins but was not in keeping with Blunt's vision of a funky blitz.

The first fruit of this new working relationship was 'Me In Time' (working title the rather presumptuous 'Hit Single Number Five'), a three-track single put out at the end of October and produced at Rockfield Studios by Hugh Jones, later to find success with Dodgy and The Bluetones. Intended to fill the gap created by the album's postponement, it was also a statement of intent. The Charlatans would adapt and survive, and by refusing to ransack *Some Friendly* (which would be a smarter move, according to some), they were still sticking to their principle of taking only one single from each album. As a gap-filler, it was a rush-release, as hasty as the official report that the band, ensconced in Wales, had completed eighteen tracks and were considering the possibility of a double album. It was all way too hurried for Blunt's liking.

'The recording of the second album was a very traumatic time,' says Steve Harrison. 'Martin was very down over personal stuff. Also, he'd not found John's leaving to be easy. But more importantly, they'd just written "Me In Time", one of the first songs written with Mark Collins, and Martin fucking *hated* it. He didn't just dislike it, he *loathed* it. If you ask him today what's the worst song he's ever been involved in, I guarantee he'll say "Me In Time". Rob didn't like it much either. I think Martin felt everybody was losing the plot.

'You know, they threw "Weirdo" out at the demo stage. Great tracks that were really popular live, like "Happen To Die" (from the "Over Rising" EP) and "Subterranean" weren't going to be on the LP. With hindsight, it was like everyone was thinking too hard about it, working too hard to avoid doing the obvious thing, when the obvious thing was the most natural way to go.'

Given the climate, it came as no shock when 'Me In Time' suffered a serious critical manhandling. Nevertheless, the ferocity of the battering took the band aback. With nerve-twanging repetition, the line was trotted out that The Charlatans were a one-trick pony, that 'The Only One I Know' had become a painfully ironic title. One review cruelly, and rather surreally, claimed the song sounded like a rejected Tom Petty demo for the Traveling Wilburys.

A few critics pointed to the toughening-up of the sound and the band's growing maturity, recognising that the single's strength lay in its insidious nature rather than its in-your-face immediacy, but most were gleefully dismissive. Burgess himself now describes the work as 'hesitant and unsure' and it's understandable that he of all people should fail to see that therein lies its charm and its inherent truth. With the band exchanging their former headlong charge for deeper, darker, more technologically complex atmospherics – they'd had their moody moments before, but they hadn't really been noted by reviewers – Tim was left, for the first time, to fend for himself. His new hesitancy, an evident lack of confidence exhibited by a formerly cocksure exhibitionist, was a revelation. Burgess was being forced to move beyond the status of simple pin-up and wasn't quite ready.

Consequently, his laboured efforts made him, vocally, into a three-dimensional character where before he stood the danger of being imprisoned in glossy A4. 'Me In Time' could never be lauded as a killer single but it is the sound of a band refusing to follow suit, desperately seeking to trump their way out of trouble. Where most of their peers continued to plough the same old indie furrow, delivering a noisome succession of contemptibly half-arsed jangle-songs, The Charlatans were swerving off into leftfield. They were asking for it, really.

And they got it. 'Me In Time' stalled fatally at Number 28 in the UK charts, a miserable showing considering 'Indian Rope', re-released to save fans paying out a wallet-walloping top dollar for the original twelve-inch, had recently reached Number 57 with no promotion whatsoever. Questions were asked, mostly by Blunt, who'd been outvoted over the choice of single (actually he'd been outvoted over 'Me In Time' ever seeing the light of day). It was even suggested that the single had not been playlisted by Radio 1 because

Burgess had earlier refused to be interviewed on their breakfast show – which had never exactly been likely, as The Charlatans are well known for breakfasting a good five hours after everyone else.

For all of the band, to a man spoiled by the crazy trajectories of *Some Friendly* and the first three singles, this was a major disappointment. All of them, that is, except the new boy. Mark Collins, after eight long years on the dole, thought going Top 30 to be a spectacular success. In his own words, he was 'doing laps of honour', and was utterly bemused by his sullen fellows, thinking that he'd 'joined The Glums'.

Mark was thrilled by the immediate use, if not unanimous acceptance, of his input – one of the B-side tracks, 'Occupation h. Monster' (the other being 'Subtitle'), which had a similar introduction to that of The Waltones' 'Smile' – and by the new line-up's debut on Mark Goodier's radio show. This was Collins' first chance to party big time and he took it. Within two years, he reckons, he had done serious damage to his nose, giving himself a permanent clinical aversion to cocaine.

By now, Blunt was not coping well at all. After the comparative failure of 'Me In Time' (of course, he himself would never use the qualification 'comparative'), all he could see were the vultures circling overhead. The band was moving in another direction, taking onboard Mark Collins' ideas and seemingly outvoting Blunt at every turn. Blunt was no longer in control, and that was as bad as it got. His need for control was a major symptom of his grievous insecurity; his only protection against flooding paranoia. As a musician with a deep-seated desire for security, he was always going to have problems. He was in deep shit.

To Blunt's mind, the press were unfairly on the Charlatans' case, the record company still harping on about continuing to tour the *Some Friendly* set, and the band, his last refuge, were broken and bickering. And the fans, well, with the single stiffing at Number 28, *what* fans? On top of this, his relationship with Toni was suffering. He was always away, touring or recording, and Blunt, like most musicians, wanted both a life in music and a 'normal' one too. He wanted his cake, he wanted to eat it, but it was all falling in crumbs to the floor.

Blunt had always been prone to brooding and the band's

increasing problems soon threw him into a full-blown depression. Ever the worrier, now he was a truly wretched soul, feeling both abandoned and assaulted, as if his life were being scripted by Edgar Allan Poe. While the others scrabbled to stay afloat, rowing and rucking and struggling with possible progressions, Blunt was paralysed by his thoughts. Already more than usually morose, his speech impeded to the degree where he was visibly fighting to talk, his words building up inside then bursting out all at once, and often, due to that pronounced accent of his, completely unintelligible (he's a lot better now, thank God). He felt inescapably hounded. No wonder, then, that in September he finally collapsed.

The Charlatans' previous success meant that their fame had extended beyond the music press, so the national tabloids were on to the story of Blunt's mental troubles like a wind-assisted Ben Johnson. Beggars Banquet stonewalled all inquiries. Blunt, in truth, *had* experienced such episodes before, but not since he'd become famous.

Burgess would later state that no one had seen Blunt's collapse coming; they had thought he was just 'being miserable' again. Laughingly he explained that Blunt had gone out to buy food for his dog then, suddenly finding himself back home clutching ten cans of cat food, hadn't left his house for the rest of the weekend. It wasn't exactly a *breakdown*: the poor bastard just didn't know what the fuck was going on. The rest would use the story to affectionately taunt him sometimes, to lighten things up, like.

Blunt himself brushed it off as quickly and tersely as possible. A proud and private man, he had never wanted to lose control and certainly didn't wish to be seen to have done so. He told the *Sun* simply that it had all been building up since August, that it was mainly to do with 'things outside the group', and that, contrary to reports in other papers, he hadn't gone to hospital but just convalesced at home for a couple of weeks.

Blunt didn't speak about the matter again for seven years, apart from some four months after the fact, when he admitted to this author that, 'I was in hospital. I was totally fucked up, seriously. It wasn't to do with the group, but I needed time out badly. It was like I was on this treadmill; it was getting like a job. It wasn't self-pity or anything, just insecurity and an attack of paranoia brought

85

on by personal stuff. It was a bad time. I was over-thinking, over-analysing and John was leaving and I always thought the main thing about the group was keeping it together.'

Even today, Blunt still prefers to skim over the matter, saying, 'I just thought everything was imploding. I went to the doctor and he said, 'You've got clinical depression,' and I went, 'Oh right' and I took two weeks off. And that ended up being reported as manic depression, which it *wasn't*. It was just this feeling of impending doom, like I was trying to juggle mercury. I had had it before, but it's just one of those things. Some people are just natural born worriers, aren't they?'

So the collapse wasn't to do with the group but at the same time it was. Blunt had felt failure creeping up on him again, a failure more painful than Makin' Time's because he had climbed so much higher, only to take a knock-back from which there would probably be no recovery. He found it more painful still because he felt he should have been sussed enough to sort it out for everyone. He even feared that maybe time would prove Baker to be the lucky one, shoved to one side before the blade fell.

Blunt, as ever, kept it all inside. No matter, really. Whether the reasons for them were hidden or exposed, the band's tribulations were there for all to see. For those cynics keenly awaiting The Charlatans' downfall, it was all grist to the mill.

On top of all The Charlatans' problems, and to the huge delight of the gloating music press, came the slow, writhing death of Madchester. This was both pitiful and predictable. Manchester had the wide-ranging and contradictory characteristics of any other major conurbation. It had its elitist green suburbs and glitzy shopping areas, as well as its run-down districts and problems with drugs and homelessness. It was buoyantly multi-cultural and keenly aware of international fashions, yet conscious too of its traditions and past triumphs. Creatively, in this three-year boom-time, it had reflected all of this and, in its carefree crossing of black and white, rock and dance had delivered an adrenalin injection straight into the frontal lobe of British music.

But Madchester wasn't about that. Madchester was the north-west experience shorn of its complex contemporary relevance and pared down to a painful simplicity, a saleable commodity. This involved the extraordinary and patently ludicrous notion that Manchester was simply a cityful of over-confident, floppy-fringed teenagers in magnificently non-functional flares, storming from club to club in a high-grade Ecstasy rush and gleefully engaging in monosyllabic conversations usually involving the words "top" and "safe". Madchester was a media construct designed to sell magazines and T-shirts, a tasty morsel to be chewed up and inevitably spat out (not digested, never that).

This was nothing new, of course. There had been the San Francisco of the sixties, as well as Liverpool in that same decade and in the early eighties of Echo And The Bunnymen and The Teardrop Explodes. New York was currently being feted for its hardcore rock and Los Angeles still for the poodle-headed variety. Even Birmingham had tasted short-lived glory in the heyday of Led Zeppelin, Black Sabbath and the fledgling Judas Priest. Every town will eventually be awarded its fifteen minutes by a media so high on self-importance that it's capable of crediting a fashion journalist, as it did, with 'inventing Barcelona'.

Manchester certainly gained from the whole Madchester furore. Youngsters were handed a flip but much-needed cultural identity, and revelled in a sense of community normally exhibited only in times of footballing catastrophe. Already buzzing, it was brought to a peak by the attention of the world. With the city prowled by predatory and increasingly desperate A&R men, with the main chance there for the taking, thousands attempted a creative self-advancement where it might have been hundreds. Lucrative businesses were built up as an international market opened up to the designers, producers and merchandisers of T-shirts now as commonplace as Frankie Goes To Hollywood's once were.

But like all media hypes (reluctant, deserving or otherwise), it had to end and, unavoidably, that ending brought suffering. Their aspirations raised to Sputnik levels, many bands too slow, talentless or simply luckless were left in the lurch as the A&R herds departed to graze pastures new. Many more, with deals already in the bag, saw their dreams wither as record company priorities changed and, baggy or not, yesterday's things were not given the financial backing to turn into tomorrow's. The so-called Second Wave of Madchester, headed by the likes of Intastella, World Of

Twist, Paris Angels, My Jealous God and even The High (despite their spacey, tremendously soulful debut LP) were denied their shot at stardom and instead sent packing back to a sorry station miles below base camp.

Autumn 1991 saw the release of Nirvana's *Nevermind* and immediately Washington State became music's latest vortex. On the heads of the cognoscenti and their attendants, floppy fringes were left to grow wild and Joe Bloggs were tossed aside in favour of dark-checked lumberjack shirts, scruffy Levis and battered trainers. Soon, Dinosaur Jr's J. Mascis would appear on *The Clothes Show*. The baggy construct collapsed like Jericho. Madchester's advanced sense of togetherness was painfully alien to this new Me Generation.

Consequently, the previously lauded Madchester icons were ripe for an almighty kicking. The Stone Roses, hobbled by their long-running court case with Silvertone, were mocked for their lack of productivity, with critics quick to forget that it had taken them a good four years to produce their first album. The regular re-releasing of their singles, coupled with a compilation of B-sides only highlighted the sense of anti-climax. Happy Mondays, after the brief triumph of the *Pills 'n' Thrills and Bellyaches,* staggered from one press disaster to another, their once-celebrated streetwise laddishness now provoking righteous accusations of sexism, homophobia and all-round boorishness. Their drug intake had also reached critical levels as they buried 1992's '...Yes Please!' – recorded in the West Indies with Talking Heads' Tina Weymouth and Chris Frantz – under an avalanche of Class As. It was a pitiful, joyless affair, to many proof positive that these were just pig-ignorant yobs using music as an excuse to get tanked up rather than knuckle down. Even those drawn into the phenomenon from outside, like Lancashire's 808 State, were being dismissed as old hat.

And The Charlatans, for all their oft-repeated claims to West Midlands roots, with Baker gone, Blunt losing it and that 'difficult' second album still to be completed, were seen by many as cynical chancers on a bandwagon which was now out of control and heading for oblivion. As far as the media were concerned, were The Charlatans to split or, better still, publicly fail and fade wretchedly away, a neat full stop could be placed at the end of the chapter headed Madchester.

03 From Sickening Defeat To Chemical Warfare

FOR THEIR INTENSELY DIFFICULT second album, The Charlatans returned to Rockfield, a studio in the countryside outside Monmouth on the Welsh/English border. Opened in 1965, it was the UK's first residential studio, run by brothers Charles and Kingsley Ward until a split in 1988 when Charles took the original mixing desk off down the road to start his own business at Monnow Valley.

Rockfield was and is legendary. It was here that Queen recorded 'Bohemian Rhapsody' and Oasis later constructed *What's The Story (Morning Glory)?* The Stone Roses were ensconced there for some considerable time, fretting over *The Second Coming*. The place was perfect for The Charlatans: quiet, conducive to both work and play (there was plenty of fishing action for Rob Collins) and also, in the fields around the complex, extraordinary opportunities for reaping magic mushrooms.

The Charlatans knew their choice of producer for this record was crucial. They also knew they had no idea who they wanted.

'I don't think there was any cohesive reason for *anything* around that time,' says Steve Harrison. 'For the only time in the band's career, there was no collective direction. We were almost clutching at straws. It was also probably the only time Beggars were really, really helpful, sending us CVs of different producers. There was a kind of Negative Option Syndrome going on, with everyone knocking everything back. You know, it's a lot easier to break things than create them, and that's what the band were up to. No one was in control, no one even knew *how* to be in control. It was like we were too confused to grasp anything, to move forward or sideways or backwards, so we kind of let things happen.'

The band's attitude was just not right.

'We'd lost something by the time we'd come to make this album,' says Jon Brookes. 'I'd loved it before, me and four other blokes in a small room, really doing something for the first time. Then suddenly we were in Rich Bitch studios in Birmingham, with Dave Hill from Slade working in a different part of the building, with people making us tea and coffee and bringing in chocolate Hob-Nobs on a plate. That's no way to live your life. It's like being on one of those weird planets in *Star Trek* where everyone's cohabiting and leading a peaceful existence, wanting for nothing. That's no good for us; we need to grind out a good result, like Arsenal do. I don't wanna be pissing about in a silken robe with a big smile on my face. I like a good fucking row.'

What was called for was someone who could latch on to the spirit of the band, recognise and isolate their best ideas and help them find a natural and painless escape route out of baggy. The experiments with David Allan and Hugh Jones having not quite lived up to expectations (though Jones's version of 'Subtitle' would make it on to the album), they decided to venture even further out into leftfield.

The man chosen for the job was Flood, who, having been pushed towards The Charlatans by his girlfriend (a big fan of *Some Friendly*), had earlier remixed 'Sproston Green' for the American market, as well as recreating 'Opportunity' as 'Opportunity 3'. His real name being Mark Ellis, Flood had earned his nickname while working as tea-boy in London's Morgan Studios in the late seventies, apparently for overfilling mugs.

After some time spent assiduously watching and learning, he'd become an engineer, moving eventually to Trident Studios where he met Mute boss Daniel Miller. This was a fateful encounter, with Flood going on to engineer for many Mute acts (Depeche Mode, Nick Cave and Erasure, as well as Soft Cell and The Jesus And Mary Chain), all the while gaining for himself a heavy (and well-deserved) reputation for innovation. Having been deeply involved in Nine Inch Nails' cult million-seller *Pretty Hate Machine* he was invited by Brian Eno to help on U2's *The Joshua Tree* (you know U2 – they do so love to be cutting edge and rich at the same time), thereby proving his abilities in the mainstream.

When he got the call from The Charlatans, Flood was just finishing up U2's *Achtung Baby*. The band had already been recording in Rockfield for two weeks, but when Flood arrived he binned the lot – which left a frighteningly short six weeks for recording and mixing. Because of the way he worked, he really needed to have been there from the start.

Flood's style was to coax a storming live performance from the band, break the recording down into parts and then rebuild with different rhythms and effects, all the while protecting the vital melodies. He would deliberately retain mistakes, when they felt good, to avoid technological coldness. He also liked to work extremely hard in short bursts, at one point nailing down eleven backing tracks in eight punishing days. The Charlatans were not used to this; they were thrown by this new approach and particularly by the intensive toil. Burgess's personal tracklisting at the studio was headed with a scrawled 'Flood is a Nazi'.

The sessions were hard-going. It wasn't that there were no ideas – if anything there were too many – it was just that no one could agree on anything. Flood found himself living in the midst of a five-man barracking contest, with Blunt especially forceful after what he considered to be the debacle of 'Me In Time', and even the happy-go-lucky Mark Collins now feeling the pressure. While trying to keep the band's best efforts from being dumped by their ruthless democracy, Flood was forced by time constraints and his own professional inclinations to lead the way and make sure *something* got done.

'We really didn't want to be in the same room as each other,' recalls Burgess. 'Thinking about it, I think there might even have been a bit of an ego problem. It's hard to admit, but we almost forgot who we were. And then Martin lost it, lost his bottle a bit, I think, got really down. Mark was pissing blood with worry all the way through. I don't think he'd ever drunk or smoked so much in his life before, because he could only afford five Silk Cuts a day on the dole.

'Lyrically, the whole LP was weird. It was like "Please get me out of this place." That's why we don't really play any of that stuff live now – bad memories. We were practising in Birmingham for a start, and we were surrounded by people who kept saying how brilliant the first LP was. Everyone had got into Nirvana too. We had one track that was 100 per cent baggy, and Flood tried to turn it into a grunge classic.'

In some respects, The Charlatans had undermined themselves. Their refusal to take more than one single from *Some Friendly* had forced them to record extra tracks for 'Over Rising' and 'Me In Time' – half an album's worth which would have been more than helpful now. Only four tracks, 'Weirdo', 'Tremelo Song', 'Can't Even Be Bothered' and '(No One) Not Even The Rain', written before the arrival of Mark Collins, were even remotely ready to go – and there were severe doubts about 'Weirdo'.

The album would be called *Between 10th And 11th*, that being the cool-sounding half of the address of the New York Marquee, venue for the band's first ever US gig, on 4 October 1990. It was also the name of an old track, recorded for a John Peel session in February 1991, but then unceremoniously dumped (and nothing whatsoever to do with the Spanish Civil War, as Burgess would later mischievously claim on Radio 1). Yet up until the last minute the working title was *Anticlockwise* (*Prefabs And Riches* was a further throwaway possibility). *Anticlockwise*, the initial title of the track 'Ignition', was Blunt's idea and referred to the band's habit of going about things the wrong way. Given the mess they had got themselves into, *Widdershins* might have been more fittingly fatalistic.

On they rushed, ever prompted by the demanding and resourceful Flood, chucking in everything but the kitchen sink – and they might have used that, too, if they could have battered an interesting noise out of it. 'Subtitle' was a seriously spontaneous affair, featuring Burgess, drunk as a skunk on cheap sparkling wine, accompanied only by Rob Collins. He'd gone in to lay down test vocals with only the vague notion of writing a song about an adolescent crush and only the phrases 'not the same as everybody else' and 'why talk to her?' completed, and come up with a precious little ditty. Now it was taken and turned into a bizarre, sub-oceanic beast of a track with bursts of Who guitar, elated New Age keyboards and a filthy bass rumble pre-dating many of techno's madder moments.

This set the tone for much of the record. 'I Don't Want To See

The Sights' saw a perky jangle swept away in a mud-slide of bass, with Burgess distant and echoing. 'The End Of Everything' was an innately violent piece, characterised by pummelling bass, punching guitar and stabbing keyboards – like the rest of the album it exchanged the sheer rush of the band's early work for a more considered, jolting momentum. 'Page One', at first titled 'Vulture' after its self-hating opening line 'Physically I resemble a vulture', had Rob Collins relegated to a faraway swirl. Even 'Can't Even Be Bothered', its big chorus the most immediate link to *Some Friendly*, used its power in bursts – an object lesson in restraint, timing and technique.

Flood was true to his word in retaining the band's, and particularly Burgess's, melodic flourishes. But the beat was clearly at the front of his mind, and the industrial idiosyncracies that had made his name. He used samples of Mark Collins dropping his amp, and the opening track saw the band taking the top off a piano, hitting the strings with brushes and twanging one with a pick. The final, dopey 'Not Even The Rain', where hypnotic, clattering percussion and a gut-deep bass eventually overpower all accompaniment, ended the album with a shattering racket. Musically, it was an intriguing collection, disappointing in its lack of cheap thrills but impressive, especially rhythmically, in its struggle to rise above the norm.

Lyrically, as Burgess explains, the album was at points painfully introspective and self-doubting, the premise for 'Can't Even Be Bothered' being, he says, 'What am I up here singing for? I only wanted to play tambourine anyway.' For Burgess, internal questioning had replaced his former certainties as he began to seek more profound influences. Given Burgess's cut-up technique, inherited from The Fall's Mark E. Smith, these are often hard to spot, but one was the pre-electric Bob Dylan and another Edward Estlin Cummings (or ee cummings, as he himself preferred it).

Cummings, who died in 1962, was along with Robert Frost the most widely read poet in mid-century America. Influenced by jazz and contemporary slang, he drew together lines and phrases of great wit and beauty while at the same time – by breaking all rules of punctuation and typography – having his lines create a visual impression that gave his poetry an extra dimension in theme and tone.

Cummings was preoccupied with the obscenity of war, the dangerous complexities of patriotism and religion, and the true power of nature relative to the desperate scuttlings of men. Burgess was touched by his abrasive belligerence and the abandon of his uninhibited Bohemianism. He loved his stuttering then wildly flowing rhythms, and took them on board (*Between 10th And 11th* is at its best when his efforts fuse with Flood's own stop-go! style). Cummings had moved Dylan and, through him, now moved Burgess, his thoughts infusing the lyrics, especially those of 'The End Of Everything' ('There's no soldier in me') and '(No One) Not Even The Rain' (the line 'Not even the rain has such small hands' being taken from the final line of Cummings' 'somewhere I have never travelled').

The very title of that poem had deep resonance for Burgess. Just as Dylan had been set on the road by Woody Guthrie's songs of hard travellin', so Burgess, now stuck in a tiny room decorated only with a *Quadrophenia* poster and a postcard-sized ad for *Bonnie and Clyde*, fantasised and constructed lyrical daydreams about permanent escape from small-town Northwich. For an age, this was The Charlatans' main point – the search for a bigger, fuller life. And it was this heartfelt longing that most touched the fans who flocked to their gigs in their rapidly increasing hundreds. No wonder Burgess and the rest would later revel in their friendship with Terry Hall: The Specials' 'Ghost Town' was a chilling expression of the life they'd wished to flee. Same goes for Paul Weller and The Jam's 'In The City' and 'Down In The Tube Station At Midnight'.

When accused once of sticking too rigidly to the guitar band format, J. Mascis of Dinosaur Jr said that he really had no choice. Using different styles and instruments, with the endless possibilities involved, would paralyse him. He could find direction and motivation only by limiting his own scope. The Charlatans were now suffering in the same way. They could try anything, so they did, leaving Flood and his vision of the band as the only constant. The results were interesting, but hardly the earth-moving experience the band felt they could have created. Still, there were important lessons learned.

'Flood taught us a lot of the technological stuff,' says Blunt. 'I mean, the man is a genius. Maybe not quite right for us, but he is a genius. I got on really well with him, I think we all did, really. We'd do a performance and then it would all get cut down, chopped and changed. It was different for us, and I tried to get used to it as it went along, but it was all done in such a short time we thought, Oh, let's go with it. It turned out to be a bit of a curate's egg, really.'

It had also lost some of the clarity of *Some Friendly*.

'We suffered from being over-subtle,' admits Blunt, 'like with "Chewing Gum Weekend". No one got that. I mean, there's only two reasons you chew gum – either you're trying to pack in smoking or you're trying to stop yourself grinding your own teeth to dust. No one ever clocked what that song was about.'

One notable success was 'Weirdo'. With Rob Collins' keyboard riding a shudderingly funky bassline, Flood picked this one up off the cutting-room floor and turned it into a compellingly fidgety expression of neurosis. Mark Collins calls it 'a marvellous job' and adds that, without it, they might never have reached their later heights. Throughout, Flood had helped them get to grips with studio technology. With 'Weirdo' he taught them how to effectively run sequencers alongside their live performances. Without this knowledge, says Collins, The Charlatans could never have later pulled off their biggest hit single, 'One To Another': 'It was the track that pointed us in that direction.'

All the band were concerned about the quality of the final product, but at the same time extremely relieved that there actually *was* one. For good and bad, Flood was the main reason for that and, being as he was as new to working with bona fide pop bands as The Charlatans were to dealing with technological frontiersmen, he should be unreservedly applauded. The album too, despite the critical mauling it received at the time, is now undergoing a more generous reappraisal. But Flood did put a final foot wrong: he broke Burgess's bloody, almost Corsican, code of loyalty.

'I remember Flood was suggested by someone at Warner Chappell, the publishers,' Tim says. 'He'd done stuff with Pop Will Eat Itself and U2 and Nine Inch Nails and we thought, He wants to do something with us? Cool. But, with hindsight, it really didn't work. We didn't have the songs for it, and he didn't tell us when he was supposed to be the producer. I mean, come on, man, you've got to tell people straight what's right and what's wrong. We were confident, but not as confident as we were with the first LP. And this was the first time we'd had someone who was supposed to be looking after us. But all we got was, "Oh, that song's great – that sounds great, you're going to be massive."

'He also told us he was going to do our third LP but he flaked it, let us down. I remember the last thing Martin said to him after *Between 10th And 11th*. He said "Flood, if there's one person we want to work with and keep working with, it's you. Will you do it?" And Flood said, "Martin, I'll do anything for you." I'm not saying Flood's a bad person, he's not, but he and Martin were best mates all the way through that, and he didn't do what he said he would. And he left us off his portfolio. I'm still pretty bitter about all that.'

'We basically just handed the album over to someone,' ends Burgess. 'We had plenty of songs but we gave it to someone else to do it for us and it was a bad mistake. I remember saying to Martin afterwards, "Do you think Mick and Keith or John and Paul McCartney ever didn't have a hand in what they were doing? We've got to do it ourselves." In the future, it led to a major paranoia about producers and about technology, and we did end up producing and mixing ourselves.'

It wasn't Flood's fault, really. Deservedly in demand, he just had other commitments, a different set of loyalties. But Burgess, like the others, deals in absolutes: you are either with The Charlatans or you are not, no inbetweens. For them that attitude is a blessing and a curse, bringing them both deep satisfaction and untold and often unnecessary grief. There would be a similar problem three years later.

Despite the near-unbearable strain of the past year – the constant interruptions, the ongoing arguments over strategy, the pressure to discard their fan-friendly principles, the break-ups and break-downs – the band were now in (fairly) high spirits. Fashion had moved on, and the band had seen the Madchester scene collapse. Baker had left, causing a radical rethink about what constitutes a 'perfect' rock career. But, fuck it, when The Rolling Stones lost

Brian Jones it only seemed to prod them into a new, ever more glorious period. And the perceived antipathy of press and public
towards The Charlatans gave them something the speed of their
success had earlier denied them – a bunker mentality where they
were forced to close ranks, put their trust completely in each other,
dig deep and, above all, fight. Like real bands do.

Burgess in particular was bubbling. Perhaps he was aware of the
damaging effects of overkill, perhaps the turnaround in press atti-
tudes had dented his confidence in his looks and natural charm or
maybe he was simply bored with his own repetitive boasting, but
he was no longer as quick to bludgeon you with his flip self-idoli-
sation. Instead, as if in his naive, childlike way he was unable to
accept the existence of ruinous, dream-shattering failure, he would
rave on and on about The Charlatans collectively – my band, our
band, the band – as if engaged in a life-long mantra, a relentless
positive visualisation. He was certainly very relieved to have got
some kind of album together.

On 28 February, 'Weirdo', before long the only track from
Between 10th And 11th to remain in The Charlatans' live set, was
released as a single (a limited twelve-inch coming with free art
prints). Though it outdid 'Me In Time' by reaching Number 19, it
wasn't viewed by their detractors as a Top Twenty smash but as
having stiffed in the lower reaches of the charts – such was the pre-
vailing attitude towards the band. Yet it was an exceptionally
strong track with a compelling accompanying video, cutting
sharply between a dalmatian, a sofa and a dancer, with the band
chopping in and out as the black and white is occasionally shot
through with colour. It was one of The Charlatans' better efforts,
but unfortunately received little airtime, and none at all in
America where the song's subject matter had been very strangely
perceived.

'When we'd done the second album,' says Blunt, 'RCA, our
label in America, said we should go over to Los Angeles for four
days to do back-to-back videos for "Weirdo" and "I Don't Want
To See The Sights" with Matt Bayer, the guy who'd just done the
video for "Smells Like Teen Spirit". Unlike Nirvana, we didn't get
the audience or the rah-rah girls. What we did get was all these

people from Venice Beach who looked like the kind of punk rockers you got on postcards from London in 1984. Because the track was called "Weirdo", you understand. And, to top it all, they had a dwarf dressed up as Mr Punch. A fucking *dwarf!* And we'd already made a video in London that was really good at a third of the price.'

The video for 'I Don't Want To See The Sights' was hardly any better. Shot in a mental institution, with a guy spinning around in a wheelchair and another assortment of oddballs, it was dreadfully embarrassing stuff that could only serve to undermine the band as they criss-crossed the States throughout that year. And it could have been pulled off with so much more aplomb – The Charlatans had come up with the idea of getting in Ken Russell to direct for them. Considering *The Devils* and *Lisztomania*, this could have been a riproaring and gratifyingly disgraceful success. It never happened.

As February turned to March, The Charlatans played two notterribly-secret gigs at King Tut's Wah-Wah Hut in Glasgow. These were intended to break in Mark Collins and their new material in preparation for what was intended to be a full year of touring. A London audience would have been too harsh, too unforgiving, Manchester safer but still pressurised. Scotland, which had always rallied to the band with unrestrained fervour, was the perfect choice.

The Glasgow shows were a shambles, with equipment breaking down and the band rolling around laughing at the chaos around them. The crowd annoyingly and relentlessly insisted upon hearing 'Indian Rope', on the first night invading the stage and further damaging the gear (on the second, crash barriers were in place). King Tut's was a pulsing sweatbox and a hell of a good time was being had. Burgess was less studied in his peacockery, moving towards a less forced showmanship. The band were cheerful but still intense, clearly glad to be back live after the scientific rigours of recording. The Charlatans had much to prove and, despite the supposed failure of 'Weirdo', still seemed joyfully resolute in taking up the challenge.

The band also threw themselves into the few interviews and photo opportunities that now came their way. One shoot in particular, in a North London branch of Safeway, proved a massive giggle. Such was the disruption to normal business that staff allowed customers a few free bits and bobs, at Beggars Banquet's expense, just to appease them. Howard Devoto, arch ex-Magazine frontman and then in Luxuria, stablemates to The Charlatans, was along for the ride and decided to avail himself of a free can of Sapporo. Sadly, the Safeway staff, unfamiliar with the more arcane reaches of indiedom, mistook the former punk guru for an undesirable skinhead interloper and had him tossed from the building.

Between 10th And 11th was released on 23 March, a week or so before the band began what would be their last major UK tour for three years. Their fans, as is their wont, all bought the record in the first few days of release, giving it the thoroughly cheering midweek chart position of Number 4. By the time the chart was finally announced on the Sunday, though, it had fallen to a disturbing 21, a week later depressingly dropping a further 22 places.

One reason for this was the reviews. A couple of them praised the album for its daring and inventiveness and the band's attempt to escape a reputation for being frivolous popsters. One perceptive critic even picked up on an underlying sadness and saw the lack of storming choruses as pointing to a new maturity, with Burgess, apparently an old head on young shoulders, taking on the mantle of world-weary and disillusioned aesthete. His sensitivity and lack of laddishness were recognised, an important point when comparing and contrasting The Charlatans with the Manchester scenes of the early and mid-nineties.

However, many more reviewers proffered the opinion that The Charlatans had used Flood in the same way as the hatefully pompous U2 – to make themselves look like avant garde risk-takers, and to disguise the fact that they had come up with no melodies. The best that was said about many of the tracks was that they started well, then meandered pointlessly off into nowhere. Flood escaped relatively unscathed but the band were slaughtered, Burgess especially getting it in the neck for supposed laziness. His lyrics, intended to evoke moods and provoke thought, were ridiculed, as was Steve Majors' cover shot of a close-to-overripe bunch of bananas.

The album jacket wasn't deliberately planned by the band as a reference to Andy Warhol's cover to *The Velvet Underground & Nico*. Just as the tracks had been recorded too quickly, so there was no time available to concentrate on the sleeve. The banana shot was picked out of a small pile of possibilities at the very last minute. It was chosen because, according to Burgess, none of the others seemed to them to refer to anything and, since this one had bananas a little like Warhol's (in that they were yellow and curved), at least it referred to *something*.

Typically, Burgess refused to complain. Almost childlike in his seeming inability to accept bad news, he'd turn to you – head bowed, chin stubbled and eyes looking up through his now longer, stragglier mop – and murmur, "Oh, mate, they fookin' *hate* us, they do!" Then, snapping his fingers with that wrist-jarring flick, he'd burst into loud gales of laughter and instantly begin to regale you with tales of newly discovered classic rock and new ideas for his next album. Even at this dark hour, Burgess – indeed, all of them bar Blunt, who acting as the band's unpaid sin-eater, would be squeezing his chin, talking rapidly and indecipherably through nervous fingers and generally worrying the life out of you – appeared to have no thought of failure. *Between 10th And 11th* was regarded as a blip, a simple delay, almost before it came out. The band were looking to America once more and, already, the third album.

With rehearsals in Scarborough over and the album at that heartening midweek Number 4, the band took off for Greece for two more warm-ups and a bit of a knees-up – The Charlatans have an old-fashioned and really quite touching affection for the seaside. Once back to tour the UK and face the music, they were beset by yet more problems, most of them revolving around Rob Collins. Collins loved his Hammonds but now they were turning against him, exploding in his hands as if booby-trapped. Two of them blew before the doors were opened at Glasgow's Barrowland, another went the next day, and yet another at Manchester Apollo. Replacements were sought desperately at £1,000 a throw. So incensed was Collins that a fight broke out after the Manchester show, with Collins quitting the band and storming off into the night (thankfully, he was pacified on his return to the hotel).

Beyond this, and a continuing series of caustic reviews, there were also problems with Beggars Banquet. With sales of the album dying off so quickly, the label were extremely keen to give it a boost by taking a second single from it. This struck the band as a serious affront: it meant breaking their word to their fans, and to themselves. Beggars also urged the band to embrace formatting and release singles in two, three, sometimes four different sleeves, with extra tracks exclusive to each one, and even collectors' packs to go with them. This basically boosted sales by forcing fans to purchase the same item over and over, and enticed outsiders with a glitzier package.

The Charlatans reacted badly to what were known as 'commodity-angled strategies'. They thought it was exploitation, striking against their working-class socialist principles by making life tough for fans who had as little spare cash as they themselves had had a mere eighteen months before. Plus it added extra pressure for the band in that all those B-sides meant they would have to come up with what amounted to another album's worth of material – unless they knocked out any old rubbish, which was, to The Charlatans' minds, even worse. This scenario would place them right back where they were after 'Over Rising' and 'Me In Time' – in trouble.

Then there was the matter of America. *Some Friendly* had sold in excess of 350,000 copies Stateside: a relatively paltry amount considering the size of the market, but nevertheless a valuable springboard to greater things. MTV had changed matters to a large degree: its airing of videos nationwide meant that the years of touring endured by the likes of Black Sabbath were no longer as necessary. Still, in order to score big time, you had to make your presence felt – *months* on the road were still imperative.

So they discussed how to approach it. The Charlatans felt that, with effective promotional back-up, they were big enough to carry off headlining tours of their own. Beggars baulked at the expense. Though *Some Friendly* had gone some way to filling their coffers, The Cult were no longer the saleable force they had been and the rest of their roster was a drain on resources. In order to cut costs, they suggested that The Charlatans engage in a double-header with Peter Murphy, the charismatic yet inexpressibly silly ex-frontman of Bauhaus.

'The pressure was unbelievable,' says Harrison, 'because both acts were on Beggars Banquet and it would have saved them a packet – more bums on seats, two posters for the price of one, two ads for the price of one. They'll try and get you sharing the same coach. On the positive side, Pete Murphy was doing quite well, so we could have played 5,000-capacity venues instead of 2,000 and, because this was America and not England, maybe some of Murphy's crowd would have been turned on to The Charlatans, and vice versa. You know, there *was* a positive side. And I remember being in a backstage room with the president of RCA pleading with us to do this tour. He was saying, "It'll be great. MTV are into it. We can make this work for everybody." But there was a negative side too – that Pete Murphy's a goth and he's fucking *crap*. The band were all going, "We're not going out with a fucking *bat*!" We couldn't do it. They would have been so uncomfortable.'

So The Charlatans refused the offer out of hand and, by doing so, annoyed the hell out of their American label yet again. In the US they like to plan. They'll think about an artist, put together a cohesive nationwide strategy, psyche up the workforce and go for it. If it doesn't work, well, it's on to the next one. The Charlatans and Harrison were unused to this. They were familiar with the notion of perseverance, with getting a few more bites at the cherry.

With Beggars, a small-scale operation, the band knew that no matter how bad it got there was usually some kind of agreement to be reached and some way of everyone coming out of it more or less happy. With the big corporations it's hardball. If you mess about, you're history, buddy. Calls are all of a sudden not returned, responsibility seems to pass from office to office, tier to tier of the organisation. From being a skyscraper packed with your closest friends, the company becomes the faceless monster of legend.

The Charlatans, with their impassioned but naive indie mentality, their belief that everything should be done their way, and no experience whatsoever in dealing with the big boys, were beginning to find themselves on hold with uncomfortable regularity.

The first leg of 1992's US tour began on 19 April at the Dallas Earth Day Edge Festival, known as the Edgefest, where The Charlatans played with the Björk-fronted Sugarcubes and Pearl Jam (still growing in popularity – by August that year their debut album *Ten* would be US Number 2 and well on its way to selling ten million copies). The concert would make upward of $150,000 dollars for local environmental groups.

As the tour progressed, it became increasingly obvious that it wasn't quite happening. Some of the gigs were bigger than they had been the year before, but The Charlatans found themselves back at the Chicago Metro again, and no one really seemed to be buzzing about the album's chances. Unsurprising, really. A week after the final date, at New York's Academy, *Between 10th And 11th* peaked at Number 173. In the UK there was at least the consolation that though record sales were down, live audiences were growing fast, and not just in the band's now traditional heartlands of Manchester and Scotland. That had them feeling that, no matter what was being said, they must be doing *something* right. In the US, the outlook was somewhat bleaker.

Still, there was a resolutely American institution to encourage the band – The Beastie Boys. Back in 1987, with their *Licensed To Ill* a worldwide smash and 'She's On It' and 'Fight For Your Right To Party' even bigger party anthems than 'The Only One I Know', Ad Rock and the gang were both critical and popular darlings. A short two years later, the sprawling, purposefully oblique follow-up, *Paul's Boutique*, like *Between 10th And 11th*, had died in the water. But now they were back. As The Charlatans slogged across the States, the Beasties' *Check Your Head* was gaining underground momentum and, no longer the squawking brats of old, the Beasties were cool again in the coolest of senses – brave, inventive, self-possessed and battle hardened. A week or so after The Charlatans had departed for a month-long drag through Europe, *Check Your Head* would rehabilitate the Beasties entirely by debuting in the US Top Ten.

Burgess remembers Jon Brookes picking up a copy of the album at a US radio station, and the DJ saying, 'Oh, you can have that. I don't even want to listen to it.'

'Beastie Boys was an example of a band going from big, to nothing, to doing exactly what they wanted to do,' explains Brookes. 'We played that CD night and day on the tour bus and the philosophy really caught on with us – that you can look into yourself and come back as you really are.'

Time had proved the Beasties right and the DJ wrong. Now liberated by recording inexpensively and easily in their own studio, they had taken their time, taken the hard blows and the cheap shots, and now were back, with a shit-hot reputation and an album in the Top Ten. It was an invaluable lesson to learn. Even in the nineties, with the market-place's voracious appetite for fresh blood and its grim habit of tossing artists aside, misunderstood and only half-consumed, there *was* a way back: but only if you stayed true to yourself. The Charlatans' inordinately powerful bunker mentality, with (naturally) a touch of historical rock 'n' roll 'tude tossed in for good measure, was proving very useful.

Tim Burgess alludes to it in his foreword to this book but, of all the band, Jon Brookes is best able to explain the depth of this communal resolution. 'The thing I always say is that The Charlatans is a thing beyond us all. You might occasionally let yourself down, you might not pull your weight or act responsibly, but you must never let the name of The Charlatans down. You must never shit on the group, never diss the band, never rubbish it. It's something we all have in common. We've fought really hard to keep this group going, to keep it special, and it's something we now do by instinct.'

After their Euro tour, taking in Holland, Belgium, France, Spain, more of France, then Italy and Germany, on 24 June The Charlatans returned for a more extensive pop at America. They were to tour for a full two months. As ever, things didn't prove easy, but this time the elements as well as social history conspired against them. They suffered earth tremors in San Francisco, and in Los Angeles they played on the cripplingly tense evening before the verdicts in the Rodney King trial.

Then, as the tour reached Seabright, New Jersey, the call came through that Blunt's wife, Toni, was about to give birth to their son, Joseph. He *had* to be there: the band all agreed. The Charlatans rescheduled their New York date for the end of the tour, and on the way down to the next show, a festival in

Washington, dropped Blunt off at JFK. Despite spending a spank-
ing £108 on a cab from Heathrow to the north-west, Blunt missed
the birth by 24 hours. He was back on-stage inside three and a half
days. It seemed his marriage would be mercilessly tested after all.

The Charlatans ground their way across the Midwest, up the
West Coast from Tijuana to Vancouver, then back to New
York's Limelight. Here the band still clung to the last vestiges
of hipness engendered by *Some Friendly*. But naturally they
didn't build upon it. Madonna, on the guest list, was invited
backstage to find Burgess, the public face of the band and the
one everyone wanted to meet, lying face down on the floor,
bottle in hand, totally off his rocker. Madonna had no way of
knowing that this is standard behaviour for Burgess. He's been
known to be prone on the carpets of residential studios and
hotel rooms across the globe at the end, and occasionally the
beginning of a long evening. He looks like he's out cold but
he's not. Even with his nose squashed into the pile he's more
than capable of holding up his – under the circumstances somewhat burbling – end of the conversation. Madonna had no
inkling of this, and swept regally from the backstage area, leaving Burgess chuckling into the rug, with a muttered, 'Ugh,
you're *gross*.'

The US tour could have continued, perhaps *should* have.
Instead, the band cut out and no more dates were arranged.

'You have to choose,' says Mark Collins, 'between another
20,000 sales or keeping your sanity. We chose sanity.'

Back in the UK, a small battle had been lost with Beggars
Banquet. 'Tremelo Song', an artful mix of seventies disco and
nineties dance marked by chiming rock guitar and a hypnotic
piano riff recalling the Stones' post-incarceration single 'We Love
You', had been released on cassette, twelve-inch and two separate
CDs. Chart success and its concomitant media interest were vital,
so Beggars thought, in keeping up the band's profile at this difficult
time. A second single from *Between 10th And 11th* was essential.
The competition was formatting like crazy; that had to be done
too.

The Charlatans hated it. All the touring meant that there was
really nothing new to offer their fans in the way of worthwhile

B-sides. There was a fair recording of the live favourite 'Happen To Die', a demo of another, 'Normality Swing', but then just live versions of 'Then' and 'Chewing Gum Weekend'. It was not enough. And the single only reached Number 44 anyway.

'Yeah,' says Burgess. 'We fell into the formatting game and it sucked. Again Martin didn't want anything else taken from the LP, and again he was right. The thing was, in avoiding it for so long, we'd set up a foundation, done things that had made us believe in ourselves, to build something solid. Very few people do it; very few have done it since. We had to have principles. After reflection, some things change a little, but that foundation is still there now.

'It wasn't as if before "Tremelo Song" we were giving stuff away. We always prided ourselves on charging as much as we could for records: we felt our music was that good that if people wanted to buy into it they ought to pay full price. But we did try to make sure it was always something new, not just dodgy live versions. We never wrote things to be on B-sides. Every song is always intended to be the best one we've ever done, so we always thought the stuff was really, really good value.'

'Eventually, though,' says Harrison, realistically, 'you do have to consider the record company's needs, and one of their main needs is to compete in the market-place. If, say, EMF are sticking out twenty-five different versions of their single and you're doing one, you're going to lose out. The industry was going mad at the time about what they called value-for-money packaging and everything – Def Leppard singles coming out like box-sets and all that. But we did always *try* to give people something new.'

Returning from America in the second week of August, The Charlatans had a few days to themselves before the Reading Festival on Bank Holiday weekend followed by a brief trip to Japan. At Reading, the headliners were Public Enemy, riding high after their *Fear of a Black Planet* and *Apocalypse '91... The Enemy Strikes Back* albums, and Nirvana, topping a grungy Sunday featuring Mudhoney, L7 and the superb Screaming Trees. The Charlatans played the Friday, second on the bill to The Wonder Stuff, who the year before had topped the charts and guaranteed their own demise with a cover of Tommy Roe's

'Dizzy', recorded with the surrealist comic Vic Reeves (a man famed for finding cold cuts of meat innately amusing).

Reading was a good gig for the band. Burgess hatched plans with Ride's own pretty boy Mark Gardener, and the show itself was further proof that the by now *de rigueur* critical slappings were not affecting a live crowd that seemed to love them all the more for partying through a crisis. If anything, to the audience this new adversity made more sense of the band; it made their search for a brighter day more traumatic, more dramatic, just like it felt inside for each of them.

And if drama was what Charlatans aficionados wanted, they soon got it. On 3 December 1992, with the band back from the East and about to embark upon an extended period of writing and relaxation, Rob Collins, along with his friend Michael Whitehouse, was arrested for his part in an attempted armed robbery of the T&S supermarket and off licence in the village of Great Wyrley near Cannock, Staffordshire.

The bizarre events unfolded as follows. Collins, at a bit of a loose end, looked up his old school-mate Whitehouse (Collins was keen to remain unspoilt by success) and visited a few pubs in the area. After a couple of pints in Cannock, Collins was driving the pair back to Wednesbury to meet up with Jon Brookes for last orders when, at around 9.15, Whitehouse asked him to pull up outside an off licence. As he clambered out of the car, Whitehouse said, with ludicrous macho bravado, 'I could do this offie over, you know,' and went inside, leaving the car door open. Collins closed the door and waited.

The next thing Rob heard was a loud bang as Whitehouse came storming out of the shop and past the car. Unbeknown to Collins, Whitehouse had pulled out a replica gun and demanded the contents of the till. The fellow behind the counter had bent down and come up with, of all things, a scimitar, sending Whitehouse into a blind panic manifesting itself in immediate terrified flight. The gun had not been fired in earnest, but went off accidentally as Whitehouse turned and ran.

At that moment, Collins, being no mug, recognised the seriousness of the situation. He knew he should have left Whitehouse to do the Headless Chicken straight into the arms of the law but he'd known him a long time and didn't want to abandon his mate. So Collins picked him up and the pair fled together.

As they drove, Collins voiced his bewilderment. 'What the *fuck* did you do *that* for?' Simple: Whitehouse needed the money. They made it to Wednesbury in good time for more beer, and Collins got home around 12.15 a.m. As he was parking his motor in the garage, a Ford Fiesta pulled up outside and its three occupants approached him. They were all plain clothes police officers and one of them pulled a gun. As startled as you'd expect, Collins accompanied them back to Cannock police station.

Collins was there for five days. For the first 48 hours he denied everything. Then, informed that Whitehouse had made a full confession, he spilled the sorry beans. He was charged with attempted robbery, as well as possession of a firearm. As a hapless getaway driver, he could at least plead ignorance if not outright innocence. Bail was set at £25,000 – paid by his father, as Collins himself was not permitted to contribute – on condition of his reporting twice a week to the police and continuing to live at his home address. His passport was taken from him.

On hearing the news, his band mates were said to be 'very angry and very concerned'. If found guilty, Collins faced five years in jail. Just as The Charlatans were being named a not-too-disastrous eighth in the Modern Rock category of US Billboard's chart of Biggest Selling Artists of 1992, they'd taken another uppercut to the chin. Worst of all, they would have to wait eight long months to discover whether it would be a knockout blow.

On 12 and 13 March 1993, the stoned and drunken plans laid by Tim Burgess and Mark Gardener at Reading Festival the previous August came to fruition in the Daytripper extravaganza. The original concept had been a home town double-header, with The Charlatans and Gardener's Ride playing in Northwich and Oxford, but there were no suitable venues. So The Charlatans took one of their childlike fantasies to its logical conclusion and invited their fans on a jaunt to the seaside. It would be a huge laugh, for Blunt like the scooter runs of old, the two sets of supporters combining first at the Brighton Centre and then at the Empress Ballroom in Blackpool.

In itself, it was an interesting bill as Ride, like The Charlatans, were under great stress. Formed at art school in Oxfordshire in 1988, they'd broken through in 1990, the same year as The Charlatans. Yet Ride were at the forefront of a UK movement in stark opposition to Madchester. Shoegazing – so called because the bands involved played standing stock still, staring wilfully downward at their flickering fingers – was intended to be a cosmic experience, a musicianly head-rush far removed from baggy's sweaty, luv'd-up party.

Shoegazing bands included Slowdive, Swervedriver and Chapterhouse (even The Charlatans got an occasional misguided mention) but Ride were the real deal, their plaintive melodies screaming through your skull on a wave of endlessly mutating white noise. 'Nowhere' and 'Going Blank Again', aptly titled both, had been big hits, but shoegazing eventually suffered the same demise as baggy, after a backlash which was not as gleeful but just as severe.

So here were the kings of two defunct scenes, both with strong fan bases (though it did seem as if the crowd was a good 65 per cent for The Charlatans), both looking for a new sound. Ride shone through in Brighton. Under the influence of guitarist Andy Bell, they were moving from a blissful sonic blitz towards a very easy country rock. Somewhere in-between they found The Who and now covered 'The Kids Are Alright', their version a real pointer to their future. Within four years they were gone, Bell going on to form Hurricane #1 – and later to join Oasis.

The Daytripper gigs were a huge success. Fans had travelled in for the occasion (and it *felt* like an occasion) from Japan, America, Europe and, of course, Scotland. There was an ecstatic togetherness about it all, reminiscent of The Charlatans' earlier days. They themselves played a stormer, with tracks from the last album seeming to open up more in the live setting (one unreleased track, 'Subterranean' was recorded and later given away with the *109* fanzine). Even the press seemed to be turning around, describing both bands as 'purists' and 'the last of the real groups'. It was said that they were rock 'n' roll aesthetes, busying themselves with idiosyncratic self-expression in their own insular worlds. They were emotional craftsmen; *important.*

After the Brighton show, in a seafront hotel, the party was liver-threateningly good. Upstairs, Burgess was sharing a thoughtful, cross-legged toke with Gardener. Downstairs, Blunt, who'd been carefully circulating, very, very quietly offering drinks to his closer friends, mislaid his room-key, an item that allowed him to mark up any expenses to his overall bill. Looking around a bar now stuffed with reeling, jabbering drunkards, he recognised that dropping this key was not unakin to tossing a peeled infant into a pool of Great Whites. *This would not do.* Blunt is exceptionally generous, but he had a wife and kids, for God's sake, and the idea of buying beer for this motley collection of hacks and hangers-on filled him with resentment.

Slowly, alone in the bar, Martin Blunt turned into a bubbling crater of disgust. Sitting with elbows on knees, fingers as ever clasped to his mouth, he stared ahead, lost in unusually murderous reverie. Thankfully, the key had been confiscated by bar staff suspicious of a particularly flamboyant order of cocktails, and was returned unused. Typically, it took Blunt some considerable time to return from Planet Problem, but he did eventually break back into the party atmosphere, secure in the knowledge that he could worry about Blackpool later.

He needn't have bothered himself. You could easily surmise the mood of the next day's Blackpool audience by looking out of the window and watching them laughing and dancing all over Brighton beach.

The band now turned to recording their third album with darker clouds looming over them – like the possibility that Rob Collins could be jailed for five years. With the trial set for August, the band decided to spend the time regrouping. They would never again allow themselves to fall into that *Between 10th And 11th* trap of being forced to write, record and release without full and soulful consideration.

They started to get it together immediately, beginning by officially altering their methods. It was clear that their much-vaunted democracy was a no-no. Members were using their right of veto too freely and songwriting was proving too stressful and anarchic. It was decided to split up where necessary or convenient: they would work on tracks individually or in twos or threes until they were ready for presentation to the others, then they would complete and perfect them as a band. This would give good ideas a chance to survive and also ensure that when they came to record they'd have the maximum material to draw from.

Burgess took to writing with Mark Collins, naturally concentrating on traditionally structured songs, with the result that for the first time the music was sometimes written around the voice. Blunt stuck with Brookes, melding the elements of funk, dance and heavy rock that would keep the resulting album *Up To Our Hips* (and also their fourth and fifth albums) on the creative edge. You can easily spot the difference in styles by comparing the pop/rock blast of 'Can't Get Out Of Bed' wth the funky technoid monster 'Feel Flows'. Rob Collins worked with both sides and, once in the studio, on his own, often playing far into the night with only an engineer for company.

Rob also brooded long and painfully on the possible effects on his family were he to receive a five-year stretch in jail. The band would twice feel the benefit of his nocturnal efforts.

He was not the only one worried.

'The whole *Up To Our Hips* LP had a sense of urgency,' says Burgess, 'but also a sense of hatred. We were thinking about Rob going to prison, and we didn't know how long he was going to get. We were thinking we had to rush the LP, finish it before he went down, because if we didn't there wasn't going to be an LP and there wouldn't be a Charlatans any more.'

'We were thinking,' says Mark Collins, 'If he goes down for any serious length of time, that's it for us. We ain't gonna go on without him.'

So they had to move it. Once again a producer was necessary and, now that the Flood experience had taught them how little they knew of technology, an engineer too. That April they met up with Dave Charles, an old-school engineer who, having worked with Elvis Costello, The La's, Jeff Beck and Edwin Starr, just had to possess an appropriately open mind. A quiet and kind man, he could also entertain them with a quite startling array of rock 'n' roll stories. He'd be an ideal professional companion in the leafy confines of Monnow Valley.

For producer, the band had been considering Boys Own's Hugo Nicolson and the remixer and brilliantly eclectic DJ Andy Weatherall, who'd both done exceptional work with Primal Scream. Then Steve Hillage was mentioned.

Hillage was an odd one, that's for sure, first finding fame with Gong in the early seventies. Gong, after Hawkwind, were the greatest and strangest of the space rock outfits. They were formed in Paris in 1970 by Australian guitarist Daevid Allen who, having disbanded them in 1972, quickly reformed the band to take advantage of a deal offered by Richard Branson's fledgling Virgin label. This was when Hillage became involved, as Gong moved into their notorious 'Radio Gnome Invisible' trilogy. These albums concerned the antics of a gang of dope-addled pixies who travelled through inner space in lurid green teapots customised (in inimitable pixie fashion) to operate as helicopters.

As the band veered off into a more sophisticated jazz rock, Hillage left for a highly successful solo career hardly damaged by the onset of punk which, of course, saw the likes of Gong as Satan incarnate. Indeed, his services as a producer were much sought after. In the early eighties, also at Monmouth, he'd produced the albums that led Simple Minds on to superstardom – *Sons and Fascination* and *Sister Feelings Call* (he'd furthermore worked with Dave Charles around the same time).

The Charlatans were aware of Hillage but not of his acclaimed solo work, nor of Gong's gnomey opus. By 1993, Hillage had managed to reinvent himself yet again. With his advanced production skills and years of experience handling and writing about absolutely anything that could be dried, rolled up and smoked, the ambient scene springing from rave culture was made for him. He'd garnered headlines with his own band, System 7, and had worked on The Orb's *The Blue Room*, all the while proving himself to be wholly in tune with the mood of the day.

Rob Collins' idea for the band, after the second album, was that they should 'stop trying so hard and loosen up again', and Hillage convinced them that he was the man to help them do it. He told them they reminded him of The Faces, said that, rarely for rock bands of the time, they had soul. He described himself as 'a musician's producer', not involving himself in the writing process but trying to draw the best from the band as if he were an organising extra member.

'We got him in because we liked his eyes,' says Burgess. 'That's the truth. We were suffering a bit from technofear and he said he'd help us get the live sound we wanted. He'd just started the System 7 thing, but we really liked the stuff he'd done with The Orb. He was also recommended by a mate of ours, John Male, who's in Republica now but was then in Airstream and had done some stuff with Steve and Martin Duffy from Primal Scream. We were producer-paranoid, record company-paranoid, everything-paranoid, and Steve Hillage was the gentlest man we'd ever met, and from his eyes he looked like he could tell a few drug stories. Which he could.'

The band moved into Monnow Valley and began to demo with Dave Charles. Two weeks later, Hillage arrived and, far from being the benignly useless hippy many might have expected, made it straightaway apparent that the live feel was exactly what he was after. According to Mark Collins, he would stop them 'going up our own arses' by replaying their demos to them and pointing out that they were beginning to lose the original feel of songs. He'd also go fishing with Rob Collins who, now intensely active, would sometimes seek peace of mind on the riverbanks.

Before long, in stark contrast to the recording of the second album, twenty songs were demoed and, as predicted, the practice of taking near-completed songs to the rest of the band worked well. Beyond this, the growing familiarity between them and the recognition of a shared struggle began to gradually (very gradually) break down a very English emotional reserve that could only hold them back. And, amazingly, given his evident communication problems, it was Rob Collins who led the way – the same Rob Collins who hated the sound of his own voice and could never bear to watch himself on TV.

'In the studio we've always worked really hard,' says Jon Brookes 'but there's always been a bit of reserve. Like, "I don't want to show too much of myself in case I embarrass myself." It's hard to go out on a limb and completely be yourself. What taught me the lesson of how it's supposed to be was Rob. He was a really quiet, unassuming person, but sometimes in the studio he'd really let it all come out. I'd be embarrassed for him, but he wouldn't be embarrassed himself.

'Rob would throw himself into his playing or his singing, let himself become really open; put himself in a place where he could have been really hurt by a comment, by people taking the piss. He had a big seriousness, something in him that he had to make come out. Tim's been doing it since Day One, and I've always been naive enough to think that that was just because it's his job because he's the singer. It wasn't because it was his job, it was just because he had the balls to do it before the rest of us.'

'There's always been that facade,' continues Burgess, 'where you're wondering, Should I let all my emotions flood out, or should I just try to be really cool? In a way, a lot of those emotions were shown on the first record, because it was such a new thing for us. The trouble was that a lot of the music was just wallpaper. The second record was all over the place, but the third one was us coming back. Tracks like "Feels Flows" and "I Never Want An Easy Life" were us tearing it out, really. And Rob was a bit of a leader in that. He really didn't like singing in front of other people, but he'd go in there and stand there and do it. People could have really humiliated him, especially when he was doing all those high-pitched backings. You know, singing like a girl and all that.'

The sessions were going spectacularly well but August inexorably rolled around and, on the 23rd of that month, Rob Collins stood trial at Stafford Crown Court. The serious charge of possessing a firearm had been dropped, and Collins had changed his plea, saying he had not believed Whitehouse seriously intended to proceed with the raid – until he heard a gunshot. He had remained in the car throughout, he claimed in his own defence, though he did admit that he'd driven Whitehouse away after the incident. Five years were still on the cards.

Despite his reputation as a hell raiser, Collins had common sense on his side. His legal team busied themselves with burying the judge under a pile of press clippings testifying to The Charlatans' bright past and future. They'd been Number 1 in the charts: why would he need to turn over a half-arsed offie for a mere couple of ton? On top of that, why would he be so foolish as to use his own car? Then there were sworn statements attesting to his good character, and a Stoke psychiatrist's report concluding that Collins was 'stable and well adjusted' and 'of average intelligence' and that 'for him to become involved in serious crime is entirely out of character'. Mercifully, the charges were reduced to 'assisting an offender after a crime', the judge adjourning the trial for further consideration of the facts.

The band were convinced Collins would receive a severe reprimand, perhaps a short suspended sentence and a few hundred hours mowing grannies' lawns or scrubbing graffiti off the walls of Cannock's playgrounds. Collins himself was more concerned. Having devoured all available articles on similar local cases, he knew it could turn nasty. Though there was no longer any mention of them on his charge-sheet, shooters have a way of increasing sentences.

On 20 September, proceedings were reconvened. The judge announced that he'd decided to hand both defendants a custodial sentence. First, Whitehouse: four years. Without the warders' rough assistance, he would have collapsed. Next, Robert James Collins: eight... Though he knew full well the potential extent of his sentence, the judge's pause still had Collins convinced he was going down for eight years. Of course, it was to be eight months.

Handcuffed, Collins was taken by bus to Shrewsbury prison, where he was strip-searched and ordered to shower before being designated Cell 13 on A Wing. Collins stood gazing at the lines of cells stretching away from him, a tea urn doing the rounds. He watched as one prisoner took a cup of boiling water and tossed it over his cell mate, the warders immediately piling in to quell the disturbance. Five minutes gone. Eight months to go.

On his first night, Collins discovered that his cell mate was in for murdering his wife and stabbing her father. He got himself transferred the very next morning. That achieved, he was in the showers when he noticed a fellow prisoner staring at him. Every jail cliché came to mind. *Shit*. But, rather than coming out with gut-wrenching threats from *Deliverance*, the guy began to hum 'The Only One I Know', introduced himself, and proved a friendly fan of the band.

News spread fast. Soon inmates and warders alike were requesting Collins' autograph (though more often that of Tim

Burgess). On the advice of the warders, he hid the bags of letters he received from his family, the band, Harrison and assorted well-wishers (plus an *Ogden's Nut Gone Flake* beer mat with an autograph and a scrawled 'Keep on keeping on' from Small Faces keyboardist Ian McLagen). He wouldn't want to look privileged. A few lags were keen to take him down a peg or two but there was nothing severe.

Collins spent his days in the kitchens, working eleven hours daily, from 6.30 in the morning, dealing in such delights as powdered eggs and lumps of liver (which were sometimes dropped on the floor, picked up, dusted down and stirred in with the rest). He noticed the 'special attention' paid to food to be consumed in the area reserved for sex offenders. The rest of the time, having declined an offer from the prison chaplain to have a go on the church organ, he was banged up, pondering every tiny aspect of being big in Japan while slumping wretchedly in a cell measuring nine feet by three. There was hardly room to swing a cat, were such a luxury obtainable.

Collins' prison wage amounted to £5.10 a week to spend on phone cards and tabs, neither of which vital currencies inmates were allowed to buy with private funds. He spent lock-up periods replying to all those letters, with a promptitude and honesty that made this probably the point in his life when he communicated most truly and regularly. He heard of a couple of suicide attempts and of one guy who, refusing to be transferred to Birmingham's notorious Winson Green, could only be removed from his cell with the help of a hydraulic jack. But it wasn't unbearable. Not quite.

After six weeks, Collins was told he could serve out his term toiling in the kitchens of Shrewsbury nick or transfer to an open prison in Redditch. Feeling that an alternative venue might prove a great deal more disagreeable than his present lot, he declined the offer of a move – until he was informed that open prison meant weekends at home and a weekly wage of £160, not that far below the national average for the unconvicted. He was off like a shot.

Redditch was, in some respects, a step up. Not in the ways Collins had been told, exactly – the home visits and extra cash were only for those serving sentences of over twelve months – but there were twelve-man dormitories, a TV room and room-sized latrines as opposed to the bucket-like variety Collins had not grown used to (prisons, like tour buses, have an unspoken rule that there's to be no shitting till immediately before slop-out time).

More importantly, Walkmans were allowed, so now he could play the material the band were working on. Days began at the ever-so-slightly more rock 'n' roll time of 7.45 and each month prisoners were permitted to wander through the town, unsupervised, for five hours. Responsibility was demanded and lapses punished harshly. Those not up, dressed and ready for action at 8.15 faced a seven-day extension of their term; those late back from town a cruel 28. Anyone wishing to watch *EastEnders* when 150 other blokes preferred *Coronation Street* did well to hand over that dope remote.

And, of course, being a British prison, there were parties. Ecstasy was smuggled in with reasonable ease, and Collins had a kindly relative who would regularly bury litre bottles of vodka in the grounds so Rob could sneak out, dig them up and instantly become a very popular fellow indeed. He'd later tell the story of how the warder would, while carrying out his morning checks, smell Rob's breath – still potent from a night's quaffing – and wink knowingly. These things were understood.

On the day prior to his release on 13 January 1994, Collins was called up to the governor's office. Apparently, his brother had phoned to find out when he was due out as he was to pick him up. Records quite rightly showed that Collins had no brother so, to avoid the media reception so obviously planned, Rob, armed with his £62 discharge grant, was next day ushered out early through a back exit. He had served four months less one half-hour – four months having been subtracted from his sentence for good behaviour, 30 minutes for being famous. Prisoner RD1533 was no longer a number: he was a free man. Nevertheless, he did not attend the party organised to celebrate his release. Despite the extra freedom of Redditch open prison, and the fact that the very next day he would be joining the band on-stage at *Top of the Pops* to perform 'Can't Get Out Of Bed', he did not yet feel up to facing a jumpin', pumpin' crowd.

Soon afterwards, Collins received a phone call from

Featherstone prison. It was Michael Whitehouse calling to apologise and ask if Rob would care to visit. Er, no, mate, not really, no. Typically, though, Rob did maintain his sense of humour. Driving north once with Jon Brookes, they found the M6 to be log jammed as ever. Brookes casually suggested that they turn off at Cannock to beat the traffic. 'Nah, mate,' replied Collins, 'last time I went there I didn't come out again for four fookin' months.'

Those four months held additional problems for Collins in that visiting access was not easy to come by. Even his wife, Joanne found it hard to get in to see him, and their relationship hadn't been a bed of roses even before this. Joanne had not married a rock star, she had married the 'normal' Rob Collins – the quiet fisherman, the pub denizen. In fact, when they were married in the summer of 1989, The Charlatans didn't quite exist. Burgess had just joined the band but they were still playing their old material. There was still no clue of what life would be like later.

Prison certainly didn't help: it changed Collins for the worse. And soon his marriage would break up, circumstances leaving him unable to see his daughter Emily as much as he would have liked. He would find it hard to deal with life apart from someone he loved and who loved him.

'Rob was such an ordinary bloke,' says Harrison. 'If you went to the pub with him in Walsall, he'd probably be talking about fishing, what lead weights and floats he was using. Really normal, almost dull sometimes. The whole prison thing really worried him, not being able to look after his kid, missing her growing up and everything.

'And he certainly got more involved in drugs as a result of going to prison, and that made him more confident, so he started doing more manic things. I think prison had an incredibly negative effect on Rob. It didn't do him any good at all and it seemed so pointless – he wasn't a big enough personality to make an example of like that.'

While Rob Collins was in jail, something truly horrid had happened. Burgess had involved himself in a Christmas single.

Occasionally, in the past, Tim had been carried away by his own rock star posing, with the result that there were a few excruciatingly embarrassing photos floating around. Not embarrassing for *him*: when asked he'd pause, consider and respond with a very unembarrassed, 'Aw, fook it, it's just a laugh, innit?' But this was different. This was a deliberate and full-on artistic contribution to a ghastly and, what with the advent of CDs, probably permanent record.

Saint Etienne, comprising Bob Stanley and Pete Wiggs, had been around for some time, having broken through with a cover of Neil Young's 1970 hit 'Only Love Can Break Your Heart'. For that they'd used as vocalist Moira Lambert from Faith Over Reason (a band noted, at least in these parts, for their hopelessly ill-advised and insultingly twee version of 'The Needle And The Damage Done'). Now they were a true trio, having employed singer Sarah Cracknell full-time, and were receiving serious plaudits for their tacky, glitzy, unwholesomely wimpy take on modern dance. Cracknell herself, for reasons known only to those who still took tissues to bed with them, had become a music press pin-up.

Burgess had met Cracknell at Granby's, a Manchester club, and got on well with her (no surprise there, as Saint Etienne, despite their horrifying output, are all extremely decent folk). They decided – Burgess feeling like a break from do-or-die recording – to embark on a project, just for fun. It would be a musical Yuletide feast entitled 'I Was Born On Christmas Day'. And so they did it, with a video and everything – wedding dress, suits, cake, the lot, first at Chelsea Registry Office and then the Cobden Working Men's Club in Kensal Rise, West London, where Burgess and Cracknell smooched on the dance floor.

With the single limping into the pre-Christmas chart at a gratifyingly sorry Number 37, you'd have thought that would be it. It wasn't. A *Top of the Pops* appearance took place, again in marriage regalia (though Burgess had mercifully discarded the cravat and top hat). Someone said it made Kylie Minogue sound like the Red House Painters. In terms of the monumental depression the single flung the listener into, that should have been the other way around.

* * *

Back at Monnow Valley, though, *Up To Our Hips* was all coming together. Where Rob Collins had been the driving force behind *Some Friendly*, now Blunt, desperate to avoid disaster, took the helm. Influenced by Can's *Tago Mago* and *Ege Bamyasi* as well as The Small Faces and The Faces (Blunt reckons the album was 'touched by the hand of Rod'), he drove the others on, in his sheer bloody effort leading by example.

'Martin had this killer riff for 'Inside-Looking Out,' says Burgess, 'but he wanted some keyboards, too. But Rob was in prison, so Martin – and this says a lot about what he's like – stayed up for three days and nights to write and learn a keyboard part. And it was a beautiful melody, too. It was even kept for The Chemical Brothers' remix. That's Martin's determination. On the album, though, Steve Hillage made it sound a bit limp and lacklustre.'

Blunt's endeavours would make the album brilliantly bass-heavy, adding to its contemporary nature and making it a God-given gift to remixers. But the rest were enthused also. Burgess was buzzing, and Rob Collins' problems had him thinking of the Stones circa *Their Satanic Majesties Request*, a prime inspiration for him. Brookes was involving himself more; Mark Collins now truly finding his feet. Mark's brother, John, a keyboardist himself, was also lending a hand. While inside, Rob Collins was listening to the tapes made and putting forward suggestions, and Hillage's expertise with sampling technology allowed the band to make full use of the riffs and thrusts Rob had recorded before being sentenced.

'He left us with a few keyboard parts for "Feel Flows",' says Burgess, 'and some other bits. He had this habit of leaving us things *just in case*. There are bits on *Tellin' Stories* that he didn't think were gonna be used.'

Burgess also found in Collins and his predicament a new and bountiful source of lyrical subject matter. Before Rob had gone away, Burgess had attempted to pick his brain; to 'juice' him in order to discover exactly what he was feeling about his impending ordeal. Collins understood this, and despite that kind of attention (any kind of attention, really) being difficult for him, he accepted it as being for the good of the band. 'Patrol', with its line, 'I want to patrol this innocent mind', is about that precisely. 'Inside-

Looking Out' is often said to have been written by Collins about gazing at the world from inside Shrewsbury prison. It was in fact written by Burgess as he imagined Collins' mindset. And then, even more obviously, there was 'I Never Want An Easy Life If Me And He Were Ever To Get There'.

'That one's about Rob,' explains Burgess. 'Me and Rob were actually getting on really well at the time. You know, everyone has their fall-outs and we used to fall out a lot. But on this LP we got on brilliantly. Weeks were spent at Monnow Valley where there'd be just me, Rob and Dave Charles the engineer. And "Easy Life" is just me saying, "You don't ever want it easy, do you, mate? It's just shoot it up and go for a ride – that's you."'

By now, Burgess was discovering a real confidence in himself and the band. Hillage's methods were hugely encouraging and Tim was finding that they could hold things together, even without Rob Collins' final sardonic or approving word. He became more shameless in his sources, basing 'Autograph' on the lines, 'Can I have your autograph? It's not for who you are, it's only for what you're not', from Danny Sugerman's *Wonderland Avenue* (Sugerman was, with Jerry Hopkins, author of the famous Jim Morrison biography *No One Here Gets Out Alive*).

Vitally, Burgess also began to come to terms with the distorted rhythms and meanings of his cut-up words, saying of 'Jesus Hairdo': 'This was rushed, and I think a bit thin-sounding, but we left it on the LP because it was good pop. Strange that, because a lot of the LP is quite bleak. I like the title, too, and the lyrics. I always got a lot of criticism for my lyrics, for them being nonsensical, and eventually I thought, Fuck it, I quite *like* them being nonsensical.'

Such was Burgess's rediscovered belief in the group's abilities that he took the wholly unexpected step of cutting himself out of 'Feel Flows' altogether. That track, its title an oblique tribute to The Beach Boys' *Surf's Up*, came about when the band found Brookes hammering out a drum pattern on his own, the engineer Charles not present. Impressed by the pulsating percussive flood, they pressed the record button and then each added their own parts: Rob Collins a mighty, mournful synth-theme, Mark Collins huge swathes of rock, Blunt that hammering undercurrent.

Burgess stepped forward as well but, blown away by his colleagues' explosive contributions, he persuaded them to erase his vocal tracks. He was right to do so. For a while afterwards when playing live, he would exit the stage and watch the others, now without a face or centre of attention, as they kicked up such a storm you could imagine 'Feel Flows' permanently replacing 'Sproston Green' in their repertoire. It was supreme encore material – pulsing, remorseless and utterly undeniable.

As The Charlatans prepared to release *Up To Our Hips*, the rapid dissolving of *Between 10th And 11th* and the extended US and European tours made them feel as if they had been away for years. They found the musical climate changed to such a degree that they might as well have been.

Madchester was now forgotten and, in the minds of many, The Charlatans were gone along with it. Britpop was now springing to the fore. In 1993, Blur's *Modern Life Is Rubbish*, their first serious attempt to reflect the state of England, had made a strong showing. Their appearance at Reading Festival had further revealed the depths of their grassroots following. Now, first with the jaunty 'Girls And Boys', then with the album *Parklife*, chart numbers 5 and 1 respectively, they were really coming into their own. Englishness in general, and Blur's prime influence The Small Faces in particular (Damon Albarn has always fancied himself as a bit of a Steve Marriott), were now the focus of everyone's attention.

Coming up on the outside were another band even more qualified for the description of a phenomenon. In May of the previous year, Creation boss Alan McGee had attended a gig at Glasgow's King Tut's Wah-Wah Hut to check out the band 18 Wheeler (or Wheeler 18, as they were called by our Cool Brittanic Prime Minister). Yet it was the support band that changed his life. Oasis, even as rough and ready as this, struck him as a cross between The Sex Pistols and The Beatles, a sure-fire winner. In Liam Gallagher they had a truly charismatic frontman with a gloriously tuneful snarl, in his brother Noel a songwriter of exceptional taste and deftness. And with *such* an ear – he was a kind of jackdaw genius.

For Oasis, 1994 was the take-off year and, unlike The Charlatans, they would not go off like the Challenger – high, wide, beautiful, then kaput. Oasis liked a beer, they liked a ruck and they loved to lip off, making them prime tabloid fodder for the foreseeable future. 'Supersonic', 'Shakermaker', and 'Live Forever' were brilliant squalls of melody, powering them towards the Top Ten and ensuring that, in September, their debut album, *Definitely Maybe,* would enter the charts at Number 1.

Very soon a competition would arise between Blur and Oasis - scheming art school popsters versus the home-grown hooligan virtuosos. The Charlatans would once again be relegated to the status of side attraction. They were called Britpop, by virtue of being British and, due to their temerity in continuing to come from the north-west, they also were tied in with Oasis and this new Manchester wave. Burgess, after all that Ian Brown nonsense, would now be accused of ripping off Liam Gallagher. Incomprehensible, really, when you think how far Burgess and his band (now quite openly struggling to overcome their personal, technical and artistic limitations) were from Oasis's brash and occasionally smug arrogance.

The Charlatans stood to gain little from this current set of trends but were, of course, in danger of being eventually dragged down with them. All of it drew the public's attention away from the fact that The Charlatans were still very much in the business of finding a sound and a reputation resolutely their own.

Oh, well, as Burgess might say, some good might come of it. After all, good things were happening again. Rob Collins was out of jail and events were taking on outrageous momentum in Cheshire where The Charlatans' exploits had encouraged the council to fund a fanzine and two radio stations, and 30 bands had formed a collective to organise gigs. Manchester too was thriving, having recovered from its baggy hangover. As before, the city was exploring all possibilities: funk metal, dance rock and grunge hybrids of all descriptions. For all their bravado, Oasis were not the be-all and end-all.

And now the time had come for The Charlatans to assault the charts once more, to test their new-found mettle against all comers in this changed environment. In their now time-honoured fashion, they made it as hard for themselves as they could. Released on 24 January, 'Can't Get Out Of Bed' was a killer single, a pop rush possessed of Flood's exquisitely timed power and the easy flow they'd rediscovered with Hillage. It had a groovy video, filmed in a rehearsal room and on a London rooftop, which featured Blunt rather sweetly planting a kiss on Burgess. The intended follow-up, 'Easy Life', was strong too.

But the marketing tactics were strange, to say the least. 'Easy Life' would be available a mere five weeks after 'Can't Get Out Of Bed', and then only for a week, presumably to persuade fans interested in the postcards contained therein to snap the single up immediately, thereby raising its chart position. This didn't really give the singles the chance to "grow" on casual listeners. You'd expect only diehard fans to cough up and, with hindsight, that's exactly what happened. The singles charted at 24 and 38 respectively (the postcards and 'strictly limited edition individually numbered' boxes clearly making no earthly difference at all). Burgess had been right about formatting. It really sucked.

Burgess was undeterred.

'I really like "Can't Get Out Of Bed",' he says. 'It was a dole-ite song with a positive message – like, "Get off your arse." It was also the one I felt proved to all the doubters that we could actually write good songs. But I do remember when it came out one journo writing that it shoudn't have been the single; it should have been "Easy Life". Then, a month or so later, "Easy Life" did come out, and the same bloke reviewed it and slagged it off! At that point I thought, Oh, people fucking *hate* us.'

The band had spent February on a whistle-stop tour of Europe, including one date at Gino's in Stockholm, where this author contrived to pick up pleurisy. The planes over and back were packed with Charlatans fans: cheerful and charming, they have a meekness that belies their ability to rave. The gig was a smoking, steaming black hole and fabulously good fun (terrible for a chap's chest, as it happens).

Burgess, accompanied by his girlfriend Chloe Walsh from the Heavenly Records press office, was rocking, aware that the band had turned a corner of sorts. He even on occasion began to sound a little like his former feyly self-aggrandising self. 'I *do* feel like a superstar,' he spouted. 'If someone's putting posters up on their wall, I feel I look pretty good beside someone like Mick Jagger. And I'm ready for it now, I'm really fucking ready.'

It's interesting to note how the It he was then ready for has changed over time. The Charlatans have always expressed a desire to record a classic LP but it was only really later that experience and confidence made that a potential reality. At this stage, Burgess, though he was clearly playing up to the interviewer's microphone, was still a tad enraptured with the pose.

In March came the acid test: the release of *Up To Our Hips*. The showing of its singles did not fill the outside observer with hope for the band but the band members themselves were upbeat. Brookes was pleased that Hillage had persuaded them to ditch the technology and 'get a bit of dirt on the tape'. Burgess liked the raw, trashy, melody-orientated feel of it all. Only Blunt had his doubts. He felt that there had been too much wacky baccy around at the mixing stage and believed this had, er, blunted the album's effect and reduced its sense of urgency. This was an important point. Where Burgess and Mark Collins were beginning to veer from a blasting pop towards a more cerebral American country-folk, Blunt, Brookes and Rob Collins were dealing in storming contemporary rhythms that rooted the band firmly in the here and now. The combination kept the band true to the open-minded spirit which motivated them. It was also essential, with the likes of The Prodigy beginning to make a mark, and the public revealing a strong affiliation to hardcore, that the band maintain its harder edge.

Blunt had other things on his mind, too. Though it had been through no fault of his own, he felt he had let the side down with his depressive collapse during the making of *Between 10th And 11th* and so he had taken it upon himself to pull them through this next difficult patch. *Up To Our Hips* is obviously bass-driven but Blunt's influence also stretched to a major say in the choosing of the album's cover.

Despite a morose, almost dour, exterior that gave the impression of his being the most parochial of northerners, Blunt was at this point by far the most cosmopolitan of the band. With the cover he wanted to say something, *artistically*, like, so he came up with the idea of a retake on a Lewis Morley photograph of a model and a hairdresser, the point being that The Charlatans – contrary to a by-now seemingly unanimous popular opinion – were 'more than just haircuts, more than just bowl-heads on the make'. It would be stylish too, as is Blunt's wont: Morley was widely lauded for his portraiture in the fifties and sixties, a non-populist David Bailey.

Blunt put a lot of thought into the sleeve – the mock-up, the reasoning – and he felt satisfied that his efforts had taken a weight from the shoulders of his band mates. Unfortunately for Blunt, for whom nothing comes easily, the band were to have big problems *because* of it. It has been the cause of much intra-band argument since, with one of the less inflammatory suggestions forwarded (others involved withdrawing all copies from the shops, rolling all the covers up and asking poor Martin to bend over) being that they should re-release the album with an entirely different cover.

'It confused everyone,' says Steve Harrison. 'When we got to the US again, because Rob had gone to prison, people were asking us if the picture was of the new keyboardist. Then, because the band weren't on the cover and there was no "UK" mentioned after the name, everyone thought it was by the original Charlatans. That sleeve gave us a lot of grief.'

Before skipping off for another shot at America, The Charlatans played one of their finest gigs to date – it's still in Burgess's top three. On 2 April, they stormed Trentham Gardens in Stoke-On-Trent.

This was a big day for the venue. Trentham Gardens had staged major gigs in previous years, having hosted the likes of Pink Floyd and The Who, but had not now seen a gig since The Jam played in 1978 (coincidentally, Blunt's first ever gig was The Jam that same year, supported by The Dickies and Patrik Fitzgerald at Birmingham Odeon). It was a big day for the band too. Hopes were high for *Up To Our Hips* and the sell-out crowd, some of them sleeping out overnight in the freezing fields, seemed to justify them. Their first UK gig since Daytripper a year before, the situation seemed to spur the band on: they were pumping, the crowd almost dangerously energised. Burgess, clad in an absurd yet strangely apt Superman T-shirt, chatted incessantly, endlessly muttering positivist mantras like, 'Got to be done, got to be done.' And it was: unlike The Stone Roses at Spike Island, the show was a triumph.

Four days later, the band played the Tramway in Glasgow, part of the Sound City festival, along with Throwing Muses and Pulp. Pulp had stepped in at the last minute to replace Hole, Courtney Love having cancelled due to problems tracking down her husband, Kurt Cobain. She didn't know how much of a problem there *was*. Cobain was actually already lying dead in his basement, having shot himself in the head, though his body would not be stumbled upon until two days later.

Cobain's death was a sickener, casting a spiritual shadow over The Charlatans' impending US tour. They also had a further problem in that Rob Collins' criminal record might mean he would be disallowed from entering the States. In fact, so sure were the band of this that they even discussed replacing him for the tour with James Taylor, their old influence from The Prisoners. In the end, this wasn't necessary. Collins went down to London with the band's lawyer and camped in the US embassy for a couple of days until it was sorted to his satisfaction. That wasn't the end of it, though. Within an hour of landing on American soil, Collins was enduring a thoroughly intrusive strip-search.

The month-long tour, titled 'Up To Our Hips In The USA And Canada' (unfortunate echoes of *Tap Into America* there), began on 16 April, and was as usual a little fraught. No real progress seemed to have been made. The band had switched US labels from RCA to Atlantic and had discussed and declined tours with both The Lemonheads and the then-burgeoning Cranberries. A support with INXS had also been refused, much to Atlantic's chagrin. The band were proving hard to push, despite the best efforts of the label, who had managed to get them on an MTV special and the popular Conan O'Brien Show. Then there was Blunt's sleeve for *Up to Our Hips*. And that 'UK' business reared its head again.

'When we joined Atlantic,' remembers Harrison, 'we convinced them that the problem with the other Charlatans had gone away. Then as soon as we released the record we got hit with another law suit, and this time Olsen had got his mates involved because *their* records had been re-released and there was a lot more activity for them. They were probably getting royalties.

'They said if we put one foot on American soil calling ourselves The Charlatans they'd sue us – for three and a half million, I think it was. So we thought it best to put the UK back on there. We had to change all the posters and reschedule the tour. I really thought we were big enough in our own right to do it, but obviously we weren't. We just confused the hell out of people.'

'Actually the best-selling album in America was the second one' adds Burgess. 'The first did about a quarter of a million copies, and the second just topped that. Then the third fell away drastically because everyone thought it was fucking Dollar on the front. We'd been forced to call ourselves Charlatans UK but when we came to record the third album we said "No, fuck that, we'll call ourselves The Charlatans". So we did, and everyone thought we were a different band from Charlatans UK.'

Up To Our Hips, by charting at Number 8 in the UK, had taken a hefty swipe back at the detractors. Gigs were booming (in Britain, at least) but reviews were still dreadful, the singles weren't scoring and America was having none of it. Though the band seemed to have got it together, in some ways it still appeared to be falling apart.

Nowhere was this more true than at the Apollo Rock Festival in Brussels in the third week of May, when it actually did. With the generator breaking down, full volume was impossible. The Charlatans were forced to play 'The Only One I Know' on piano, then departed after four songs, narrowly avoiding a barrage of bottles, bricks and booing. It hadn't happened before, and it hasn't since, yet Burgess will even now admit to a recurring nightmare where his band is jeered from the stage.

But there were bright signs too, extremely encouraging pointers to the future. Before the UK shows earlier in the year, the band had tested the reaction of the crowd to a remix of 'Patrol' put together by The Dust Brothers. This pair, Tom Rowlands and Ed Simons, who'd met at Manchester University, were among the first DJs to promote themselves with an identifiable image. To those in the know, they were considered poor mixers and their DJ sets were mocked for their clumsiness, but the pictures told the true story.

Scruffy and long haired, they were rock boys and would find their strength in collaborating with rock bands. Paring their tracks down to the essentials of melody and power, often leaving songs fairly intact, they'd play with rhythms and pull bands into new stylistic arenas.

Burgess had met The Dust Brothers (soon to change their name to The Chemical Brothers after complaints from the well-known American production crew) on the first night of the Heavenly Social Club, at the Albany, near Great Portland Street, London. Heavenly, run by Jeff Barrett, was a label – they'd put out records by Manic Street Preachers and Saint Etienne – and also an independent press office. Now they were staging a weekly club event (later staged in the East End and monthly at Deluxe in Nottingham) where a variety of DJs would mix and match ragga, hip-hop, techno, reggae, indie and classic rock and soul. Burgess loved the variety and the rush, which took him back to his earlier days, and he became involved via girlfriend Chloe Walsh. He'd even DJ for a couple of hours, once clearing the dance floor with 'Uncle Ernie' from The Who's *Tommy*. With Keith Moon as a bug-eyed paedophile sadist, and the song's infuriating 'Fiddle *a-bout*! Fiddle *a-bout*!' refrain, people just weren't quite ready.

The Chemical Brothers had a field day with 'Patrol', basically returning it to the kind of state Blunt felt it had lost in mixing. The Charlatans were the first major rock band they had worked for, and the two teams clearly learned from each other. Leftfield were employing John Lydon ('Open Up') and Curve's Toni Halliday ('Original') to great success, and The Chemicals would outstrip them, first in August 1995 with 'Life Is Sweet', sung by Burgess, then in October 1996 with the Noel Gallagher-featuring Number 1 single, 'Setting Sun'.

With The Charlatans, the Chemicals would become something of a perennial feature, later producing thrilling remixes of 'Toothache' and 'Nine Acre Court', contributing loops to their fifth album, *Tellin' Stories* and probably (definitely if the band have their way), being deeply involved in the mixing of the sixth (at Hendrix's Electric Ladyland studio, if all goes well).

The Heavenly connection would also bring the band some high-class support acts in FC Kahuna and Jon Carter from Monkey

Mafia, each charged with taking the audience to a peak before the band's entrance and each playing a blinder – though Carter was once asked by a panicked tour manager to desist from playing the Chemicals' 'Nine Acre Dust' (which appeared on the *Live At The Heavenly Social* album) immediately before the set, as 'Nine Acre Court' was the band's opening salvo.

After Brussels and the Pink Pop Festival in Holland, the band played three more UK dates (their last for another year), then cancelled everything. They had been down to play that June's Glastonbury Festival but decided against it. The reason given was that they had prior US tour commitments, but this wasn't strictly true.

The trouble was Blunt. Actually, it was Blunt's backside. For a while he'd had a growth on his 'lower back' and now it had become a fully fledged cyst. He had it gutted of its core by a district nurse but, due to constant refilling, it needed daily packing for three full weeks. The band were as sympathetic as ever, taunting Blunt for 'growing a tail'.

Rob Collins was chuffed. He hadn't wanted to play Glastonbury anyway. In fact, he didn't want to play anywhere. The band's recent US tour, concentrating on the East Coast, had been intended to be only Part One, but Collins had had enough. He refused point blank to accompany them across the western states so the band took a few weeks off and then went straight back to South Wales with Steve Hillage. This left the single, 'Jesus Hairdo' – its title taken from Douglas Coupland's Generation X novel *Shampoo Planet* – and its B-sides, including remixes of 'Patrol' and 'Feel Flows' by the Chemicals, Luvdup and Vanbasten, out in the middle of nowhere. It only just scraped into the Top 50.

As an aside, Rob Collins would soon be suffering a cyst himself, when the band were in Brighton around the release of the fourth album. It was under his arm – a hot and uncomfortable location. Never one to piss about with social niceties like district nurses, he lanced and cleaned it himself. What a *pussy* that Blunt was.

*　*　*

It was Hillage's idea that The Charlatans should re-enter the studio straight away as he thought they were on a roll after *Up To Our Hips*. On a brief trip to the Mediterranean with their wives and girlfriends, they considered their options and, deciding there would be no downers on the album, they went for it.

Once ensconsed back in the studio, there was a noticeable change in the atmosphere around recording. According to Blunt, each member would contribute to the playlist of what he terms 'our own club'. Between the hours of midnight and four in the morning, they would sit around drinking and smoking and playing each other their top tunes of that particular day. This was partly for the sake of entertainment, but each member was also possessed of an ulterior motive: by bombarding the others with their own personal favourites, they could surreptitiously alter the sound of the tracks the band were presently recording.

Blunt, for instance, had noticed that Burgess and Mark Collins had formed a C&W axis that was having a notable effect on the tunes, moving them away from the funk, contemporary technoid groove and flaming mod attack he preferred. Consequently, he took on the role of anti-country policeman, initiating a series of exasperating rows that could flare up at any moment, bullishly refusing to ever back down until a solution was found that satisfied him.

'That's the Martin Blunt effect,' explains Burgess. 'You come up with something that's fairly straight and then Martin puts his bit in and completely throws it.'

'He doesn't think like normal people, Martin,' continues Mark Collins, 'and he's not easily swayed. If something's coasting along quite nicely, he knows how to uncoast it and make you think about it. He's got this funk thing to him. Me and him argue till we're blue in the face. It's both him and Jon Brookes, really. They've been playing together for so long that when Martin starts up, Jon knows exactly where to go.'

Fuelled by cocaine, E and plenty of blow (despite Blunt's fear of dope's dampening influence, they even had a shrine to their bong), The Charlatans piled back into Monmouth life. They would regularly visit The Griffin pub – and all the others, just for variety, like. Then they would lie around watching *The Rutles* (no *This Is*

Spinal Tap for these northern lads) and, especially and often, Arnold Schwarzenegger's mighty *Predator*. Battling against terrible adversity is, of course, a band obsession.

But they were also very, very busy. With the album's working title changing between *Nine Acre Court, Smiling, You Start A Riot* (a lyric from 'Just Lookin'), *Live It Like You Love It* (from 'Bullet Comes'), *Look At Us* and *Crashin' In, Crashin' Out*, they got straight down to it. The first tracks recorded were 'See It Through', 'Green Flashing Eyes' and 'Backroom Window', then 'Crashin' In' (the middle pair eventually constituting the B-side of the last tune). 'See It Through' was a big pointer to Burgess's lyrical concerns. With its line 'I wanna free all the monkeys, don't wanna live in the zoo', it was an appeal to and an anthem for all the outsiders, the misfits, the northeners, the ugly, the Scots, the weirdos. It came right from the centre of the band's psyche, and aimed directly at the hearts of a potential audience of multi-millions.

Each track came naturally now. 'Nine Acre Court', the thudding, howling instrumental opener, came about after the band had just returned from clubbing in nearby Bristol. An A&R man from Beggars had arrived to check on their progress so the ever-friendly Burgess was sent out to occupy him while the others pretended to be working. They were just messing about but, with Blunt and Mark Collins loving the heaviness of it, and Rob egging Dave Charles and Brookes into joining him in that screaming vocal refrain, it turned into a winner. The title was taken from the block of flats (in Salford, near Old Trafford) where Mark's girlfriend Claire lived, and Mark had been staying as he wrote for the record, and the intro was from a tape made by Brookes on London's Oxford Street as he was approached by both a bus and the Jesus Army. A little later, Burgess played the song to a few mates back at his flat on Eton College Road in Chalk Farm after a punishing all-nighter. As the bright morning sun began to pour into the room, he sang along, dancing maniacally around and over the clutter of empty record sleeves and bottles. It was unbelievable and, at that hour, a very welcome burst of energy.

Mark Collins was now really enjoying himself. Much to Blunt's disgruntlement, he was using the band's internal 'club night' to push big rock and American folk. His guitar began to deliberately lag behind the beat, creating a lazy, laconic feel and turning his compositions into bona fide gems. 'Just When You're Thinkin' Things Over' was a take on Led Zeppelin's 'Ramble On' – its lack of drums purely down to Brookes breaking his foot in a game of soccer, tackle courtesy of Laurence O'Keefe (then of Levitation, now Dark Star).

The filthy-dirty swamp rock of 'Toothache' was an attempt to capture the spirit of 'When The Levee Breaks' from *Led Zeppelin 4*. Collins now hates to hear this one, believing himself to have executed it poorly. When you hear him live, torturing every filthy nuance from the riff, you know why. Even so, the track, with its summarising mantra, 'You can have it all, you can have it all', had a truly sexual voodoo feel, even more so than 'Bullet Comes', which Burgess claims to have been influenced by Dr John's *Gumbo* album.

On top of these there were more destined to become live killers, the soulful, almost hymn-like 'Here Comes A Soul Saver' for one.

'There's quite a Neil Young, kind of country vibe to that,' says Burgess, who at the time had given up smoking but replaced cigarettes with amphetamines, 'and it suited the situation. Loads of country songs are about struggle and survival, you know, trouble and joy, and that felt like what had happened to us over the years. The sound was right for us. We loved it and we could say something with it, and it said something about us. Which is what rock bands should be about.'

This reaching for some kind of inner truth spread through the whole album, and clearly infuses the title of 'No Fiction'. This track had emerged almost complete from a jam between Burgess and Mark Collins. It took them four months to convince Blunt of its merits. 'Because he worries all the time,' explains Burgess, 'and he thinks it can't be any good if you haven't really worked on it.' 'No Fiction' meant a lot to Burgess. To him it was about the necessity of total immersion in life, as well as the full and final coming together of The Charlatans.

'In 1990, Rob Collins sold himself to this band,' he reflected. 'Martin too. Mark did as soon as he joined, but me and Jon have kind of been dipping our toes in. And now we're completely in it too. I love this band, I love what we do and I wanna die for it. It's like we put a rucksack on at twenty-two, spent all that time putting things in it that we really liked, and we're emptying it out now.'

The subject of loyalty was a vital lyrical source too. 'Tell Everyone' concerned Burgess and his fidelity to Chloe Walsh (she's pictured on page two of the sleeve booklet). 'I don't like shagabouts,' he once muttered darkly. And then there was the closing 'Thank You', like 'Feeling Holy' written by the two Collinses. This, a simple acknowledgement of their supporters that might have been trite and unctuous, is somehow rendered resolute and charming. The appeal of the track is its very simplicity.

'It's little but it's really strong,' says Burgess. 'I just walked up to the mike and said "Thank you". That's about all that needed to be said.'

As an album, The Charlatans – so named because the band finally felt themselves to be in control – was a stunning surprise. Up To Our Hips had had its great moments, but this was a consistent corker, drawing on all their previous influences as well as their deep knowledge of Americana. There was Rob Collins' sometimes panicked, sometimes soaring excesses, the keyboardist tinkering till he tumbled into the groove. There was Mark Collins' super-distorted wah-wah, ever backed by Blunt's funky rumble, with Burgess occasionally singing through what sounded like a blender on slow, and Brookes hammering away, rapidly turning himself into one of the most respected drummers in the land. With it all coming together like this, it seemed that The Charlatans were finally really living up to the potential of that earlier Manchester melting pot, truly and thrillingly exploring the possibilities of their psychedelic pop, just as pioneers like Leftfield were doing with dance and Renegade Soundwave with dub.

The first release from The Charlatans was 'Crashin' In', a massively upbeat yet also oddly melancholic rush of a single, the lyric a wake-up call to the youth of the nation. Aside from the example set by their own personal lifestyles, The Charlatans' main political thrust is their ongoing war with apathy (although they do assume that most of the people they might wake up will be Labour voters).

Its video features Charlie, the studio cat, who the band had helped nurse back to health when she turned up with worms, fleas and, hideously, cigarette burns on her ears.

The single was to be released on Boxing Day, 1994, but was held back a day due to the Bank Holiday. 'It was the start of our date thing,' explains Burgess, 'where we have to do things on particular days. Like, we'll do something on Mods' May Day. "Just Lookin'" came out on my birthday.'

The album was not scheduled for release until the next September, so 'Crashin' In', a superb single, was seemingly being tossed away (it hit Number 31). Furthermore, there were problems with the final mixes of *The Charlatans*. Hillage had done his stuff, putting together an untold number of different versions for the band's delectation and delight, but now he was away to projects new, specifically to a long-confirmed date with an Algerian artist in France. This was not unreasonable considering the band's search for perfection had taken the album well over its deadline, but it still pissed them off mightily, just as Burgess had earlier pissed off Hillage by dissing *Up To Our Hips* – though he was only comparing its quality to that of material yet to come. But this was different. This was a crime against loyalty. They did not react well.

'Here we started a new thing,' explains Burgess. 'Writing and immediately releasing, so we had two singles out, this and "Just Lookin'", miles before the fourth LP came out. Beggars Banquet didn't want to do it but we felt we knew better – we were really getting back the confidence and belief we had in the first place.

'I remember all of us sitting around the mixing desk one midnight and doing this one, and all of us saying, "This is it. It's a bit rough and ready but it's just right." Then Steve Hillage came in and said, "Well, technically it's not much." And we thought bollocks, and we sacked him. Well, actually we sacked him later. He gave us eight different mixes of the LP to take home and listen to that Christmas, and we hated every one of them. So then we sacked him.

'It wasn't good because we wanted to get into a situation where we would always work with the same people, people we could trust. Because, on the second LP, we really felt like we could trust no one. But it worked out OK. Co-producing with Dave Charles was good. The results weren't technical genius, but the spirit was at full force.'

'After learning about technology with Flood,' adds Blunt, 'and having loosened back up with Steve Hillage, we had a real air of confidence. We really felt that we could do it on our own.'

Between 12 and 25 January, the band took the album to London's Strongroom for mixing but the results, despite a cost of £15,000, were unusable. They returned to Monnow Valley, then spent two weeks at Rockfield before finishing up back at Monnow in the first weeks of March.

From here it was straight into rehearsals for a tour that would last the year, the only pause being due to a change of heart over the choice of the next single. This was to have been 'Bullet Comes', backed with 'See It Through' and 'Floor Nine'. Indeed, on 7 March Dave Charles, Blunt and Rob Collins had gone down to Metropolis Studios in London to cut the track, along with its intended B-sides. They'd slept overnight on a barge on the Thames. Three days later it was decided to risk shooting their wad entirely and couple 'Bullet Comes' with the equally ferocious 'Just Lookin''. This was another of Burgess's teen anthems, and concerned the death of youth spirit in the UK. The message was 'Get up and *do* something'. It was also a personal reaction to the singer being told at school that he'd never amount to anything. Burgess had wanted it to capture some of the righteous anger of 'Blowin' In The Wind' though lyrically it was more similar to Lennon's 'Bring On The Lucie (Freda Peeple)' from *Mind Games*, released in the autumn of 1973.

And so it was on to the first UK leg of a crippling tour, where it soon became apparent that Rob Collins, altered by prison, drawn from his shell by drugs and missing his little daughter, was going slowly out of control.

After the very first gig, at Newcastle University on 29 April, Collins went missing. With another lad, he had returned from the venue to the hotel bar where his friend's behaviour had merited expulsion. Ever loyal to his mates, Rob stood up for him and, despite being a paid-up guest, got thrown out too. The pair went in search of beer, a search so fruitful that Collins failed to make it back to his room by the time the band were due to leave for Glasgow Barrowland the next morning. As the tour bus waited on double yellow lines, arguments raging with pouncing traffic wardens, Harrison was forced to clear out Collins' room, load his gear on to the bus and depart for Scotland, leaving Collins a message bluntly demanding, 'Get to Glasgow, you bastard.'

Rob did get there and, in his usual infuriating fashion, it was before everyone else. But the signs were there.

Though neither 'Crashin' In' nor 'Just Lookin''/'Bullet Comes' had managed to crack the UK Top 30, The Charlatans were quite sickeningly confident about the prospects of their next album. And with good reason. They knew in themselves that they had managed to successfully incorporate country rock into their sound (the next single, 'Just When You're Thinkin' Things Over', would let the world know that), and their latest efforts on their springtime tour had opened up a new can of whup-ass. Audiences loved this new stuff, recognising the stadium-filling power of it. Indeed, so strong was the reaction to the likes of 'Crashin' In' and 'Toothache' that the old songs they replaced in the set would never return.

The album would enter the UK charts at Number 1, justifying their efforts and making sense of all the bullshit. But then they already knew that.

'By the time *The Charlatans* came out,' says Burgess, 'we were supremely confident. We had a review saying we'd stopped sounding like the Roses and started sounding like Oasis, but we knew better. We thought we'd done something like The Beastie Boys did with *Check Your Head*, really come back. We thought we're never gonna get back that original euphoria, so let's just do what we wanna do. We knew all the way through recording that it would go into the charts at Number 1. It was a real "Told you so" and a huge relief to us.'

So confident were the band that after that spring tour, instead of spending the summer spreading the word across Europe, entering on to the standard festival circuit, they sat back, playing only six festivals in the space of four months. These included Glastonbury (on the second stage with Goldie, Elastica and Veruca Salt),

Phoenix, Brighton and a headline spot at Benicassim, an odd little musical fiesta taking place yearly, just south of Valencia on the east coast of Spain. The band flew across from Heathrow, along with quirky indie band Salad, one of the other acts on their bill, and travelled by coach down to the little town hosting the event.

On the first evening the bar was assaulted with exceptional gusto. The brevity of the respite from recording made appearances in foreign climes seem more like vacations than work. Cocktails were being tested out long before the afternoon ended. A meal had been organised at a waterfront seafood joint, and both bands attended, The Charlatans and their crew filling one long table, Salad half-filling the next one along.

Halfway through this jovial event, with the sangria flowing like, er, wine, it became noticeable that Rob Collins was playing with his food. Strike that – that makes it sound like he was sending peas spinning with his fork, which was way too tame for Collins. What he was actually doing was building with his food. A less flamboyant but infinitely more intense version of Richard Dreyfuss in *Close Encounters of the Third Kind*, he was moulding it into an ever-taller, ever-crazier semi-edible edifice. Starting with a raised dessert bowl for a base, he used leftover rice and chopped vegetables for a strong foundation then began building upward with ice cream and fresh scallops. He used recently deceased prawns for gargoyles – a nicely inventive touch. Halfway up, a silver teaspoon stuck out, as did a couple of semi-smoked Rothmans and some shells. Atop it all, he carefully placed bent and burned fag butts, their ash being carried down the sides by the swiftly melting vanilla ice.

It sounds disgusting and it was, but there was a strange architectural beauty to its mad lines and curves, and the intensity Collins lent to creating it was wholly compelling. His concentration was only broken by a stray roll tossed from the next table. With both hands, Collins grabbed his untouched plate of paella and tipped it backwards over his head on to the guilty and innocent alike. Clearly he had to be the heavyweight champion of everything.

The gig the next night was another good one. The festival was held in a stone stadium usually devoted to cycling. The street outside was filled with record stalls, the air with smoke from burning torches. Despite their few appearances in Spain, The Charlatans were greeted like returning heroes (as Cranes would be, headlining the next night). Afterwards, loved-up to a man, all bar Burgess were taken out to a sweet all-ages-welcome fiesta in a huge wooden bar on the shore (Burgess preferred to return to town, where he sat drinking lager in the tiny square, watching the world pass by). More beers were sunk, and a little paddling indulged in (this was the seaside, after all), then the band were called back to the coach for the trip back to the hotel.

All of them obeyed that call except Rob Collins. As you stood on the beach there, you could hear the dull thud of distant drums. Around a mile away, you could discern the flashing, multicoloured glow of some kind of rave. No one paid it any heed but Collins seemed almost transfixed. He turned towards the far-off fun and, accompanied by his ever-present friend and keyboard tech 'Mad' Johnny Clark, he started walking, visibly taken by the beat, like a stern and determined Baloo the Bear. Gone for the night, obviously.

Back at the hotel, Burgess was now in the bar and Blunt joined him there, as did Salad's singer Marijne van de Vlugt and their guitarist Paul Kennedy. This pair were pleasant enough, very much so, but Kennedy was in band-bonding mode. First to Blunt, then to Burgess, he went on and on about his band's problems with the press, how Marijne had been an MTV presenter and everybody hated that but it didn't matter anyway because they had soul and everyone should realise that and on and on and on. Blunt left the room, as did Marijne herself, but Kennedy continued until finally rashly declaring that Salad were just like The Charlatans. That was too much for Burgess and he let Kennedy know it, for the first and only time exhibiting real anger in front of this author. Some bands were a little like The Charlatans, he ranted. The Verve, maybe. Pusherman, even Oasis, but *not* Salad. You don't say that.

The very next day, The Charlatans flew to Scotland, to the T In The Park festival. There's no longer any point mentioning the receptions they receive in Scotland – euphoria is a given. Two weeks later, they were in Stockholm, for the Waterfestival. Here Rob Collins was in trouble again, this time through no real fault of his own. Spotting a man hassling two girls, he went over to offer his assistance, only to be attacked for his pains. In the ensuing tussle he broke his hand and consequently, refusing to allow any gigs to be cancelled, he took to carrying around a can of painkiller, spraying his digits whenever the pain became too great.

This was a telling little story. Despite all the drugs and the madder-than-thou bravado, Collins was still capable of this kind of gallantry. He also liked to hang around with Steve Harrison's son, Martin. Maybe because he was missing his own kid Emily, he'd buy the boy huge bags of sweets and pay for him to join in on the slot machines. As a wind-up, he'd tell the cigarette-loathing Harrison that he'd 'have young Martin smoking tabs before he's ten'. For obvious, painful reasons, young Martin still can't watch the video for 'One To Another', Collins' last with the band.

This was another side to Rob Collins. He was decent and compassionate: just not a good communicator. He struggled to understand why anyone was interested in him and refused to do interviews. By now, though, he knew the power of his reputation as jailbird and hardcore daredevil, and he used it to control the situations around him. He also had a total lack of physical fear and an innate ability to quickly suss people out. He recognised Harrison's efforts to create an easy atmosphere and liked to undo them; he also liked to occasionally unbalance the other members of the band, particularly Burgess and Blunt.

Harrison believes that Collins was deeply anxious and, not being much of a talker, he would deliberately make others even more anxious. Only in music was he comfortable. There he knew where he stood, felt equal to or better than everyone else. When that certainty slipped, there would be trouble. 'When he was concerned about his ability within the band,' says Harrison, 'he became destructive again.'

Outside of the music, when it came to drink and drugs, Collins was indisputably pack leader. He had an amazing constitution and kept his tolerance high through constant indulgence, schooling his body to take more than any prospective challenger.

'I think Rob was a genius,' says Harrison. 'On keyboards he was a genius. And one thing that people never mention is that he also had a beautiful singing voice, a really special voice.

'I honestly think Rob spoke to more people in the last eighteen months, two years of his life than he had done in total before. But they weren't talking to Rob, they were talking to the drugs. And it was just one more all the time with Rob. He'd always go one more than everyone else, even to the point of once drinking bleach. James Pearson [the band's driver and official all-round helper] used to say that you'd meet all these hard people, hard nuts, but that Rob genuinely had no sense of fear – you could see it in his eyes.'

In August, The Charlatans released 'Just When You're Thinkin' Things Over', an invigorating slice of country melancholia (how did *that* one slip through the Blunt net?) that, reaching Number 12, was the band's biggest hit single since 'Then' five years before. It might have gone higher but that week the nation was held spellbound by the big stand-off between Blur and Oasis – would 'Country House' or 'Roll With It' take the top spot? It mattered little to The Charlatans. High chart positions were nice but, having now found a strong, identifiable and mutable style, they were more concerned with moving towards that long-threatened classic album. Besides, their album was Number 1. Who *cared* about singles?

As the first Charlatans single in five years to reach Radio 1's daytime playlist, 'Just When You're Thinkin' Things Over' earned the band a spot on *Top of the Pops*. They went down to London, did the show, then got seriously caned. In the dead of night, back at the hotel, the fire alarm went off. Some water had found its way on to electrics somewhere and there genuinely was a fire. Everyone was evacuated from the building. Sharing a room with Rob Collins, Blunt was deep asleep. Before the bells could wake him, Collins had got up, smashed the alarm off the wall above the door and tossed it into the wardrobe. Next morning Blunt, who like many of us has never hankered after being burned alive, was horrified. Collins' excuse that he couldn't sleep with all that racket hardly seemed sufficient.

Maybe Rob felt he needed his sleep to escape the pain from his hand. It can't have been easy, and certainly kept him from contributing to The Charlatans' next mini-project. This was to be the recording of a song for the *Help* album, a project organised by Tony Crean of indie label Go! Discs for the War Child charity which was gathering funds for the children of war-torn Bosnia. Inspired by the double-quick writing, recording and release of John Lennon's 'Instant Karma' single in 1970, Crean's idea was to have a collection of bands put together and mix an album's worth of tracks in a single day.

Blur were involved, plus Suede, Manic Street Preachers and Paul Weller. Noel Gallagher would record a version of The Beatles' 'Help' with Paul McCartney. On the same day, 4 September, The Charlatans recorded a version of Sly Stone's 'Time for Livin'', the track being immediately mixed by The Chemical Brothers. Burgess and Mark Collins had earlier tested the song out in a pub in London's Soho, at the Acoustically Heavenly evening. They had also covered East Village's 'Silver Train', and run through 'The Skies Are Mine' (a B-side to 'Just When You're Thinkin' Things Over') and a few tracks from the new album.

Help was an unqualified success. Released a few short days after the recordings, it proved to be the fastest-selling album since The Beatles' *White Album*.

Now, for The Charlatans, it was off to America once again, with the tour shortened as juice merchants Ocean Spray had pulled their sponsorship due to Rob Collins' criminal record. Yet it wasn't Collins who got them arrested on landing in the US.

The in-flight incident was absurd. The guy sitting in front of Burgess and Mark Collins was a moaner (no one knows if he was a Taurus) – a middle-management type resentful at being in economy. The Charlatans wouldn't keep silent to order, so the guy casually reached round and blocked Burgess's little TV screen with his hands – naughty hands, the lads decided, and hands they ought to tickle. The guy leapt up, shouted a general '*Fuck off!*' and took a swing at Burgess. It all got a little heated, with Rob Collins taking the opportunity to playfully strangle Johnny Clark on account of his forgetting to bring some valves for the organ.

On landing, the band were told to stay where they were – all of them bar Brookes who was sitting further down the front. They were each cuffed by the police and humiliatingly forced to look away as the other passengers passed them, some of them stopping and offering their addresses should the band need witnesses to attest to their reasonable behaviour. From the plane, they were taken to the New York Port Authority cells, where their passports were taken away, as were their shoelaces, lest they chose to hang themselves in shame. They were told they had been swearing and spitting and smoking on the flight: 'lewd and indecent behaviour.' Three hours later, after questioning Rob Collins extensively, the FBI declared the situation 'ridiculous'.

Despite this unpromising start, this US tour was better for the band. Their mélange of mature rock, dance techniques and a still teenlike ebullience was a great deal easier to understand. Burgess was now friendly but tight-lipped, wary of making the same mistakes as in 1990 and '91, no matter how confident he felt in himself. Also, he had come to realise how much he liked America and how much its music had influenced him, so he didn't wish to appear a jerk.

The reaction was good. The Charlatans were now rebuilding, making up for the ground lost over the last four years. It helped that many reviews of *The Charlatans* were mentioning 'the dirtier parts of the Stones' *Exile On Main Street*' – a real thrill for Burgess, that one. He dearly loves The Rolling Stones, even having a good word for their *Black And Blue* album. Well, for the track 'Memory Motel', at least. He was having a great time, even, in Toronto, allowing himself to be photographed in a wedding dress. It was the second time Burgess had blown it in wedding gear, but fook it, it's just a laugh, innit?

On tour with The Charlatans this time were Menswear, heirs apparent to the Britpop crown. This was a typical choice, the band having risked being supported by many of the UK's most explosive young acts (at least, by acts that were *said* to be explosive). Mansun, Gene, Whiteout, Daytona, Northern Uproar, The Bluetones and The Dandy Warhols: all of them shared the same stage over the years yet none of them managed to blow The Charlatans away.

The Charlatans got on well with Menswear. Aside from Rob, who was up to his old tricks again.

'Rob's reputation had gone before him,' says Harrison, 'and you could see that this band – they looked so young – were dead scared of him. Rob knew it, and for some reason he'd decided to pick on

the guitarist. I was standing there at the side of the stage at sound-
check and I saw Rob watching them. I thought, What's going on
here? They hardly ever show any interest in the support band.
They're always thinking about their own performance. Then I
realised he wasn't watching them, he was staring at this guitarist.
The poor guy couldn't tune up his guitar, couldn't play. Whatever
he tried to do his eyes were always drawn back to Rob. And Rob's
eyes weren't moving. I said, "Rob, will you leave him alone?" and
Rob got that smile on and said "I'm not doing anything," all innocent like. And I said, "I *know* what you're fucking doing."

'So Rob walked off and I followed him and the next thing I
saw is the singer, Johnny, coming over, a really nice bloke. He
said, very tentatively, "Hiya, it's Rob, isn't it?" And Rob said,
"All right, Jarvis?" And the guy went to bits. He said, "Er,
Johnny. My name's Johnny." And Rob said, in that big Walsall
accent, "Yeah, but yaow *wanna* be Jarvis, don't yaow?"
Completely killed him and kept on walking.'

Britpop hadn't been going over too well in the States, partly
because most of it was purposefully parochial, namby-pamby
nonsense, but also because there was a lack of a concerted
focus. Americans actually look forward to the occasional
British invasion – it takes them back to the good old days
(there's a little bit of Oliver Stone in all of them). But now was
the big push. Pulp and Supergrass had had a go. Now
Menswear were there, as were Blur, and Blunt and Rob Collins
ended up with them on a 'Britpop breakfast show' on San
Franciscan radio. Having nothing to do with the scene, the pair
had very little to say. It was ludicrous that they were there at
all, when you think of where The Charlatans were headed
musically.

Still, in the States this confusion might be useful. *Rolling Stone*'s
David Fricke, who had been a supporter of the band for some
time, said that Burgess might well be the face and voice of this new
movement, and while Britpop had a long way to travel yet, 'The
Charlatans' boat has definitely come in.'

After those ten dates in the US, there was a brief European excur-
sion, concentrating mostly on Germany, then their longest UK tour

in years. After returning to Number 1 after five years in the rock wilderness, this was like a triumphal march through their kingdom. At Glasgow's Barrowland, where (as in a fair few other venues) they had broken the record for the number of sweaty bodies shoe-horned into the place, they took the stage with Burgess theatrically miming to The Zombies' 'This Will Be Our Year'.

It was a great time; a truly joyful celebration of their own abilities. Rob Collins was already in the spirit of things; along with the others he had had a hell of a time with light entertainer/comedian Joe Longthorne, who had shared their hotel early in the tour. Now he went further. With Pearson, he engaged in what they called chemical warfare, seeing who could outdo the other in the popping of multiple Es. Pearson was enjoying himself, but he had responsibilities too. It wasn't helping that Collins had taken to covering his eyes as they sped down the motorway.

The show at the Southampton Guildhall on 21 November was a tremendous rush. Burgess had done a little DJing for the crowd beforehand (he is occasionally flown to Sweden to do the same), and during the show he was a compelling presence. Confidence had slowed him down and allowed him to visibly enjoy the band. It was infectious.

After the gig, back at the hotel, Rob Collins and Pearson were hilarious, achieving new peaks in post-gig entertainment. In the bar, Collins sat down at the piano and endlessly repeated the introduction to 'Heart And Soul' as Pearson, standing beside him, hand on his shoulder like some louche old-school cabaret artist, burst into their song for the tour – 'He Really Loves Those Es'. With the title, repeated a few times, serving as the chorus, the song itself began, 'He went down to Aberdeen/Took more Es than you ever seen' and continued on through the tour itinerary, carefully listing the pair's inglorious exploits.

There was another song doing the rounds, one not quite so popular with Collins. Sung to the tune of 'Winter Wonderland', it went:

Robbie Collins, are you listenin'?
Don't you know, your eyes are glistenin'?
You know it's no joke,

You've done too much coke,
Walkin' in Robbie Collins Wonderland.

Then a brief break, a deep breath, and on into a verse that used
to wind the proudly imperturbable Collins up big time.

Everybody knows that you are mental.
And of all the things that you have done.
Like the time you went into the supermarket,
And tried to turn it over with a gun...

Rob Collins had always enjoyed pushing his tour managers to and
over the edge of distraction. On one occasion, on the way to
Heathrow at the start of a US tour, he'd tossed his laminates out of
the car window then, while at the airport, torn his personal tour
itinerary to shreds, thereby giving himself an excuse for maximis-
ing the tour manager's headaches over the weeks to come.
Pointless questions and unnecessary requests, mostly made
between the hours of three and five in the morning, were a speciality.

He also liked to wind up night porters, a species that, as a nocturnal creature himself, he had come to know well. Most nights,
particularly in the UK where hotel services are not geared towards
rock 'n' roll bacchanalia, the band would stay late in the bar – usually until the bar was closed due to licensing restrictions and the
porter was forced to bring drinks through on a tray. Eventually,
they would all drift off to bed. And that's when Collins went into
overdrive, ever-so-politely running the poor sod into the ground.

On this tour, he was beginning to perfect his methods, turning
badgering into something of an art form. With demonic subtlety,
he'd get to the porter via an unsuspecting middleman. One night,
he used Paul Draper, singer and guitarist with The Charlatans'
soon-to-break support band, Mansun.

Draper had retired fairly early for a few quiet drinks in his room
with his nearest and dearest, then bed. Collins, having got hold of
his room number, called him up, pretending to be the night porter,
and asked him to keep the noise down as his neighbours had been
complaining. There had *been* no noise, and Draper told him so.

Again Collins called, sterner this time: Mr Draper really should take other people into consideration. Again Draper denied the charges. On and on this went, deep into the night, until Draper, by now furious that he was being rudely woken up and even more rudely told to shut up, marched down to the lobby and boxed the unwitting porter's ears.

Naturally, these interminable nightly japes made it hard to get up in the morning, and Collins would do so in his own sweet time. Any attempts to rush him were futile. The morning after the Southampton show, things were running a little behind schedule, yet finally the tour manager John Gibbon's persistence saw everyone slumped, bleary but cheerful, on the lobby's homely sofas. Everyone but Rob, that is. The bus was revved up, coffees were sunk, but still no Rob. A request was made of the receptionist: could he please call Mr Collins' room? 'Already done that, sir,' came the slightly sheepish reply. Well, could he please call up again?

Now the receptionist began to look concerned. It was clear that for some reason he would really rather not disturb Mr Collins again. Gibbon insisted, so the call was made. The phone must have rung twice before the receptionist's head jerked away from the receiver and he turned to the waiting assembly, his face covered in a triumphant told-you-so smile. He held up the receiver and, from right across the room, you could hear the high-pitched backing vocal tones of Rob shrieking, 'LALALALALALALALA.' It was a new peak in irritation: imagine Cleopatra's Needle tipped up and scraped down some monstrous blackboard.

Collins didn't stop either; wouldn't stop for breath till the phone was put down. It was another little victory over both himself and whoever it was trying to tell him what to do.

On 28 November, after the major leg of the UK tour (they would return for three final dates in December), the band left for a five-date jaunt to Japan. The Bluetones, who were supposed to be co-headlining, would later publicly comment on The Charlatans' standoffishness.

This was more to do with The Bluetones themselves. With a Top 5 single, 'Slight Return', and a hugely well-received debut album, *Expecting To Fly* (produced by Hugh Jones, who'd also

worked on 'Me In Time'), they, like The Charlatans before
them, had hit big fast. And they, again like the early
Charlatans, were bragging like crazy, telling and retelling the
tale of how they had shared digs with the fledgling Dodgy (if
all went well, a neat slice of rock history – please stop snigger-
ing at the back), and endlessly testifying to their own talent and
potential. Insecurity was rife: was this the good life or just a
single golden year followed by a lifetime of dashed hopes and
cheek-burning humiliation? Clearly The Bluetones too were
engaged in that monotonous rock mantra of positivism. Say it
enough and it will come true. Say it enough and it will come
true. Say it. Yes, yes, fine, we believe you.

What The Bluetones missed was that The Charlatans, in
some respects, were similar to them, only much further down
the line. But they did have a point: The Charlatans were not
always the easiest of bands to get along with. As a unit,
Burgess and company were still possessed of a bunker spirit
that was second-to-none. Outsiders were welcomed and treated
well but at some points necessarily ignored. As individuals they
were bigger, brasher, infinitely more intense than their Bluetonic
counterparts, yet – with the exception of the big-shouldered
Brookes who will good-naturedly barge through any situation –
they could be shy, as intimidated on their own as they were
intimidating en masse and by reputation.

No doubt another factor making this tour less than a delight for
The Bluetones was the little matter of co-headlining. Up until this
point, the Burgess-fronted Charlatans had not and would not support anyone else, with no exceptions (aside from that grim gig
with Cactus World News in 1989). Aside from festivals (which
don't count because people aren't just there for the headliners),
over hundreds of gigs they had stayed true to the spirit of Ian
Brown's notorious comment about playing with The Rolling
Stones ('They should be supporting *us*, man'). They wanted shows
to have a Charlatans atmosphere, with DJs and support band simply adding to this idiosyncratic, special mood. Again, it was conscious myth-making. Festivals were there to pick up stray
converts; gigs were there to be remembered for ever, and remembered specifically for The Charlatans. There would be no co-head-

lining. No matter how much it annoyed The Bluetones, they could make their own myth elsewhere.

The next August, The Charlatans would betray this principle, once and once only. The extenuating circumstances would drip blood.

ust When You're Thinking Things Over', Maida Vale, 1995

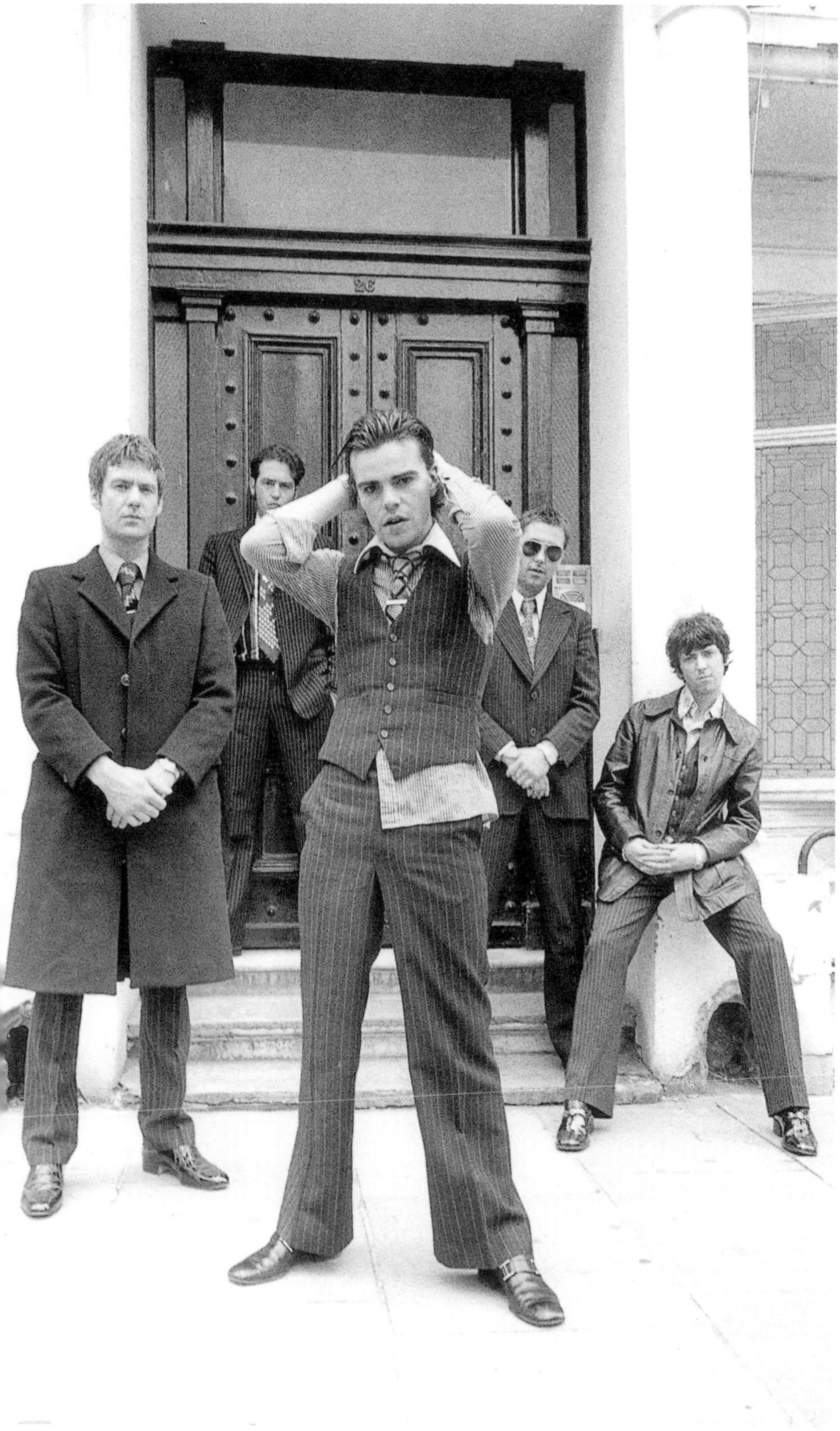

Tim with Tom Rowlands – Chemical Brothers

Knebworth

Wales

Stockholm, 1997

SET V98 CHELMSFORD

WITH NO SHOES
NORTH COUNTRY BOY
TELLIN STORIES
TOOTHACHE
A HOUSE IS NOT A HOME
JUST LOOKIN
SOUL SAVER
ONE TO ANOTHER
AREA 51
BLONDE WALTZ
CLEAN UP KID
JUST WHEN YOUR THINKIN
WEIRDO
HOW HIGH

THEN
SPROSTON GREEN

Martin, V98

Mark

John Anson Ford Amphitheatre, Hollywood

04 The Bright Light Beyond The End Of Everything

NINETEEN NINETY-SIX FOUND The Charlatans in bullish mood. They had found their own way now and seemed to have guaranteed the escape from baggy they had been engineering for years. The ultimate goal, a place in rock history, seemed in sight. The Stone Roses were breaking down, John Squire announcing his departure in March. Shaun Ryder's Black Grape had entered a downward spiral after the success of *It's Great When You're Straight, Yeah!* – but none of that seemed to matter any more. The Charlatans were outside and beyond it all.

It wasn't just that they had managed to stick around the longest, that they were clearly genuine survivors. What The Charlatans had done was stay true to that original Manchester spirit and had succeeded where the others had not: they had grown, become competent in different styles and in melding those styles. In short, as a band they had artistically progressed. Burgess knew that. He claimed not to have been hurt by criticism because it sometimes contained an element of truth, and that was helpful. His attitude was mature and it would soon stand him in extraordinarily good stead.

In terms of musical output, the year began and continued slowly for the band. They contributed a version of 'I Feel Much Better' to a Small Faces tribute album. They planned a UK tour of smaller, more obscure venues, 'for people who usually have to travel to see us'. And they also decided, after bitter arguments, to break their rule about supporting people, agreeing to play with Oasis at the huge shows they had announced at Loch Lomond and Knebworth. There was a touch of history in the making to the gigs, at Knebworth especially. It had to be done.

The band spent some time writing and relaxing at home then, at Easter, took themselves off to South Wales once more. Work was slow; very slow. The clubs of Bristol, Cardiff and Swansea seemed so much more attractive. But some progress was made, particularly on the track intended to be the next single, 'One to Another'. This was a definite step beyond *The Charlatans*, with a searing hypno-riff and Burgess now finding vocal rhythms which were evidently all his own. The release date was set for August (inevitably, months before the album) and a shoot arranged for the sleeve.

The plan was to go down to the South Wales coast. Locations had been scouted and things were looking good. But as the day progressed the band became less and less keen on the idea: it was too much of a pain in the arse. Why not just do it in the studio's garden? So a new concept was born. They could all sit around the bench-sided table which could be loaded with pertinent materials: CDs, magazines, wine, beer, perhaps lobsters now things were on the up. There could be a bit of a low-key *Beggars Banquet* vibe to it.

Rob Collins, Burgess and this book's photographer took themselves off to Waitrose in Monmouth to obtain the relevant props. They had stopped off for a couple of beers in a pub garden when Collins announced that he'd suddenly realised *just* what they needed. He rushed off into the town, then returned to say that they would have to wait another hour as the shopkeeper couldn't oblige them till he closed up for the day (this may have just been an excuse for staying in the pub).

As it turned out, Collins had spent a pound on a frozen pig's head (you can see it next to Rob's left buttock on the single sleeve). They picked it up, took it back and, as the light was fast fading, got on with the shots. The session didn't last long. Brookes, finding himself assaulted by a God-awful stench, guessed that the head was thawing fast (note his expression in the photo). He leant over for a closer nasal inspection – as you do – and reeled backward, eyes watering, retching up bile, close to vomiting wholesale.

That was enough. The pig was shot for posterity then bade a less than fond farewell as Rob Collins took it off into the woods where it could fester and supply him with maggots for further angling exploits. The band set about nailing the wine and barbecuing the lobsters, along with the trout Rob had recently hooked. Happy happy joy joy.

On the afternoon of Monday 22 July, everything was progressing as usual. True to their principle of never rushing anything ever again, the band had taken up residency at Monnow Valley studios, with each member turning up as and when inspiration or duty called. Jon Brookes, at home that day, remembers receiving a call from Rob Collins. Ordinarily, such a call would entail Brookes being deluged with thoughts, plans and questions – Collins, despite his reputation as a wastrel, was probably even more concerned than the rest with the minutiae of The Charlatans' career. No matter how pissed he was, he always prided himself on staying on top of it all.

But this call was different. Collins seemed strangely restrained, as if in 'a semi-coma or something, like it was one heartbeat per hour'. He told Brookes he was about to leave for the studio, and they began to discuss Collins' ideas for the tracks in progress. Brookes, typically forthright, said he found Collins' recent efforts a little 'wishy-washy', and Collins, ever a reluctant recipient of criticism, at first argued his case then gradually kind of-almost-maybe agreed. The conversation ended with Brookes telling Collins to 'get stuck in', knowing full well that he would, and saying that they would meet at the studio in a few days. They would never speak again.

Collins arrived at Monnow Valley at around 6 p.m. Burgess remembers him as being 'miserable as ever. No more or less so than at any other time. He was just Rob, you know, slagging everything off, taking the piss. He was ready for work as far as I was concerned.' Work, though, had to be briefly postponed. Some friends were at the studio, keen to celebrate the birthday of Ric Peet, who was engineering for the band (he would later be credited with co-producing 'Area 51' and 'Rob's Theme'). Along with Burgess and Mark Collins, they had been awaiting Rob's arrival with a view to continuing the festivities in the pubs of Monmouth.

By 9 o'clock, it was becoming raucous. Even Rob Collins, never much of a social butterfly, was joining in. Where you would often find The Charlatans, along with girlfriends, crew and assorted entourage, packed in tight in bars and restaurants, pulling tables together to create the uproarious familial atmosphere of a medieval banquet, Rob was generally to be found on the outskirts. He would sometimes separate himself or sit aside with one or two close friends, watching proceedings like some spectral host – quietly musing, delivering the occasional hilariously rude aside – or simply enjoying his own internal buzz. If there was a friut-machine in the room, he could be relied upon to attempt to master it, placing his pint-glass precariously on top and glaring balefully at the spinning icons. This evening he'd already chanced his arm on the machine and had come up trumps – £60 to the good. He was in a better-than-average mood.

As Burgess recalls, 'It was fucking manic, man. We were all just mad for it. Everyone was having a great time. Even Rob was more social than usual. I mean, he was off his head, having a top night out, and he won all this money. He was jumping about all over the place, dead happy.'

Around ten, Burgess decided to return to the studio, the thought of vocals to be laid down preying on his mind. Mentioning this to Rob Collins, he was told to take Collins' red BMW back to Monnow Valley, then to call a cab to pick Rob up from the pub at around eleven. Burgess went out to do just that but found the BMW's handbrake to be faulty, causing him to shunt the car parked in front. Not having driven in five years, and a little perturbed by this minor accident, he decided he didn't trust himself behind the wheel and returned to the pub to hand back Collins' keys. He made it back to the studio alone and immediately commenced work.

At closing time, an hour or so later, Rob, Mark and the rest finished up, thinking to down a few more back at the studio. Mark chose not to ride with Rob. Along with Tim, he had recently seen an advert for the GTI, spoofing seventies' cop shows. As one of their friends was in possession of an old Granada, the like of which Detectives Carter and Regan had used to hound seedy crims in *The Sweeney*, they'd spent the previous weekend screaming round the winding, leafy lanes of Monmouthshire, shouting, 'Shut it, you *slaaaag*!' and exhibiting their prowess with the shrieking handbrake-turn. So Ric Peet went with Rob, Mark picking the Granada over the flash crimson Beamer. That, he believed, would be more of a thrill.

Like Burgess, Rob Collins found moving the car difficult – he was boxed in. Aggressively resourceful, he shunted the vehicles front and back, setting off their alarms. Moments later, Rob's lights were to be seen in the Granada's rear-view, catching up fast, drawing closer and closer. Everyone thought Rob was messing about: he did like 'to drive at things or creep up on you'. Then, just as the headlights had sprung upon them without warning, on Rockfield Road they suddenly disappeared. No one thought twice about it. Rob had either taken a short cut to beat them back to the studio, stopped to buy cigarettes, or maybe, in one more wicked wind-up, broken off the pursuit simply because they'd never expect him to.

When the Granada reached Monnow Valley, the BMW had yet to show. After a while, they became convinced that Rob had stopped in to visit friends at the nearby Rockfield studios, or shot off on a midnight spin through the countryside, as he was known to do from time to time. Then, at around twelve, they received a call from a friend who, out on the road, had spotted the wreckage of a car with attendant police vehicles and ambulance. Guessing the truth, he had raced into Rockfield to call the band. Rob Collins, he told them, had crashed his motor and been taken to hospital.

Then the police turned up. Burgess, drunk and somewhat dazed, remembers them asking him what must have been how old Rob was, which he heard as 'How bald was he?', the misunderstanding adding to his confusion. Recalling the scene, he says, 'I still wasn't thinking the worst. The police were just asking a load of questions. Mark was doing his usual bit, walking round casual as fuck, trying to bully the police and take the piss out of them.

'I did kind of get an inkling. I remember them saying, "What instrument did he play?" and I thought, They're using the past tense, so I said, "He fucking *plays* keyboards." But it was only fleeting. It came at me but I didn't really realise what they meant. I did but I didn't. I don't remember dwelling on it.'

Checks completed, the police told Burgess and Mark Collins that Rob had been 'a naughty boy' and that they should get to Neville Hall Hospital in Abergavenny as soon as they could. The journey took around an hour, with Burgess silently singing 'One To Another' to himself, the song that would, in a matter of weeks, take the band to that longed for 'other level'. It was a successful attempt to block out thoughts of the nightmare scenario. Drawing heavily upon that irrepressible optimism, by the time they arrived at the hospital Burgess had convinced himself absolutely that everything was OK.

Everything was *far* from OK. Tailing the Granada through narrow, hedge-lined lanes that make you feel like you're inside an arcade racing game from the early eighties, Rob had lost control. Not by much, but down there you only get a few feet's grace. The BMW had ploughed through the hedge on the right-hand side and careered up the bank beyond, the sudden, shuddering rise sending Rob flying through the sun-roof. Where a seatbelt might have seen him, like Peet, jarred savagely yet safe, he shot upward then slammed back into the summer-baked earth, beside the battered car. It was rumoured that, unbelievably, Rob had struggled to his feet before collapsing again.

He didn't: never could have. In a nearby cottage, Linda Williams heard the crash, called the emergency services and hurried to proffer what aid she could to a broken body pouring blood from the scalp, mouth and ears. She bravely but uselessly blew life into him, then simply held him and awaited the cavalry.

Mark was first inside the hospital, Tim a little way behind. On identifying himself, Mark was led with frightening discretion by a nurse into a quiet room and informed that Robert Collins had died in the ambulance. It was for Mark to tell Tim and, having said it once, he repeated the terrible phrase all the way back to the studio, knowing the truth but unconvinced in his heart that this could really be happening.

Jon Brookes was still up when the phone rang. Deciding on an early night, he had found it uncomfortably hot in bed and gone back downstairs, hoping a book and a warm drink might soothe him into sleepiness. Around midnight, the telephone rang. Brookes' first thought was that it was Rob Collins who, true to form, had made a habit of calling him at unreasonable hours to shoot The Charlatans breeze, particularly if he'd had a few. But it wasn't Rob this time, it was Steve Harrison. There had been an accident. 'Yeah,' said Brookes. 'Rob.' Obvious. The other guy in the car was hunky-dory but Rob was in a bit of a state. Harrison would call back when he knew more. Wholly out of character for a thoroughly worldly, non-believing pragmatist, Brookes sat down on his settee and *prayed*.

'I just knew something terrible had happened. I mean, I've seen Rob do a lot of crazy stuff. I've seen him have fights. I've seen him in a lot of scrapes. I've seen him in violent arguments. I've seen him kick stuff about and smash things up and chuck shit out of windows. I've seen him doing all sorts of mad stuff, but never once did I ever think he would wind up dead. This time it was different.

'I envisioned him lying on one of those stretcher things, a bit cut up, a bit fucked up, and I thought, Rob, if you're still there, hang in, fight it, you'll be OK. The doctors will sort you out. Just fight it.'

Twenty minutes later, Harrison called back to tell him Rob was dead.

Rob's girlfriend, Rachel Quick, heard the news from the police in the very early hours of Tuesday 23. She couldn't believe it, wouldn't believe it. It had to be another wind-up – more of Rob's trickery. He'd played dead before, many times; used to slump there motionless, impervious to pleas or poking. He knew his reputation and recognised that everyone thought he might one day push it one step too far. But he would always sit up and laugh like a drain when you began to worry, when you *really* began to worry. That was Rob – more Captain Black than Scarlet but indestructible nonetheless. This just had to be a hoax, the most elaborate to date; a Collins classic. Christ, he'd even got the police running around – he'd *love* that. The reality must have hit her like a train.

Usually when people close to you die you at least have the opportunity to escape into your work, your relationship, your life. There will be some solace somewhere, some tiny respite. For The Charlatans, everything was coloured by the accident. The band was their work and social life. It was their past, their present and their future. To a large extent, probably too large, the band defined what they were as people.

For six years, they had constantly told anyone who'd listen that the band *meant* something. Now they had forced upon them the petrifying realisation that it really did: it meant *everything*. Aside from the fact that Rob Collins was their friend (Christ, as if that wasn't bad enough), he was the keyboard wizard, in the eyes of many the very soul of The Charlatans' sound. He could never be replaced, not Rob. And that meant they would never be as good as they were. And that meant they would never make that classic album. And that meant they wouldn't be remembered in twenty years' time. And *that* meant there was no fucking point in any-thing – they might as well pack it in right now and get on with the other life available to them, on the dole with the dead meat.

With a single ready to go, the video completed just seven days before the crash, and an album half-finished, plus the massive gigs at Loch Lomond and Knebworth scheduled, some hard decisions had to be made. They had to get it together fast, Harrison too. He was spending time with Rob's parents, both of them shredded by this dreadful thing, helping to organise the necessaries, trying to relieve them of their painful burden as best he could. He would later drive them to the inquest, though he couldn't find it in him-self to go inside with them. An openly emotional sort, he remem-bers crying, in his office, at home and in his car, suddenly realising that his eyes were running and his face was wet with tears.

Harrison arranged a band meeting at his house. There would be more over the next couple of days. With Mark Collins they had found what they considered to be their classic line-up. This was now ruined. In terms of rock history, it might be better to split up entirely. If they continued, it was possible that they might do their past a disservice. They could each imagine a future visit from a spectral Rob, just as in life laughing uproariously at their failings. They could hear the ghostly muttering: 'This is *bollocks*.'

On the Wednesday, they got the call that decided it. Rob Collins' father, Les, in an extremely admirable show of bravery and thoughtfulness, phoned the band. It was important, he said, not to let Rob's death destroy their lives. They had all worked hard together to reach this point and they should continue. Rob would carry on were he alive, and would want them to do the same. Carrying on would make sense of the past: throw it into a clearer, brighter perspective. Future success would further glorify Rob's past contributions. And it would generate an income for the child Rob had left behind.

This they understood all too clearly. They knew how Rob had felt when facing the possibility of a five-year term for robbery. They knew themselves, through hours and hours of morbid contemplation of failure, that to die leaving nothing of import behind would be grim beyond belief. They knew now that they had to continue; they had to make Rob a hero and elevate themselves in the process. Perhaps unknowingly, Les Collins had given The Charlatans what they most needed in this dark time, the thing they would react to best. With unbelievable kindness, he offered his dead son as a reason for the others to live on, and thereby gave The Charlatans a *cause*. And by giving them something new to fight for, he also reminded them of their main motivation in past times of trouble – themselves, The Charlatans. His call convinced them that, even without demon Rob, the Hammond King, they were good enough to do it all over again.

That call went much of the way towards taking away their fear and giving them back their hope. Then there was another – a call informing them that Martin Duffy, the brilliant keyboardist with Primal Scream, was willing to make himself available to them. Primal Scream were in something of a hiatus – and he was pretty much ready when they were.

Within 24 hours, the band had decided on a course of action. They knew that the recording of the album had already stagnated: more time spent pissing about could only be damaging. They knew that in order to survive they needed to hurl themselves into action. Loch Lomond would have to be cancelled – there was the funeral, and there would be no time to rehearse. But still there was possibly the cruellest, most unforgiving testing ground of them all: Knebworth.

In front of 125,000 people, most of them there to see Oasis, they could stand up and see if they still had it in them. Believing everything to be on the line, the crazy bastards decided to go for it. On the Friday, they released a statement to the press, just to burn their bridges and ensure their progression by denying themselves a way out:

> *'The band, their management and associates are naturally devastated with the loss of not only an influential member of a brilliant rock 'n' roll band, but more so of a great and loyal friend. The decision has been made to carry on because we have to continue in his memory – it's what he would have wanted. He lived it like he loved it and he ran out of time. There will be no change. We are fuckin' rock. We've lost our mate.'*

It was a brave statement, and interesting in that it revealed the bloodiness of their mindset. Knowing that they had lost such a vital element of their sound, to term themselves 'a brilliant rock 'n' roll band' was a heavy-duty self-affirmation. That they would 'continue in his memory' was a simplistic cliché, but offset by, 'He lived it like he loved it', a line from their own 'Bullet Comes' that at this point seemed as much consolation as youthful war-cry. 'We are fuckin' rock' – an expression used often and loudly by Burgess and the Heavenly crew when out on the town – now pointed to the band's revitalised ambitions. 'He ran out of time'? Again a little blithe (it was actually an epitaph Collins suggested for himself in an interview with *109* fanzine, along with the possible alternative, 'Yes he did, he does, he really did like it'), but that impression would be exploded within days by Jon Brookes, a born enemy of stultifying misery, who publicly proffered the alternative explanation: 'Technically, he ran out of road.' It was a macabre crack perhaps more typical of Rob Collins himself. After all, with his pug expression and put-upon air, his eyes glinting wickedly out from deep beneath those dark, bushy eyebrows, Rob had borne a passing resemblance to the doomed comic master, Tony Hancock.

But of all the band, Brookes was the one who could best see this coming. He was, after all, sitting beside Rob Collins at the dress rehearsal. The pair were once sailing along in an MG, Collins driving, when a car crept out in front of a line of parked vehicles. Brookes was convinced Collins must have seen it then, his stomach suddenly filled not with butterflies but thrashing black eels, he realised this was not so. Slamming his feet down on to non-existent brake and clutch, he surrendered to the whiplash as the collision took place. No one was injured but it was a bit of a mess: they had to use an iron bar to prise the front of the MG off its wheel.

Collins would later crash again, this time accompanied by another friend. Again it was fairly minor, but the omens were not good. Testing fate, running out of luck, third time unlucky, they all seem to apply.

On Thursday 1 August, Rob Collins' funeral was held at Short Heath Methodist Church, Wesley Road, Walsall, Rob having until recently lived in Bloxwich Road, close by. Once again the band met up at Harrison's house (all branches of Omega were closed, most of them filled with flowers from friends and fans), and drove down from there. They had a quick, very quick beer, in a pub near the church where those up from London had gathered, then Blunt, Brookes and Mark Collins took their places in the front pews alongside Rob's parents, Les and Maureen, his ex-wife Joanne and his young daughter Emily.

All three band members looked dour: smart, straight-backed and stoical, almost military in their outwardly calm demeanour in the face of this terrible event, like survivors of some moon launch gone wrong. Inside it was different. Blunt and Brookes were both scared and hurt but fast coming to terms with what had to be done. Mark Collins was in shock – completely aware of his surroundings but in no way certain of what it all really meant.

Around 200 people were jammed into the chapel to hear the Reverend Derrick Lander deliver his sermon. It was suitably respectful in some ways. He pronounced that Robert had been 'a loving son, a wonderful brother, a great partner, a caring father and a loyal friend to everyone', and that his musical talent had 'given joy to thousands'. However, looking out over what he pointedly referred to as a 'varied and unusual' congregation, he couldn't stop himself from undermining the memorial speech by taking occasional swipes at an 'unconventional lifestyle' that Rob Collins loved but he himself clearly vehemently despised. It must be hard to write a fitting and charitable Christian eulogy for someone you neither know nor understand, but it has to be easier than *listening* to this one was.

Having tarried in the pub a little longer than his band mates, Burgess had arrived at the church just before the ceremony began, and chosen to sit up in the little balcony at the back, where extra wooden chairs had been placed to accommodate the large, 'varied and unusual' congregation. In the pub, he had seemed chirpy; his usual self. Popping those fingers, hacking out that deep-rooted laugh, he'd greeted each friend and acquaintance jovially, devouring every snippet of news and consoling or congratulating with a heartfelt, 'Oooooh, *mate*!' or '*Brilliant!*' Now, in the church, he was different; fidgety and noticeably restless. As the service began, he huddled down, leaning forward on to the rails around the balcony. His hands were clasped and his index fingers were pressed together against his chin and lips, as if he had to manually silence himself as he stared down over the bowed gathering.

The stare became a glare became a look of bemused hilarity. You could see hurt and happiness, desperation and determination, as the mutating expressions passed across his face. This was a Christian funeral, specifically designed to publicly and permanently stamp a full stop at the end of one more chapter in the lives of everyone present. A funeral is a celebration of life, sure, but it also demands that we accept the inevitability of change, the hard fact that our circumstances can alter beyond our control and against our wishes. It demands that we accept death as real and, at least as far as our existence in this world goes, *final*.

These were thoughts that previously had no place in the mind of Tim Burgess. This was not something you could struggle against. He couldn't pull together with his mates and courageously forge a way through. Death is not a team game. There's no point arguing or shouting or sulking, you can't make it go your way by threatening to withdraw your labour or sign to another label. Everything in Burgess rebelled against this despotic accident casting a perpetual shadow over a hitherto faultless dream-world. It was so hard to believe that this could really be the end; so hard to maintain focus on this profoundly unpalatable reality. Look, down there, there's Mart and Mark and Brookesy sitting with all those old people and they're *in suits*. Totally surreal, man: they must *hate* it.

Burgess laughed. And up in the balcony there's Chloe and a big bunch from London up for the day. Oh, it'll be top: loads of beers, a few lines, ooooh *mate*, it'll be fuckin' *brilliant*. Burgess chuckled and chattered to himself, adrift.

And then the mood would catch him again, as if it were wafting up over that balcony like clouds of incense. He'd go silent, tightly clasp his hands before his face once more and, rocking slightly but intensely in his seat, gaze down, drawing the truth in through his eyes and ears. Robert James Collins was in that box – a loving son, a caring father, a loyal friend. Our prayers were with his parents, his girlfriend and his baby daughter in this distressing time. They would find succour and strength in the arms of Jesus, forever and ever. Rewind – *Rob Collins was in that box*, Rob, and when they had all finished talking they were going to take him off through this glaring bright afternoon to a quiet place where they would burn him in a fire so fierce there'd be nothing left, *nothing*.

His hands squeezed white and hot red over his mouth, Burgess rocked harder, the movement turning to a violently restrained bucking as suffocated sobs emerged victorious from that massively constricted chest and throat. Burgess wept like he laughed, the hacking sounds coming from deep in his guts. It was awful to see and hear, awful. Bad to see a man inevitably losing his pointless struggle with tears. Bad to witness someone seized, then abandoned, then seized again by a lucid realisation of tragedy. Worse that the tragedy was so obviously a vicious crime against the child-like dream informing every aspect of Tim Burgess's life. We're Number One, us. No one comes back, but we did. You don't mess with the indestructible five musketeers. *We are fuckin' rock.* Charlatans *forever*. Charlatans *forever*.

The drive to the crematorium seemed long in the blinding sunlight. Outside the main building, an ugly place squatting low amid the flat green fields, men stood smoking, cigarettes cupped in that ex-army fashion. The gap between funeral and cremation is strange. Faces are set in cold stone. When eyes meet there's a distant glimmer of friendliness and the faintest of half-smiles that seems to say, 'Halfway there, old son, halfway there'. Everyone's in the same boat and they know it.

This service was mercifully terse, a quick reiteration of blessings already given and hopes already expressed. Johnny Clark, Rob's keyboard tech and so often his cohort in craziness, was finding it tough, his burst of coughed-up sobs briefly masking the heart-breaking ever-presence of wretched whimpering. They played 'Can't Get Out Of Bed', Rob's dad's favourite Charlatans track, and one of Rob's, partly due to Rob's major vocal role. The curtain drew back and the remains of Robert James Collins slid slowly from view.

Outside, the relief at it all being over was palpable, with every-one blurting out their best wishes at treble pace, as if having just emerged from a six-month stretch in solitary confinement. It was stilted and weird; a distance was needed from this place. Everyone duly piled down to Jon Brookes' local in Wednesbury. The drink-ing and laughter were manic, everyone thoroughly glad to be there with friends and strangers who'd shared in this and would under-stand.

Burgess reckoned that when he went he'd have them play the theme to *The Benny Hill Show*. Rob would have liked this do – that was repeated endlessly – even though he would probably have said it was shit and ignored everyone as he pumped change into the fruit machine. He might *not* have done, of course, but that was the whole thing with Rob Collins, the contrary bastard.

For Oasis, Loch Lomond and Knebworth were intended to be a Roman-style triumph. Since losing to Blur in the Battle Of The Bands, when 'Roll With It' was beaten to the Number 1 slot by 'Country House', their progress had exceeded all expectations and even come close to matching their own spectacularly boastful pre-dictions. Their second album, *(What's The Story) Morning Glory?* had entered the UK charts in top spot in October the year before, spawning major hits with the Number 2 'Wonderwall' and Number 1 'Don't Look Back In Anger'. There had been two sold-out shows in London's cavernous Earls Court (you know you've cracked it when people are willing to pay top dollar to peer myopi-cally at you across a 300 yards-wide, acoustically wretched aero-drome). Rarely for a British group, genuine international success was on the cards too. Mainland Europe had fallen for them, as was evinced by a tumultuous tour at the beginning of 1996, and so popular were they in the Antipodes that a petition had been started to convince the band to tour Australasia, the number of signatures now racing towards six figures.

Best and rarest of all, it looked like Oasis had cracked America. Britpop had been heavily covered in the US but, after mulling it over for a while, they'd pretty much decided against it. Yet *(What's The Story) Morning Glory?* had gone US Top Five in February, its sales driven ever higher by 'Wonderwall' entering the Top Ten in March. By August, the album had sold over seven million copies, three of those millions in America, and was on its way to becoming the biggest-selling UK album ever, even beyond monster successes like Fleetwood Mac's *Rumours*, The Bee Gees' *Saturday Night Fever*, Pink Floyd's *Dark Side Of The Moon* and The Beatles' hardy perennial *Sgt Pepper*. And it's worth noting that the total sales of each of *those* particular albums had been boosted by people updating their collections to CD.

So Knebworth and Loch Lomond were huge triumphs for Oasis, the laurel-strewn welcomings home of populist heroes, as well as being (vulgar) displays of power in themselves. At Knebworth, they would play to 125,000 people on each of the two days. Tickets alone, sold out within eight hours, would generate over £5million. Millions more would be made flogging T-shirts, hot dogs and crummy burgers. Beer could be purchased only with patience and burrowing techniques inventive even by the standards of the inmates of Colditz. There would be a radio broadcast live to 34 countries, a potential audience of 300 million people.

Like Woodstock, the Isle Of Wight festival or The Beatles at Shea Stadium, Knebworth was to be a generation's defining moment. With Oasis backed by Manic Street Preachers, Kula Shaker, Cast, Dreadzone and on the second day The Charlatans (no women, you'll note – for some reason Oasis never liked female artists on the bill), the place would be packed with fans loyal to the point of infatuation. For The Charlatans, it carried a further historical weight in that this had been the venue for the last UK show by Led Zeppelin, taking place in August 1979, a month before the release of their final studio album, *In Through the Out Door*, and a year before their drummer John Bonham choked to death in his sleep after one last hefty session. Better still, at that show they been supported by The New Barbarians, a notoriously shambolic outfit brought together by Keith Richards and comprising of both Stones guitarists in Keith and Ronnie Wood, Stanley Clarke on bass, Ziggy Modeliste on drums, Keith's brother in havoc Bobby Keyes on sax, and on keyboards Ian McLagen who, you'll remember, later sent that signed beer mat to Rob Collins in Shrewsbury nick. Knebworth carried a heavy rep and The Charlatans were proud to enter its pantheon. Even without Collins' death it could have been pivotal for the band.

As it was, Collins' passing placed The Charlatans at the very centre of proceedings. The Gallaghers were friends and at Loch Lomond had dedicated 'Cast No Shadow' to his memory. In fact, death was very much to the fore of everyone's mind as, during preparations for that same show, truck driver James Hunter had been fatally crushed between a lorry and a fork-lift. Whether genuinely sympathetic or just keen for an emotional freak show in the midst of a long day's proceedings, all present were intrigued by The Charlatans' latest challenge.

The band themselves were out in the middle of nowhere. After a punishing week of rehearsals where Martin Duffy had to learn the set from scratch, Harrison had sequestered them in an extremely discreet hotel deep in the countryside. He had also booked a helicopter to take them to the site an hour or so before show-time. This was not, as you'd normally assume, an attempt to make themselves seem as important as the headliners. It was simply the manager dealing in a little man-motivation. 'More than ever,' he says, 'I wanted them to feel like kings, because I knew that walking out on to that stage was gonna be the hardest thing they'd ever done.'

When the band arrived, you could see they were feeling the pressure. Clambering out of the helicopter, they seemed stern and determined, intimidatingly capable, more like some crack commando unit than the usual ambling gang of Black Country layabouts. You can see the difference in the pictures of Burgess snapped upon landing. Where ordinarily he'd be revelling in such a high-powered arrival, spreading his arms like slightly off-kilter rotor blades and leaning into the camera to have his precocious pout dwarf the chopper in the background, now he let his sheer presence do the talking. Just as the others were that day, he was coldly confident in his ability to slay this audience: knock 'em dead, like.

You'd expect the sight of a band as convivial as The Charlatans getting out of a helicopter in a backstage area crammed with celebrities, media, industry types and all-round starfuckers to produce a stampede. Normally, everyone would have taken the opportunity to be seen with an arm wrapped around Burgess's shoulder, half-hidden beneath hair perfectly dishevelled by the gusts from the spinning blades. That didn't happen this time. Only those professionally involved approached them.

This was mostly because of the band's own demeanour – they clearly weren't up for small talk – but also there was The Death Thing. The bereaved can look small and pathetic, or can seem inflated by anger and their own rekindled desire for life. But they always look different, set apart. Not even the most buccaneering, live-to-ride party animal wants to be marked with that particular black spot. Despite rock 'n' roll's grotesque and often dangerous pretence, there are so very few who could be truthfully described as death-defying.

And that's exactly what The Charlatans were at Knebworth on Sunday 11 August. It seemed perfectly in keeping with events that, as they took to the stage, four Jobs and a single Samaritan, an unseasonably cold rain began to fall. All eyes were on those five distant figures. Everyone there was aware of the rites of passage being endured before them, the red badges of courage to be earned. The Charlatans themselves looked solemn and determined yet distinctly vulnerable. The sheer size of that massive stage seemed to distance them further: it decimated the impression of them as an impregnable gang and left them each to deal with their bleak thoughts alone.

Then they started up, Blunt rapt and pumping, a new aggression making him seem less like himself than Billy Gould from Faith No More. Mark Collins was eerily static, appearing to use his music to massage and blast the bad thoughts from his mind. Jon Brookes stared ahead, dead ahead. Far from simply holding the beat, he was drawing the sound and the others onward through this trial. And Martin Duffy was superb. Under the circumstances incomprehensibly well practised, he was already adding flourishes of his own, the tension in the atmosphere lending him a manic attack to match that of Rob Collins. But there was no need for comparisons. They were equal but different.

The big difference, though, lay in Tim Burgess. Where before he might have bounced on, excited by the occasion and the realisation of another rock 'n' roll fantasy, now he took centre stage and stood stock still. Pasty-white and unshaven, his face took on a dark, almost sinister, intensity within the hood of his anorak. There was nothing cheery or boyish about him. He looked small out there but he burned dangerously and disturbingly, turning your thoughts more to the likes of *Don't Look Now*, Cronenberg's *The Brood* or maybe even Bergman's *The Seventh Seal*. There was a stark individualism here. Burgess's cute, casual insolence had turned to compelling, commanding nerve. This was no time for talk: it was a clear-cut 'let's *do* it' moment. With a curt, muttered, 'New tune,' they were away. Where the others were piling in, communicating with quick sidelong glances, Burgess glared around at his band mates, his fists pumping in short, vicious movements, demanding that they each live up to their collective claims to greatness.

As the performance progressed, with the magnificent melancholia of 'Crashin' In' at last being allowed to the fore and the as yet unreleased 'One To Another' revealing its deadly serious groove, it became clear to all present that this was a band deserving of far more than mere sympathy. Oasis were undisputed champions of the Good Time – in this, they'd even been compared to Status Quo – yet The Charlatans were one step beyond that. Their upbeat 'Time For Action' alarum had been undermined in the most damaging way possible. Their message, wholly underpinned by a teenage feeling of indestructibility, was being challenged.

Where Oasis were like a wave of euphoria, a great big grinning rush that came easily and without effort, The Charlatans were struggling against all odds to live life the way they wanted to, recognisably fighting for their right to party, their right to grow in any manner they chose. There was a work ethic to be appreciated here that most Brits would understand on a very basic level. But it wasn't a traditional view, not to do with working nine to five, holding your tongue in the face of fascistic bully-bosses and spirit-sapping rulebooks. This was a joyful battle with a personal point to savour. You should work your arse off to maintain your dreams despite the ruinous attentions of brute life. Treat your trials with respect, take it all on and become what you are. Live it like you love it: it's the real thing.

Up on stage, Burgess finally looked the part. Before, while the others were locked into some instrumental groove, he'd taken his chance to slip off behind the speakers and, much to the annoyance of Brookes who could see what was going on, indulge in a few slugs of beer, wine or something stronger, perhaps a line. From this moment on, such mood-breaking actions would become ever more rare. Now Burgess stood alongside the players, feet stamping, his microphone clasped in a piston-fist, watching the fingers blur and the sweat fall, concerned purely with the music around him. Pushing, questioning, admiring, it was as if he'd come so close to losing *all this* that only now did he appreciate what it all meant, who the band were and, more desperately, who they would be if they quit.

Knebworth was a revelation for The Charlatans, and a revelation for a crowd impressed and involved even more by the band's new, more insular approach. It was like The Charlatans had become rock stars before our eyes. They were a serious proposition. The crisis had become a clear and definable turning-point. They were coming through, because of Rob Collins and despite him, their passion being drawn from their missing him and their anger at a foolishness that now bordered on betrayal. Amidst the chaos caused by Collins' accident, they had found a new order and, quite naturally, evolved.

Leaving the stage, Mark Collins was struck by what they had lost. What with the planning and the funeral and the rushed rehearsals teaching Duffy to trade riffs in that singular Charlatans style, he hadn't come to terms with any of it. Now, the power of the band's performance and the crowd's reaction to it had shown that they could still do it, and do it without Rob. So suddenly there was a future stretching out before him, a future with no Rob in it. Ignoring the back-slaps and excited buzzing of the well-wishers, and passing up the chance to drink free liquor till unconsciousness stopped the flow, he returned to the dressing room and sat for two hours in quiet contemplation of change.

Burgess joined him for a while then moved on to the backstage beer tent – not to take the plaudits but more to hang with some friends and take the edge off a killer adrenalin rush. The Heavenly people were racing around with bunches of raffle tickets. Noel Gallagher had put up a flash Italian scooter, a collector's item, as a prize, and all proceeds from the £10 tickets were to go to the family of Rob Collins (there was some dismay a few days later when it was discovered that the proceeds were also supposed to pay for the scooter itself).

Burgess seemed more relieved than cock-a-hoop, curious to know if onlookers had enjoyed a show that for him had swapped brief elation for a deeper sense of satisfaction. In a neat parallel, behind him at the bar stood the soccer player Stuart Pearce.

A legendarily uncompromising full-back for Nottingham Forest, Pearce was nicknamed Psycho, but recent events had revealed in him a vulnerability that had made him the darling of the nation – if 'darling' may be used to describe a man notorious for leaving his opponents in a crumpled, groaning heap. In a shoot-out to decide one semi-final of the 1990 World Cup, Pearce had missed a penalty that might have taken England to their first final in 24 years. Instead, God help us, Germany took our place.

That night, and for weeks afterwards, a population that had found rare unity in inexpert but enthusiastic discussions about the merits of the sweeper system was plunged into dispirited apathy. Pearce had taken the setback like a trooper and hurled himself back into the fray, but no amount of club success could erase that career-defining moment of heartbreaking international failure.

Then, after six years carrying this monstrous sporting stigma, came the Brit-hosted European Championships, a few short weeks before Knebworth. Another penalty shoot-out, this time against the much-fancied Spanish. Success would earn us the right to take on Germany once more in the semi-finals. And Pearce stepped up straight away to take the first shot, his stance and expression brooking no argument. As he paused before his run-up, the awful realisation of what he had just volunteered to do dawned upon the boisterous crowd and a TV audience of millions. For a chance to gloriously wipe away shame, he was risking a humiliation never before suffered in the game.

A dreadful silence fell, with everyone (well, everyone who wasn't either Spanish or Scottish) sharing the same thought: Oh, please, please, *please* score. Then up he ran, and score he did, sending the stadium and the country into a screaming uproar of gratitude. And he turned to the howling, frothing crowd and, with his chin jutting proudly, his fists clenched hard at his sides and his eyes burning with combative tears, he mouthed the perfect expression of his nation's feelings. '*Fucking come on!!!!*' It was an unmistakable and unqualified moment of redemption.

That Stuart Pearce should be here beside Burgess – revelling in separate but similarly spectacular comebacks, each of them now secure and untroubled in his own space and time – was absolutely correct. Pearce, Burgess and The Charlatans had put it all on the line to lay claim to that fabled brighter day. Knebworth was Oasis's event but they were not the true heroes of the hour. And it is increasingly likely that their festival, their triumph, will *not* be best remembered for them.

A week later, The Charlatans took to a major stage once again, this time at the Paul Weller-headlined V96 festival at Chelmsford (V for Virgin – this was back in the days when Richard Branson was known for more than plummeting out of the sky and annoying the hell out of the world's coastguards). For the band it was another riotous success, as important in its way as Knebworth. For where Knebworth had demanded their acceptance of what they'd lost, thereby forcing them forward, Chelmsford was a far less tense affair, allowing them to concentrate fully on what still remained to them.

The Weller connection had an importance of its own. After his *Wild Wood* and *Stanley Road* albums, Weller had been enjoying a popularity he hadn't experienced since the break-up of The Jam. He had furthermore been publicly endorsed by Noel Gallagher, and cited as a vital influence by Ocean Colour Scene and a host of Britpop artists who appreciated the simple songwriting and overt Englishness of his earlier work. There were others too: retro artists who, looking for a sharp style to rework for the nineties, had come across Weller's own prime influence, Steve Marriott and The Small Faces.

Weller was back with a vengeance, lauded once more as The Modfather. Due to his age, and the musical tendencies of himself and his younger peers, he was seen to be at the head of a new movement, rather cruelly labelled Dadrock because music paper hacks thought it was offering kids a pale imitation of what their parents had listened to in their youth.

The idea of Dadrock was partly a journalistic conceit, wilfully ignoring the fact that every band harks back to its influences. But it did pick up on one serious point: many of the bands involved lacked urgency, a sense of youthful anger or pain or panic. There was a feeling of smug complacency to it all, as if they'd studied the sixties and taken from them not the rush of revolution but just the smarmy, doped-up beneficence. It was all so far from The Charlatans' present predicament, yet once again they were roped in with a scene which had little to do with them.

The band didn't mind this time. In fact, they enjoyed the revival of Lambretta clothing, polar fleeces, Harrington jackets, fishtail parkas and desert boots. And hanging with Weller was OK, not only because of his track record as a writer of classics, but also because they *ought* to be there, engaging in mutal respect with guys like that. They were, or were soon to be, equals.

On 26 August 'One To Another' was released and, reaching Number 3 in the UK charts, became The Charlatans' biggest hit yet. A cyclone of Led Zeppelin guitar underpinned by Rob Collins' Stonesy electric piano, and a Bomb The Bass beat, it deserved its success. Tom Chemical had messed about with the drums but really all the technological advances were down to the band. Finally and completely, they had justified their efforts with Flood back in 1991. It also made sense of Burgess's stated liking of The Wu Tang Clan and the Swedish experimental R&B merchants, Soundtrack Of Our Lives. It was all over the place but, like, *right there*. And the thought was inescapable – Rob would have *loved* this.

* * *

Going back in to finish the new album at Monnow Valley was terribly hard, yet talking to James Dean Bradfield had convinced them it had to be done. The Manic Street Preachers felt they had made a mistake by taking time off just bumming around and getting fat when Richey Edwards disappeared. Their advice was worth taking.

Besides, no matter how bad it would be working with Rob's tapes, with every new chord a reminder that he was no longer there, they had to get on with their own lives. Knebworth had proved they could do it. Martin Duffy was coming along to help out (though he would not be credited for any tracks specifically, the band felt it to be better that way). So better get on with it and immediately explode the dangerous and degraded Cult of Rob that had sprung up.

'I hated it,' says Burgess. 'There were so many fucking scumbags coming down and jacking up and everything. All these people would turn up, the Bristol contingent, people you'd never met in your life before, every night, shooting up. It was bad enough with the Rob thing, but they were doing this in tribute to him. It was fucking horrible.'

Thankfully, a fair amount had already been done. Back in the summer, Burgess and Mark Collins (continuing the songwriting trend) had taken a cottage near Lake Windermere for a week or two to write, with an eight-track, an acoustic guitar, a drum machine, a bass, a record player and 'lots' of records. Inspiration was needed after the drain of touring. Burgess had been listening to a lot of Dylan, examining his vocal rhythms as he had done with ee cummings, and for the same reason scrutinising the work of the various members of The Wu Tang Clan.

When they returned, they discovered that Blunt, Brookes and Rob Collins had outscored them, having pretty much nailed down three songs.

'After *The Charlatans* tour,' says Burgess, 'we pretty much went straight back into the studio and had a session in Rockfield like our "Indian Rope" one. We did "One To Another", "North Country Boy" and "How High" in the same session. Brilliant. Then Rob left us again, and again he left himself well covered. Again there was stuff we could use. And stuff we couldn't. He

173

didn't like the track "You're A Big Girl Now", so he put bagpipes all over it, and French harmonium or something. And he ruined the track "Tellin' Stories", though he left us with a good riff. And he left "Area 51", which sounds like an alien descending from space. What a mad-head. Really funny.'

Also recorded in that Rockfield session was 'Only Teethin'', its drum intro pilfered by Brookes from Marvin Gaye's 'Inner City Blues' from *What's Going On?*

The band had known Martin Duffy for some time. Quiet, modest and personable, he was also more than capable of matching their excesses. They got on brilliantly and it was truly heartwarming to see them do so. Duffy, furthermore, being as sharp on the musical uptake as he is, served to spur them on. He would play Rob Collins' instruments superbly, so they could pick and choose the parts they wanted from each of the two keyboard players when they came to lay the tracks down (though Duffy alone would have to face the incredibly difficult task of adding the final touches). There was no excuse for continuing in the slump they had suffered prior to Rob's death.

Once they were going again, it was even kind of fun. For 'You're A Big Girl Now', they borrowed Brian Wilson's technique and persuaded Duffy to press drawing-pins into the pads of the piano, for that authentic bar-room feel. This was originally a full band track then, when Mark Collins and Burgess were going through it in the control room, Collins dropped to an open G and it sounded perfect. They got miked up and nailed it straight away.

Loops were provided by Tom Rowlands for 'With No Shoes', 'Tellin' Stories' and 'One To Another', and by Richard March from Bentley Rhythm Ace for 'With No Shoes'. Rowlands would appear again at the end of recording to deliver his opinion of the album's tightness. The rest was managed more than competently by the band and Dave Charles.

Burgess in particular was enjoying this new test. In his listening habits he was now attracted to a more literate breed of songwriters – Kevin Rowland of Dexy's Midnight Runners, Neil Young and particularly Bob Dylan. Lyrically, he began to truly attempt to emulate them – check 'You're A Big Girl Now' and 'Get On It' for Dylan's influence, then investigate further.

Continuing his theme of escape into a brighter day, Burgess's words took on a religious feel as he began to treat life not just as a thrill-packed teenage pursuit but as a sometimes painful but always rewarding learning process leading (hopefully) to redemption. Throwing in some cult references like Itchy and Scratchy from *The Simpsons*, Caine from *Kung Fu* and Thomas O'Malley from *The Aristocats*, plus a few grim cracks, like 'a side of beef should see you off to sleep' in 'With No Shoes' (surely the first comic BSE line to make it on to CD), he finally seemed to be enjoying his writing rather than seeking to come up with something clever or profound. He also looked to the unashamedly quirky approach of the likes of De La Soul, who had talked of a wise ole crocodile and various cool furry creatures on the track 'Tread Water'. Burgess claimed to have had a lyric-inducing vision of being a squirrel high up in the trees, watching the human commotion below, and this was a fitting concept as Burgess, often innocent and simple, would usually consider the importance of a song's point to override any danger of being laughed at for the metaphors contained within.

For Burgess, 'How Can you Leave Us' was a tough one. He had actually written it some time before and originally the lyric was about a girl. He'd even shouted the title at Blur's Damon Albarn as he left the stage in Toronto in October 1995 (The Charlatans were playing that town the next night). But now, after Rob's death, the words just had to be made harsher: 'I would give you mouth to mouth', 'How can you leave us, how can you bleed on us.' For Burgess the song concerned a loss of faith and love, fairly new concepts for a guy who, until pretty recently, had seemed congenitally happy-go-lucky. Now he was moving on, really reaching into himself, and becoming more himself for what he found.

Other songs were tough for more direct reasons. 'Area 51', containing, as Burgess puts it, 'Rob's best out-of-his-head solo ever', had to be completed. Then there was 'Rob's Theme'. Collins had come across a tape his aunt had made of him when he was three years old, chatting to her about putting on his shoes, and considered using it on the album. He suggested to Burgess that they might use it as the intro to a track, or even to the album itself. Burgess had thought it was just Rob messing about but, during his nightly workouts with Ric Peet, a drum machine and his Hammond, Collins had actually recorded the bones of a track around it. The band didn't hear it until a week after his death but decided to go with it, turning it into an angry mixture of rock and rave. There was a strange and quite beautiful circularity to it that they couldn't fail to appreciate.

It was odd that Rob Collins wasn't there, having the last word on every track. But, in a funny way, he still was. That was The Charlatans' biggest problem in recording *Tellin' Stories*: trying to satisfy someone who was no longer there.

Towards the end of recording the album, with Duffy in full flow and hi-jinks at their height, the band took a single day off. They drove down to London with Steve Harrison and signed to MCA/Universal for £1million. Their contract with Beggars Banquet who, despite the success of The Prodigy on their XL label, were no longer remotely big enough to serve the band well, would be terminated with the hits and oddities compilation *Melting Pot* in 1998.

A million was not a great deal of money given the band's current standing. It seemed like sod-all when you read the reviews afforded to *Tellin' Stories*. Where *The Charlatans* had been treated as an acceptable semi-comeback, this album was considered to be the real deal. Then there was the inevitable Other Stuff.

'We had to buy ourselves out of the deal with Beggars,' explains Burgess. 'I think we'd signed up for six LPs but we'd only given them five. So the deal was we had to let them do a compilation LP and give them £500,000 to release us. So when we signed for a million we had to give half to Beggars, lawyers fees took up another £100,000, then there was management's share. So the group was left with £250,000 ... which the accountant took.

'I'm not bitter about it, but I could've done with that money in my pocket. It would've made it easier to find a place in LA. I mean, it was supposed to be our pay-off for three Number One albums. But it is only money. I don't like to talk about it, really, because I think that kind of story puts people off wanting to be in a group.'

All reviews of *Tellin' Stories* noted the collision of genres – country rock, sixties garage, baggy rhythms, ritualistic chemical beats, swamp rock, the Stones, The Small Faces and Dylan. One reviewer pointed out that the album was what The Stone Roses' *The Second Coming* ought to have been, and it was a good point though, with hindsight, it might be said that it was actually what *The Stone Roses* ought to have been.

Of course, there was a good story to tell now. The death of Rob Collins and The Charlatans' efforts to survive made for good, easily digestible soap and gave people something obvious to think and write about. In its reaction to death, the album was now compared to the Stones' *Let It Bleed*, Neil Young's *Tonight's the Night* and Patti Smith's *Gone Again*: flattering indeed. But the focus was on the band's survival rather than the reasons for it. Death overshadowed their real achievement – their tortured and tortuous growth. Perhaps next time, with no robberies or depressive collapses or deaths or faddish scenes to consider, they will be taken simply for what they are. The Charlatans are big enough and brave enough now to stand or fall on that.

On 24 March, 'North Country Boy' was released and hit Number 4, proving 'One To Another' to be no fluke. It was also available on the Internet for 60p from Cerberus Digital Jukebox. The Charlatans like to stay on top of the changing times.

The song itself evoked Dylan's 'Girl From The North Country', a track about Dylan leaving Minnesota and a passionate affair with Echo Helstrom. Burgess, naturally, had his own agenda – he only ever borrows lines that mean something in his world – but he doesn't mind admitting to the influence, knowing that Dylan himself would happily name check Woody Guthrie. 'I did take that title from "Girl From The North Country",' admits Burgess. 'I just thought "I love that song. I'll take the title, change the gender". I never thought that I would be identified so strongly with the North Country. Maybe I was naïve, maybe it was just meant to happen, but suddenly everyone from Manchester and Middlesbrough and everywhere took it as an anthem. So I became the North Country Boy, just when I was getting to the point when I was going to move away.

'When we started' he continues, 'I used to listen to Dylan a lot. In fact I almost got to the point of obsession, and had to fuck it off.

177

Dylan's big for me, and The Stones, in some respects The Band, and the later Beatles. And now Tom Waits. I love Dylan, I love the way that as soon as he went electric he was suddenly a country artist, and seemed to do it just to piss people off. He was so literate, and so ... *artistic* I think is the word. He did not give a fuck. That was the main thing, he just did not give a fuck.'

The single sleeve, shots in the fields around Monnow Valley, was Mark Collins' idea. He wanted to appear like Bob Dylan on *Nashville Skyline* and so, bearded in his furry hat, watched by Burgess and a hugely disinterested Charlie the Cat, he held his acoustic guitar left-handed in front of him for an age, moving it imperceptibly in and out until he'd achieved the correct angle.

For the video, the band were thinking about classic movies rather than albums. Where 'Just When You're Thinkin' Things Over' had seen them in gangster chic, Burgess with slicked-back hair like James Fox in Nic Roeg's *Performance*, now they went further afield.

'We'd just finished the album,' says Burgess, 'and fancied going to New York, so most of the budget went on flights and hotels. The label wanted us to do it in Blackpool with all the illuminations then, because it was out of season, they suggested Southend. We said no, it had to be New York to get that *Mean Streets/Midnight Cowboy* vibe.'

It wasn't a very good video, really. Just the four of them striding through New York neon and riding in yellow cabs, Blunt grinding his teeth with terrifying intensity. Still, it made a change from five guys strolling purposelessly through a wood, which they've also done.

'We do read all the scripts we're given,' says Burgess, 'but they always say things like "Tim is nailed to a cross and the bass player, what'shisname, is walking slowly towards the tube station." But I liked the video for "North Country Boy"; I'll defend that one. It looked like we'd gone over there and taken the whole place over. It was great – one for the future.'

Rehearsals for the 1997 world tour took place at Stanbridge Farm, a fourteenth-century barn-cum-studio between Brighton and Haywards Heath.

While there, Mark Collins dreamed of having conversations

with Rob, always ending, 'I've got to go now, Mark.' He still has them sometimes. Burgess daydreams of him too, whenever things go wrong. He can actually see Rob laughing at him as the inevitable worst occurs.

As the tour began, the band, having a taste for the high-life after Knebworth, hired a twin-engined Piper Chieftain aeroplane to fly from Manchester to Dundee. This was also to celebrate *Tellin' Stories* going to Number 1, and making them (along with REM) the only band to have three Number 1 albums (excluding greatest hits packages) in the nineties. They had been clever about it this time. Having been in direct competition with Supergrass's *In It for the Money*, they'd lobbed out the cassette version (generally bought by only the casual listener) for an attractive £4.99. This ensured victory. It may seem a tad sneaky but casual listeners deserve the best too. And, hey, like the man said – you snooze, you lose.

In Dundee, at Caird Hall, cigarettes, demo tapes, one orange beany hat (in case they were looking for one) and one bra landed on the stage – proof positive that, to their fans at least, The Charlatans had not changed a jot. They were on a roll again. With *Tellin' Stories* shifting 300,000 in the UK by August, with a further 100,000 sold in Japan, Burgess was comparing their career to Tim Robbins' plight in *The Shawshank Redemption*. Mark Collins, considering the cruel taunts of old, added, 'I think we almost *are* the bandwagon now.'

Collins was having a rare time of it, even feeling confident enough to involve himself in a football single. With Manchester United looking like they might actually win the European Cup, he got together with Bez (the notorious dancer with Happy Mondays and Black Grape), The Clash's Joe Strummer (a London based Man U fan – how *odd*), and an old friend Paul Wagstaff (Paris Angels, Black Grape and the reformed Mondays) to record a song entitled 'We're United, Man United'. What pleased Collins the most was that his contribution forced Harrison, a life-long Manchester City fan, to become involved. Burgess was asked to join in too, being a fan, but after deliberating long and hard over whether he should be involved in something as innately tacky as this, he declined.

No matter. United got their arses booted by Borussia Dortmund and the demos were shelved.

Back on the tour, The Charlatans played Liverpool Royal Court on election night, 1 May, Burgess wearing a T-shirt in support of the dockers' strike. It was a memorable show, boosted for the band by the ongoing landslide for Tony Blair and the Labour Party.

Event-wise, something *special* was also lined up for one of the two dates at London's Brixton Academy. The Charlatans had agreed to headline a show for the National Missing Persons Hotline, with a bill put together by Jane Cotter, whose sister Sandra had sadly taken her own life. The hotline had been useful to Cotter and she wanted to help out. When this book's author handed over her initial letter of inquiry to Burgess and Mark Collins in a pub in Monmouth, he got another lesson in the band's methods. Burgess read it once, thought briefly, then said quietly, 'We should do this.' Collins took the sheet from him, scanned it and nodded. Later, Brookes and Blunt glanced over it and did the same. Within days it was sorted.

With The Charlatans on board, the rest was easy. Peter Hook's Monaco played, as did the Kahunas (Brookes would later drum on their 'Bright Morning White' single), Paul Weller, James Dean Bradfield (poignant in the light of the disappearance of Richey Edwards) and Noel Gallagher. The Charlatans stormed it. Simultaneously driven by pain and determination, empathy and regret, 'North Country Boy''s moving line, 'What are you sad about?', took on a new relevance.

Brixton also marked the London debut of the band's new keyboardist, Tony Rogers. It had been thought that Duffy might join up, what with Primal Scream being so inactive. But the Scream – purely coincidentally, you understand – suddenly became very busy indeed.

Rogers was born in Walsall. He has two sisters and two brothers, both musicians. He attended Stafford Polytechnic but only ever wanted to go into music. He joined The Charlatans direct from the band Jobe, a group he'd formed with his brother, Don. They had released one album, *Rosaries & Ice Cream,* on Viceroy, through Rough Trade. The band thought it 'too soft' but, asking if they could re-do it, they were turned down. They also released two singles, 'I Know' and 'Earth', both unavailable in the UK, though 'Earth' was playlisted in Germany.

Strangely, three or four months before joining the band, Rogers had been sitting in a London pub, drowning his sorrows having just had his own material rejected by a record company, when someone told him not to worry as The Charlatans would come knocking at his door some day soon. The call came via a mutual friend named Tim Ison who ran The Varsity Club in Wolverhampton, where Rogers had played two or three times with Jobe. Scouring the country for Hammond players, Martin Blunt had heard Rogers' name mentioned a few times and called Ison to see if he thought he would be interested in applying (he'd have to apply – there are no easy rides on Planet Blunt).

Ison called Rogers and soon after so did Blunt. They talked for an hour or so about influences and the like, Blunt no doubt checking Rogers' funky credentials, and an audition was arranged. 'It had to be through word of mouth,' says Blunt. 'The straight audition thing is too antiseptic.' Three, maybe four, days after the jam, Rogers received a further call, this time from Brookes, saying that if he was interested, he was the man.

Rogers had seen The Charlatans play a couple of times, first pre-Burgess, supporting The Stone Roses at Walsall's Junction 10, then in 1995 at London's Astoria. He'd never dreamt of playing with them; he was happy doing his own thing. In fact, doing his own thing was imperative. Once ensconced back in Walsall, about three years before this, Rogers had built up an eight-track studio in his flat. It was the first time he could play his Hammond whenever he felt like it, so he did, for eight hours a day, sometimes till his fingers bled. He would rather do that than get a session job.

'I've never, ever done session work for anyone,' he says. '*Never*. I play in the way I play. I've been sat on my arse being poor for a good few years because of that. About three years before I met the lads I moved into a house in Fullbrook outside Walsall – it was the first time I was able to have a Hammond at home rather than in a rehearsal room – and I just sat there getting a good groove going, for myself.'

It was possible that Rogers might be a temporary fixture, but he quickly proved himself capable (and absurdly charming). Very quickly he found himself at the front of Charlatans photos, just as Mark Collins had before him. Initially, he found it hard to be apart from his brother and strange not to be sleeping in a van, and he was reprimanded by roadies for moving his own gear about the stage, but he clearly fits in well. Indeed, his very Irish story-telling (he has claims to gypsy blood, if you believe that) is a refreshing change, and will be good for the band as they continue to come out of themselves. More importantly, he's a shit-hot player. Where Rob Collins was a study in demonic concentration, Rogers rides the Hammond like it's a foaming bronco. He also, as he says, has his own ideas. He owns the requisite Hammond and Wurlitzer, but enjoys the Melotron too. We can expect changes.

As 1997 progressed, there were more shows for The Charlatans, but now it was headlining all the way – first at T In The Park, then the Phoenix Festival. Here, it was notable that Rogers was in and fully accepted but Collins was not forgotten, Burgess pointing out that the following Tuesday would be the first anniversary of Rob's death. The band dedicated 'One To Another' to his memory.

Then it was yet again back to the States which, as *Rolling Stone*'s David Fricke had predicted, was now coming around. More at ease with their lot, the band settled into the schedule. They enjoyed taking the New York Roxy stage once occupied by The Sex Pistols, took time out to watch millions of bats leave their nests beneath a bridge in Austin and had a blast filming a video for 'How High' in the Los Angeles drain where Arnie had saved Edward Furlong from being crushed under a juggernaut in *Terminator 2*. It was all hard travelling, but finally it seemed to be paying off.

Back in Blighty, a final single, the title track, was taken from *Tellin' Stories*. With the sleeve, Blunt was making a personal comeback of his own by returning to the work of Lewis Morley. This one, though, was a safer bet than the shot that so hampered *Up To Our Hips*, with Blunt utilising Morley's signature shot of Christine Keeler perched provocatively on that turned-around stool.

'There's so much media these days,' he says. 'It can all get con-

fusingly subtle, and we just wanted something that would immediately summarise what the song was about – the idea of things
you do and say coming back to haunt you – something everyone
would understand. We were initially thinking of using a shot of
David Mellor and Antonia de Sancha, but then decided that might
take some explaining.'

The shot was a dubious decision in many ways. Involving sex,
spies and the aristocracy, the Profumo/Keeler affair had kept a grip
on the public imagination for three decades, even being turned
into a successful movie, *Scandal*. Blunt was right that the sleeve
picture had a relevant story to tell. But it wasn't good that The
Charlatans, so concerned with building a popular mythology of
their own and having gone so far towards actually pulling it off,
should choose to co-opt a signifier as over-familiar as that. They
were in a position to say something for themselves; they had no
real need to make use of the hoary work of others.

A picture of Mellor and de Sancha would certainly have been
more entertaining and thought-provoking. That story, concerning
a chubby, bespectacled Conservative official's fumbling liaision
with a young lady of very little repute threw the social changes
between the sixties and now into the sharpest of reliefs. Where
Profumo was ruined, his government shaken and Keeler forced to
disappear, de Sancha hired PR guru Max Clifford to boost the
story out of all proportion, the salacious clincher being that
Mellor had allegedly enjoyed sex more when togged up in a
Chelsea soccer kit.

Mellor was forced to quit his post but was immediately rein-
vented as a TV and radio 'personality' – an amazing turnaround,
given that previously he'd just been a nondescript, moonheaded,
slack-jawed enforcer for Margaret Thatcher. De Sancha, too, from
tabloid payments and guest appearances, did OK out of it though,
for sleeping with Billy Bunter's slimy cousin she, as a dancer, might
have expected at least a mansion in Belgravia and a hyped reputation as the next Margot Fonteyn. It was a good story involving
sex, soccer, politics, disturbing changes in public morality and
manipulation by the tabloid media. Perfectly contemporary, very
Charlatans really.

There was another bright side to the single, as well as the quality of the main track. The B-sides, 'Keep It To Yourself' and 'Clean Up Kid' (recorded in Monmouth in July), were the first tracks to be credited to Tony Rogers, and they were no step backward. A new chapter had been opened.

On and on ground the world tour, with all the usual attendant shenanigans. In Dublin, a drunken Brookes, looking for the hotel's urinal, wandered through an emergency exit and set off the alarms. As the manager came haring out to see what the problem was, Brookes, by now relieving himself on some steps, turned and showered the poor man in piss. Later, Rogers got into an argument with Brookes, stormed out into the city and embarked on a one-man pub crawl. Wound up and by now extremely drunk and confused, he started complaining that he couldn't find the band, leading to next day's bathetic headline: 'Charlatans go missing and leave Lonely Tony on the streets of Dublin.'

Then finally the tour was over, but not before one final triumph. At Manchester *Nynex*, in front of 16,000 now hardcore fans, The Charlatans built up an intensity Burgess felt they hadn't reached since the show at Trentham Gardens. More than just a fervent welcome home, this was like being ushered up on to the throne. Burgess couldn't believe it: people were on their feet and leaping like raving salmon all the way to the back, a quarter of a mile away. *That's it*, he thought. *We've done it.* He was so blown away by this realisation that he couldn't face the after-show party, instead going home with a few close friends to quietly savour the feeling.

After this, three sell-out shows at Barrowland and a performance before another 12,000 fans at London's Docklands Arena were almost an anti-climax. After the London show, Burgess again stayed away from the party. This time he was up in his hotel room, with just a couple of mates, already talking about the next project: the achievement of real, full and lasting self-expression.

Epilogue

WHERE THE CHARLATANS HAD ended 1997 on an outrageous high, with *Tellin' Stories* up there in the end-of-year polls alongside The Verve's *Urban Hymns* and Radiohead's *OK Computer,* they started 1998 on something of a low. Ian Brown was back, a really quite astonishing press campaign having levered his half-arsed *Unfinished Monkey Business* album into the charts. Brown was loving it, lipping off big time about pet hates like cocaine and John Squire and, at one point, having a go at Tim Burgess. Claiming his family still laughed at Burgess whenever he appeared on screen (supposedly because Burgess was in some way aping Brown), he came across as snide and vindictive, far from the humble professor of comparative religion he made himself out to be. Nevertheless, Burgess was unimpressed, even a little hurt. This was not the kind of behaviour he expected from someone he knew and respected. It was that loyalty thing again.

As if karmically struck down, by the end of the year Brown was in Strangeways for causing a disturbance on an aeroplane and threatening a hostess. He might well have simply been drunk or joking or both. He may have hamfistedly attempted to calm the situation and only made it worse. Whatever the truth, it's hard to feel any sympathy for him. As soon as he saw his face in the papers again, when it looked like he was back on top, he revealed himself to be smug, surly and, as one listen to his album will tell you, arrogant way beyond his ability to back it up.

Others did not feel the same way about Burgess and The Charlatans. They were being cited as a prime influence (usually and notably above The Stone Roses) by a welter of keen new acts – Casino, Dreamswallow, Houdini, Mainstream, Monroe, Jaguar,

Jel, Vapour Trail and the superbly monikered Runston Parva (they just have to mean it) to name but a few.

On 23 February came The Charlatans' final release for Beggars Banquet, *Melting Pot*, released on what would have been Rob Collins' 35th birthday, another significant date. Rather than a greatest hits package, it was a collection of hits, rarities and other recordings that might now be hard to get hold of. *Between 10th And 11th* was only represented by 'Weirdo', and the 'Me In Time' single was absent altogether.

Originally the cover was to have been a shot of a girl blowing a bubble of gum. Then the idea came up of using a cafe full of rastas, bikers and young girls – a melting pot, like. Finally it was decided to just have a cafe, and a bloke in an overcoat to remind the faithful of 'Crashin' In'. The cafe would be The Weaverdale in Northwich (the "Melting Pot" sign being made up for £500 at the request of this book's photographer by a maker of neon signs in Norwood, south London, and hung on the inside of the window).

Opened in the 1930s, The Weaverdale, on the corner of Witton Street and Meadow Street, was popular with teenagers in the fifties and sixties, then became a biker haunt. The Charlatans used it regularly when Omega Records was based at 70 Witton Street and had their first meeting there after signing to Beggars Banquet. The cafe's manager, George Olmi, has a signed photo of them on the wall. A good move, as The Weaverdale has now been added to the fans' list of Charlatans tourist sites, along with Sproston Green and Wincham Park, home of Burgess's favoured Witton Albion.

In May, 'North Country Boy' turned up on the soundtrack to *Twentyfourseven*, playing over a sequence where Bob Hoskins takes a gang of kids off for a bonding session on the moors before a big boxing contest. Actually, it's more like the movie is suddenly acting as a video to the song. Around the same time as *Twentyfourseven*, The Chemical Brothers' mix of 'Toothache' appeared on the soundtrack to Bruce Willis's *The Jackal*. It made a nice change from having their songs used to back frenetic football highlights – though they do work well – as 'One To Another', 'Tellin' Stories' and even 'Weirdo' had recently been (just as 'Sproston Green' and 'Then' were in 1991).

* * *

Aside from the *Melting Pot* release, there was one big event in the Charlatans' 1998 diary – V98. This was a two-day festival, where The Charlatans and their under-cast (including James, All Saints, PJ Harvey and Ian Brown) would play Leeds one day and Chelmsford the next, and The Verve would start in Chelmsford and move on to Leeds. It was big: 110,000 people in two days. Despite the much-reported collapse of the music industry, with the Phoenix Festival and outdoor events featuring New Order and the Lighthouse Family cancelled due to poor ticket sales, V98 sold out months in advance.

The Charlatans played a warm-up date at the Hanley Theatre Royal in Stoke-On-Trent. Tickets were sold in Hanley, but most went to the readers of *109*, who travelled from all over the country to attend the gig and the free party afterwards at the Stage club opposite the venue. The band stated, with becoming modesty, that they hoped the festival dates would keep people interested in them until the next album. The gigs themselves were excellent, though problems in Leeds, where the band felt thay had not played to their abilities, meant that by Chelmsford a degree of that old anger was back – Burgess especially is at his best under such circumstances. The massive downpour during their set didn't help, but it couldn't douse the enthusiasm of crowd or band. The fans had always considered Charlatans shows to be an event. Now this opinion was unanimous.

The next day, the band jetted off to Los Angeles. There would be one gig, at the John Anson Ford Amphitheatre in Hollywood, and a couple of DJ sets from Burgess, at the Blue Cafe and Johnny Depp's Viper Rooms. It was more of a holiday than anything; a band debriefing. All they had to think about now was how the hell to follow up *Tellin' Stories*.

Towards the end of 1998, it was decided that, for convenience's sake, the band would have their own studio built in Middlewich (er, just south of Northwich). It would be residential, in case anyone needed to stop over, but it was close to home for everyone. It would also save the massive expenditure of spending months pottering about in Rockfield or Monnow Valley.

While the building was going on, Burgess went back to Los Angeles for seven weeks at the end of 1998, and again at the beginning of 1999. He had a new girlfriend there and, fully intending to live it like he loved it, he wanted to spend time with her. They went camping together, out in the middle of nowhere. Typically, Burgess was far from adequately equipped. They spent nights huddled together for warmth, drinking and laughing at the absurdity of it. It was a fantastic time – even the bits when they were menaced by bears and rattlesnakes. Burgess, no longer a simple north-country boy swearing by his birthplace and ignoring everywhere else, now finally took America to his heart. He even had his first day without a drink since the death of Rob Collins.

Once back, and finding that the studio was not yet completed (recording was now scheduled to begin on 25 January), he threw himself into crazed activity. He bleached the interior of his house in Didsbury, quite badly splattering himself and wandering unselfconsciously around for a while with what seemed like slapdash highlights in his hair. He waded through the 50 or so classic Chess CDs sent to each member of the band by their new label. There were all the bad-boy greats – Howlin' Wolf, Muddy Waters, Sonny Boy Williamson, Bo Diddley, Chuck Berry, John Lee Hooker – but also Etta James, Minnie Ripperton and, to Burgess's unconfined joy, Sugar Pie DeSanto. He hadn't heard of her before but was thrilled by the irreproachable authenticity of her name. One blast and he was greedily reading the inserted booklet, discovering that she was still operating in San Francisco and vowing to hunt her down on his next trip to the West Coast. He immediately went in search of further DeSanto material at Goldmine, a much-loved singles emporium in Manchester.

While engaging in this frenetic activity, Burgess was thinking about The Charlatans. Each member of the band presently had his own concerns. Blunt's marriage was finally ending. All the questions first raised in 1991 had now been answered – band life was too much for his relationship to cope with. Mark Collins was ensconced with Claire in their place in Chorlton, enjoying baby Ella and awaiting their second child. Rogers was high on this new life, but also working closely with Blunt and Brookes, knowing he had yet to prove himself on the main stage. And Brookes, well, Jon Boy's so solid, so completely committed to the band, you wonder if he's not the real reason it all stayed together.

Burgess was also thinking about himself. His recent experiences in America had him wondering whether he shouldn't sell up and move away from the cosy north-west. He was considering moving back to London but this time steering clear of the party circuit. He was thinking of making new artistic acquaintances, with people who would feed his mind. As mentioned, the lyrics to the *Tellin'* *Stories* album pointed to a sea-change in Burgess. Previously, he had expressed himself mostly in a teen-pop roar. He was calling to his listeners to get up and escape their given lot; to veer deliberately away from the paths of workaday drudgery stretched out before them. But his alternative for them was to simply have fun with no real thought of deeper satisfaction. His was an important, enlivening message – apathy is a life-taker and a gift to social controllers – yet now it was changing.

With *Tellin' Stories*, Burgess was looking deeper into himself and others, following the example of Dylan's 'Ballad Of A Thin Man' (from *Highway 61 Revisited*) in attempting to refine and strengthen his insights and promptings. Rob Collins' death was a driving force behind this, demanding an extra seriousness, but Burgess had been moving in this direction anyway. He was getting real beyond the 'realness' attributed to the band purely because of simple death and disaster. Lines like 'Your boss is quietly hounding as he creeps into your sleep,' and, 'No voice or poet's pen can touch what hits you in the morning,' both from 'Get On It', were examples of truly graceful writing, and were at the same time obviously personal expressions. When it came to borrowing lines and titles, Burgess was a jackdaw, but he had become very much his own jackdaw. And now, as he looked towards the next album, he was up for just being himself.

'People have talked about my lyrics as if they were some big slobber of unconsciousness,' he says. 'But they always spring to mind for a reason. I write it all down ... then I lose the piece of paper and have to recreate everything.

'In the past I've been called a magpie, and to a point that's true. I have stolen lines, but only stuff that's meant something to me and that will scan perfectly with the line before and after. I get annoyed when I see people stealing lines that mean nothing to them.'

Burgess was talking about, in his own words, 'being a man' – as opposed to being a kid. Strangely, his writing having matured so much, he was in a sense having to catch up with and supersede his own lyrics. He talked of going to visit his parents to explain to them, for the first time, exactly who he was. He wanted to expose his frailties and fears. He wanted to understand himself and be understood. After years of being largely organised and shunted around by others (not that he hadn't needed it), he wanted control over his own life. That's what the idea of a move to London, or even Hollywood, was all about. He wanted to grow into himself, accept himself as an artist, and be *respected* for it.

'Michael Stipe,' he says, 'has become a superstar on his own terms, in his own way, not by changing but by becoming his full self. I mean, I used to love New Order, still do in some ways, but they've not moved on. Bernard Sumner's so satisfied with being the lead singer. He's like a forty-year-old boy where Michael Stipe is *Mister* flippin' Stipe. He'll be in a room, totally aware of what's going on around him, totally commanding. He might've have made a couple of shit LPs but so what? We'll make a couple of shit LPs too, probably, after we've made some great ones.'

'Being in a band does inhibit you,' he continues, 'it does shelter you, it lets you be a permanent teenager. But now's the time to be a proper person, to grow up. There was a song that never made it onto the *Us & Us Only* album (the follow-up to *Tellin' Stories*) that had the lines "I rely on you, you rely on me" and the chorus was "Goodbye". The band had become like an institution and the song was saying goodbye to that. You know, the idea of the band being the be-all and end-all and there being no life outside of it. I already feel the weights coming off my shoulders and the ropes of my ankles. In the future we'll still be a band but also a set of real separate individuals.'

Brookes too – solid, big-shouldered Brookes – was on a voyage of self-discovery. Speaking of his and the band's potential trajectory a little before the demoing process began for the next album, he was very clear in his ambitions. He too was explaining himself with a new-found lucidity.

'I'm just trying to treat it with more maturity now,' he said. 'Trying to listen more to the people around me and learn more about music. You know, when we started we were pretty naive about what a band can be. We were given everything really quickly and then had it all taken away again, and we had to work to get it all back. And now we have it back, ten times what it was, and if we want to go to a new level we have to really think about it.

'To be a drummer was the only plan I ever had, the only ticket I ever bought. If anything had gone wrong it would've been a complete fucking disaster. So I feel really lucky. I don't feel like I've done this myself. And now I want to build on the luck I've had, learn, get better, make something that's not just for me but for all the lads in the band, all of our futures. I really want the band to be the biggest thing in my life.

'I don't think any of us believe it's what it could be. We're nowhere near that yet. It's not about fame for me any more. I had a taste of that, being in the papers and on TV and all that, and it's not what I want. I just want to be a great player, prove to myself and the people around me that I can realise the talent I know I've got.'

Once the studio was completed and recording sessions for the next album finally began, it all went more smoothly than anyone had imagined. The demos had been exceptional and Burgess was still absolutely involved. Sitting in his front room in Didsbury, flipping endlessly from new releases to Charlatans works-in-progress that were, to him, evidently of carotid importance, it was clear he was still possessed of those twin defining characteristics – an appreciation of the brilliance of others and a desire to match them that overrode all else.

The new set-up worked well, the studio being appointed mostly for business (it was called Big Mushroom Studios, the name having been inspired by the first line of this biography). The ground floor consisted of studio, storage space and a rehearsal area large enough to accommodate the band at their most frenetic. Upstairs was pretty functional too. A narrow corridor lent entry to a series of tiny bedrooms. The main room had a long table for card games and drunken intra-band discussions, settees were gathered around a smallish TV, and there was a pool table – tiny and unusually tatty with tip-less cues that looked like they might've been employed by Clint Eastwood in *Coogan's Bluff*. Very cheap and cheerful, notably so for a band of their stature. Mr Williams had done his work well.

'The heartache of it for me,' says Burgess, as a final word on that dire financial mismanagement, 'was the moral issue. I grew up with two rules given to me by my mum – no-one takes your woman and no one steals from you. And if anyone does that's it, I'm finished with them, forever. So someone stole from me, big-time. And I can't forgive that'.

With all the to-ings and fro-ings and frustrating delays, the band found themselves even more keen to re-enter the fray. Rogers was especially enthusiastic, as this was his first real opportunity to write with the band, and he dragged Blunt and Brookes along with him (not that they needed much dragging), the trio producing a series of searing backings, beyond even 'One To Another'. Burgess, by now utterly taken by his new relationship, enjoyed the fact that the studio was completed, that the band's attitude was far more professional and that he could jet in from his lover's hometown of Los Angeles, fully engage with his work and then return across the Atlantic (he would soon make the move to the States permanent). To him, this was growing up and being in a *proper* band – a band that was strong in itself, almost wholly unaffected by where its members chose to live their lives.

'It's strange the way it turned out,' he says. 'I mean, I really didn't want the studio to be built. I'd been trying to get away from there since I was a kid, and this seemed to be tying me to the place for good. But we made the album there and I was still able to sell my house and organise getting away.

'I think I did worry everyone,' he continues, 'But it was the first little bit of controversy I caused since I joined. You know, someone died, someone had a nervous breakdown, someone left, someone joined and all the time it was "Oh, Tim, he's *always* available". But then I wanted something for myself. Everybody's come to terms with it now though.'

So it was off to America, for the two things Burgess has always held most dear.

'Personal freedom is important,' he states without a blink. 'America's big enough. And I really like the supermarkets with those wide aisles. I don't like people touching me, people brushing my shoulders. Over the last two or three years in England I've become really claustrophobic. I really felt at times like standing there with my hands up in the air shouting "Don't touch me!"

'It's a small example but being jet-lagged and falling asleep in a pub in Middlewich is frowned upon, because they've got nothing else to think about as being right or wrong. In America, you get guys wandering around with tattoos all over their faces and people just go "Oh, *that's* unusual". It's taken as natural, people expect the unexpected. I find it really liberating.'

Personal freedom ... and love. In the late Summer of 1999, Burgess was married to his American lover, Michelle, the ceremony taking place in Los Angeles. 'The ultimate reason why I moved to LA was that I found my woman. I never thought it mattered where anyone came from, it was just about finding the right person, and it took me the best part of 32 years.

'When you love somebody you find yourself being interested in what they're about. And I just love the smell of Los Angeles, I love the taste of it. I go up in the hills there and look down over this sprawling metropolis and think "This is where I do my thing. I wanna live my life here". The memory of that smell really kept me going while we were recording *Us & Us Only.*'

As the recording progressed, so did Burgess' drive towards adulthood. He was even buying his clothing from J. Crews, a chain dealing in a smooth and well-groomed look that managed to be hip and simultaneously recall the Kennedys at their stylistic zenith. The records he loved were made by adults, their soul born of experience; the pain was real, the celebrations hard-earned. So Burgess, really for the first time, began to *sing*.

At a secret show in Liverpool, a few weeks before the release of the album on October 18th, the results were there for all to see. The band had checked into their hotel under such *Carry On* monikers as Mr T. Watt and Mr J. Meoff. They spent the hours before the show ensconced in a bar mobbed by friends, family and fans of ten years' standing, and the hours afterwards knocking them back with massively enthused record company executives (discussing how best to spend the £200,000 earmarked for the video to the next single, 'Forever'). Nothing out of the ordinary there.

The big difference was in Burgess himself. In a packed and dripping club, he challenged himself to exhibit live the soul he had been seeking. Looking out across low-hanging dry ice that made the crowd look like extras in Vincent Ward's mediaeval plague flick *The Navigator*, he moved with a new confidence. Not with the swaggering Manc monkey-walk of before, but a cooler, deeper groove. On three or four occasions, all of them involving renditions of never-before-heard tunes, he was, at last, transported onto a higher inner plane, noticeably unaware of his physical surrounds. This was not just about conviction in the strength of the songs (though as usual the likes of 'The Only One I Know' sent the audience into steaming paroxysms), it concerned a new-found comfort in his ability and role.

This change could be heard on the record too. Produced by the band themselves at Big Mushroom, it was mixed with James Spencer at Great Linfield Manor near Milton Keynes. All The Charlatans' strengths – the innocent, frenzied pop, the huge and solemn Hammond rock, the warm, sometimes searing Country – were drawn upon, reinterpreted and creatively combined, making the album their most powerful to date. Burgess was particularly stirring on the melancholic, magnificent 'The Blond Waltz', the swampy, 'Toothache' – recalling 'My Beautiful Friend', and 'Senses', this last being unarguably The Charlatans' finest moment, the band at last lying back and allowing the orchestral sweeps, massive strums and wailing harmonica to flood over them. Elsewhere, there was the overtly Dylanesque 'Impossible' and the thudding, stadium-filling country rock of 'A House Is Not A Home'. And, though Dylan was an obvious influence, The Stones came through even more clearly. The closing 'Watching You', with its sweet piano, its multi-layered vocals and its guitar flipping out way back behind, was heavily reminiscent of 'Coming Down Again' (from *Goat's Head Soup*), while the keyboard opening of *Let It Bleed*'s 'Monkey Man' was recalled by 'Good Witch, Bad Witch 1' – a track that, when reprised later in the album, saw Burgess employ a Tom Waits-style voicebox and the music turn to a menacing drive not unlike '2000 Light Years From Home'.

Burgess openly admits to a deep love of Tom Waits' work, and also to a deep appreciation of a newer star, Elliott Smith.

And now, with *Us & Us Only*, the first Charlatans LP to feature the mellifluous orchestrals and scorching rock of keyboardist Tony Rogers, you can feel the soft conviction of another of Burgess' recent favourites – Elliott Smith.

'I respect him and I've seen him two or three times. I sort of met him once and I really wanted to talk to him, but he was surrounded by Courtney Love and Michael Stipe. He's kind of coming from the same place as us, he obviously likes Big Star too, which is probably why you think we sound similar. But we never copy anyone. There are certain styles that you might pick up on without knowing it.

'We actually only listen to American music. Right now I'm listening to a lot of Woodie Guthrie, Leadbelly, Johnny Cash. And those influences are coming through in the music. So *Us & Us Only* wasn't deliberately tailored for the American market but, on the other hand, we can't see any reason why they wouldn't like it.'

All in all, *Us & Us Only* is a fine effort, a record that, had it not worn its influences quite so clearly on its sleeve, might have been truly great. Burgess was particularly pleased with his vocal performances, and the resulting reaction of the press. To play that secret date in Liverpool, he had just returned from Japan where he conducted a brain-draining 50 interviews in five days. He said he didn't mind, appreciated the interest, though – perhaps for the first time – he admitted to growing bored of the sound of his own voice. What really made it special was the final interview, with Japan's harshest critic, from *What's In ES* (Burgess had always wrongly thought that was E's). Apparently, after years of hardcore sniping, the guy had been won over by The Charlatans' latest LP, even suggesting that Burgess should be given an award for his vocals.

'I was relieved,' admitted Tim 'but I still spent the rest of the interview trying to make sure he was going to actually say that in print. I still care about being in magazines; I see them as being about education. You know, I really loved those TV programmes about Fleetwood Mac and The Band and the making of their classic albums and, because we've always wanted to be talked about in the same terms, we like it when we're treated that seriously.'

For a variety of reasons, Burgess had begun – just begun – to match his idols' rampant individualism, throwing himself in where, before, fear of fucking up had always lent him a charming hesitancy.

'That's true,' he says 'A lot of it was always about performance and action, about getting the notes right, really. But on the album it was deeper than that. I could feel a pain in my gut and I knew I was getting it right. I'm kind of aiming at an unashamed expression of myself, and I think at the moment that "Senses", which is all about devotion – it's both biblical and personal – is the pinnacle of that.'

And, as said, this is down to love.

'Yeah, and all the openness that comes with it after waiting so long to find it. That made me more observant of everything else too. Like the song "A House Is Not A Home". That was originally about our split with Beggars Banquet but slowly became more about Martin who was going through a divorce. "The Blond Waltz" was kind of about him too, about how he's so fatherly to his kids and his friends. So in the song he's walking through the desert and his son or his friend falls ill and there's nothing he can do about it. And the rest is like a letter, or an e-mail, to my woman. You know, I find her words coming out in my lyrics and that's good because when you're in love it takes over your body. I'm 5,000 miles away from her but she's inside my soul, my heart, my mind. It's hard to talk about, but that's the truth. Whether she's with me or not, I use her every day.'

Surprisingly, or maybe not so surprisingly given the crazily idiosyncratic nature of their career thus far, The Charlatans' major label debut was not accompanied by a fearsome burst of activity. Naturally, the album charted high in the UK, opening up at Number 2, behind the burgeoning Shania Twain, but they failed by only one single place to become the only band of the Nineties to take four separate studio albums to the top. The band headlined

1999's big festivals at Reading and Leeds, then looked immediately to America. A tour of 20-odd US dates, supported by recent UK superstars Stereophonics, took them into April 2000, then it was back to the UK for a set of Easter dates called *The Chewing Gum Weekend*. In keeping with this retrospective title, the band would play once more at the Empress Ballroom in Blackpool, scene of one of the *Daytripper* shows with Ride back in 1993 (coincidentally, Ride's frontman had returned only weeks before this Easter gig with his new band The Animalhouse, while ex-guitarist Andy Bell was now a member of Oasis). These dates were followed by a major craic in Ireland, when the band, backed by Gomez, played at Dublin Castle.

The album was promoted with three singles – 'Forever', 'My Beautiful Friend' and then 'Impossible'. But though the reception received during the US dates was the best since the very earliest days, sales were a tad disappointing. The Charlatans reacted in the only way they know how – they tried again. With Burgess now happily married and settled in Los Angeles, within view of that famous Hollywood sign, Mark Collins took Claire and the kids over for an extended working holiday, continuing his close and mightily successful writing relationship with Burgess. Back in Middlewich, Blunt, Rogers and Brookes cranked up the groove machine once more. The plan was to be back in the studio within months, recording gladly and cheaply at Big Mushroom. Cheapness was still important, personally and professionally. Trevor Williams had worked them over good and proper.

The new-found spirit was the key. Being classic meant being soulful. Being soulful meant being yourself. Being yourself should come fast and easy. The confidence built up through the recording of *Us & Us Only* should mean that the follow-up would come quickly, and that its reference points should not be quite so obvious. This was a great time to be starting another offensive, and The Charlatans were ready. Soon they would be back in America where, with luck, proper bands can gain an improper reward.

This is the big challenge. Considering their history, it's the only one left.

'I come from a very structured family,' says Burgess, 'who

involve each other in everything they do. Whether it's a wedding or whatever, all the family members turn up, except me. My sister's got two kids and lives in a house right behind my mum's, and I can't understand that, why people don't want to experience more. I don't blame anyone for not looking but some people don't question their heart or their mind and I think, once you do, it becomes like an addiction.

'I'm still singing about independence, from the start right through to the "Forever" single. Only now that idea of independence has changed for me. I've been asking myself why I answer the phone when I don't want to. That's not about paranoia, it's about being what you want without people judging you. I'd really like to make people think about their own independence. I was once asked if I thought I'd changed anything and all I could think of was that I was part of a movement that told people it's alright to wear your shirt outside your jeans. I think I can make more of a difference than that.'

No one talks to drummers. But this is the story of The Charlatans, a band who have, for better or worse and throughout a full decade, bloody-mindedly endeavoured to do things their own way. So we'll leave the last word to Jon Brookes.

'Because of where we're from, we've always found it hard to come to terms with the idea of being artistic, of using your emotions and what you are to make something bigger than yourself. And that's exactly what we need to do now. We've got to stand up there in a place where we can get shot down. That's what made us one of the top three bands of the Nineties, and its gonna take us even further.'

They've come a long way – and still not far enough.

Index

203

Discography

Singles

Indian Rope/
You Can Talk To Me/
Who Wants To Know
GOOD ONET

Indian Rope/
You Can Talk To Me/
Who Wants To Know (reissue)
GOOD 1T
Indian Rope/
You Can Talk To Me/
Who Wants To Know
GOOD 1CD

The Only One I Know/ Everything
Changed
SIT 70
The Only One I Know/ Imperial
109/
Everything Changed
SIT 70T
The Only One I Know/ Imperial
109/
Everything Changed/
You Can Talk To Me
SIT 70CD

Then/Taurus Moaner
SIT 74
Then/Taurus Moaner/
Then (alt take)/
Taurus Moaner (inst)
SIT 74T
Then/Taurus Moaner/

Taurus Moaner (inst)/
Then (alt take)
SIT 74CD
Then/Taurus Moaner
SIT 74C
Over Rising/Way Up There
SIT 76
Over Rising/Way Up There/
Opportunity Three/
Happen To Die
SIT 76T
Over Rising/Way Up There/
Happen To Die/
Opportunity Three
SIT 76CD
Over Rising/Way Up There/
Happen To Die/
Opportunity Three
SIT 76TC
Over Rising/Way Up There
SIT 76C

Me In Time/
Occupation h.Monster
SIT 84
Me In Time/
Occupation h.Monster/ Subtitle
SIT 84T
Me In Time/
Occupation h.Monster/ Subtitle
SIT 84CD
Me In Time/
Occupation h.Monster
SIT 84C
Weirdo/Theme From 'The Wish'
SIT 88

Weirdo/Theme From 'The Wish'/
Sproston Green (US version)/
Weirdo (alt take)
SIT 88T
Weirdo/
Theme From 'The Wish'/ Weirdo
(alt take)/
Sproston Green (US version)
SIT 88CD
Weirdo/Theme From 'The Wish'
SIT 88C
Tremelo Song (alt take)/ Happen
To Die/Then (live)/ Chewing Gum
Weekend (live)
SIT 97T
Tremelo Song (alt take)/ Happen
To Die/Normality Swing (demo)
SIT 97CD1
Tremelo Song (live)/
Then (live)/
Chewing Gum Weekend (live)
SIT 97CD2
Tremelo Song (alt take)/
Then (live)/Chewing Gum Weekend
(live)/Tremelo Song (LP version)
SIT 97C

Can't Get Out Of Bed/ Withdrawn
BBQ 27
Can't Get Out Of Bed/ Withdrawn
BBQ 27T
Can't Get Out Of Bed/ Withdrawn
BBQ 27CD
Can't Get Out Of Bed/ Withdrawn
BBQ 27C

I Never Want An Easy Life If Me
And He Were Ever To Get
There/Only A Boho/
Subterranean/Can't Get Out Of
Bed (demo version)
BBQ 31CD

Jesus Hairdo/
Patrol (Dust Brothers mix)/ Feel
Flows (Luvdup mix)
BBQ 32T
Jesus Hairdo/Stir It Up/ Patrol
(Dust Brothers mix)/ Feel Flows
(Vanbasten mix)
BBQ 32CD1

Jesus Hairdo/I Never Want An
Easy Life If Me And He Were Ever
To Get There/ Another Rider Up In
Flames/ Up To Our Hips (last three
from radio session)
BBQ 32CD2
Jesus Hairdo/Patrol (Dust
Brothers mix)
BBQ 32C
Crashin' In/Backroom Window
BBQ 44

Crashin' In/Backroom
Window/Green Flashing Eyes
BBQ 44T
Crashin' In/
Backroom Window/Green Flashing
Eyes
BBQ 44CD
Crashin' In/Backroom Window
BBQ 44C

Just Lookin'/Bullet Comes
BBQ 55
Just Lookin'/Bullet Comes
BBQ 55C
Just Lookin'/Bullet Comes/ Floor
Nine
BBQ 55CD

Just When You're Thinkin' Things
Over/Frinck/ Toothache/Nine Acre
Dust (last two Chemical Brothers
remixes)
BBQ 60T
Just When You're Thinkin' Things
Over/Toothache (Chemical
Brothers mix)/ Frinck/Your Skies
Are Mine
BBQ 60CD
Just When You're Thinkin' Things
Over/Frinck/
Your Skies Are Mine
BBQ 60C

One To Another/Two Of Us
BBQ 301
One To Another/Two Of Us/
Reputation
BBQ 301CD

One To Another/Two Of Us
BBQ 301C

North Country Boy/Area 51
BBQ 309
North Country Boy/Area 51/ Don't Need A Gun
BBQ 309CD
North Country Boy/ Don't Need A Gun
BBQ 309C

How High/Title Fight
BBQ 312
How High/Title Fight/ Down With The Mook
BBQ 312CD
How High/Title Fight
BBQ 312C
Tellin' Stories/ Thank You (live)
BBQ 318
Tellin' Stories/ Keep It To Yourself/ Clean Up Kid/ Thank You (live)
BBQ 318CD

Forever/A Great Place to Leave/When Your Ship Comes In
MCSTD40220
Forever (edit)/Forever (full length version)/Sleepy Little Sunshine Boy/Forever (video)
MCSXD40220

My Beautiful Friend (edit)/ Scorched/Your Precious Love
MCSTD40225
My Beautiful Friend (Lionrock mix)/My Beautiful Friend (Jagz Kooner remix)/My Beautiful Friend (edit)/My Beautiful Friend (video)
MCXD40225

Impossible (radio edit)/Don't Go Giving It Up/Impossible (Aim remix)
MCSTD40231

Impossible (radio edit)/You Got It, I Want It/Impossible (full version)/Impossible (video)
MCSXD40231

Promo (12" unless marked)

The Only One I Know/ Imperial 109/ Everything Changed (test pressing with stamped white sleeve)
SIT70T

Polar Bear (test pressing)
SIT74T

Then/Then (alternate take)
CHAR 1

Happen To Die (7")
CHAR 2

Opportunity Three
CHAR 3

Me In Time/ Occupation h.Monster
CHAR 4

Feel Me Love Me (Japanese tour book)
CHAR 5

Weirdo
CHAR 6

Subterranean (free CD with *109* fanzine)
CHAR 7

Can't Get Out Of Bed (also CD)
CHAR 8

I Never Want An Easy Life If Me And He Were Ever To Get There (also CD)
CHAR 9

Jesus Hairdo/Stir It Up
CHAR 10

Jesus Hairdo/
Patrol (Dust Brothers mix) (also
CD)
CHAR 11

Patrol (Dust Brothers mix)/ Feel
Flows (Luvdup mix)
CHAR 12

The Chemical Brothers Remixes –
Nine Acre Court/
Toothache (Dub)/Toothache
CHAR 13

Melting Pot
(CD hits sampler from 1995)
CHAR 14

Crashin' In (radio edit) (CD)
BBQ 44DJ

Bullet Comes (radio edit) (CD)
BBQ 55DJ

Just When You're Thinkin' Things
Over (CD)
BBQ 60DJ

One To Another (radio edit) (CD)
BBQ 301DJ

Between 10th and 11th
box set with CD,
cassette and video

Up To Our Hips
box set with CD,
cassette and video

October '89
Indian Rope
You Can Talk To Me
White Shirt (demo cassette
sold at gigs)

Albums

Some Friendly
You're Not Very Well
White Shirt
The Only One I Know
Opportunity
Then
109 pt 2
Polar Bear
Believe You Me
Flower
Sonic
Sproston Green
SITU 30

Between 10th And 11th
I Don't Want To See The Sights
Ignition
Page One
Tremelo Song
The End Of Everything
Subtitle
Can't Even Be Bothered
Weirdo
Chewing Gum Weekend
(No One) Not Even The Rain
SITU 37

Up To Our Hips
Come In Number 21
I Never Want An Easy Life If Me &
He Were Ever To Get There
Can't Get Out Of Bed
Feel Flows
Autograph
Jesus Hairdo
Up To Our Hips
Patrol
Another Rider Up In Flames
Inside-Looking Out
BBQ 147

The Charlatans
Nine Acre Court
Feeling Holy
Just Lookin'
Crashin' In
Bullet Comes
Here Comes A Soul Saver

Just When You're Thinkin'
Things Over
Tell Everyone
Toothache
No Fiction
See It Through
Thank You
BBQ 174

Tellin' Stories
With No Shoes
North Country Boy
Tellin' Stories
One To Another
You're A Big Girl Now
How Can You Leave Us
Area 51
How High
Only Teethin'
Get On It
Rob's Theme
BBQ 190

Melting Pot
The Only One I Know
Then
Opportunity Three
Over Rising
Sproston Green (US Version)
Weirdo
Theme From The Wish
Patrol (The Chemical Brothers Mix)
Can't Get Out Of Bed
I Never Want An Easy Life
If Me & He Were Ever To
Get There
Jesus Hairdo
Crashin' In
Just Lookin'
Here Comes The Soul Saver
Just When You're Thinkin' Things
Over
One To Another
North Country Boy
BBQ 198

Us And Us Only
Forever
Good Witch, Bad Witch 1
Impossible
The Blond Waltz
House Is Not A Home
Senses (Angel On My Shoulder)
My Beautiful Friend
I Don't Care Where You Live
The Blind Stagger
Good Witch, Bad Witch 2
Watching You
MCD60069